VOLUME 577

SEPTEMBER 2001

THE ANNALS

of The American Academy *of* Political
and Social Science

ALAN W. HESTON, *Editor*
NEIL A. WEINER, *Assistant Editor*

REFORMING WELFARE, REDEFINING POVERTY

Special Editors of this Volume

RANDY ALBELDA
ANN WITHORN
*University of Massachusetts
Boston*

 Sage Publications   *THOUSAND OAKS   LONDON   NEW DELHI*

The American Academy of Political and Social Science

3937 Chestnut Street   Philadelphia, Pennsylvania 19104

Origin and Purpose. The Academy was organized December 14, 1889, to promote the progress of political and social science, especially through publications and meetings. The Academy does not take sides in controverted questions, but seeks to gather and present reliable information to assist the public in forming an intelligent and accurate judgment.

Meetings. The Academy occasionally holds a meeting in the spring extending over two days.

Publications. THE ANNALS of the American Academy of Political and Social Science is the bi-monthly publication of The Academy. Each issue contains articles on some prominent social or political problem, written at the invitation of the editors. Also, monographs are published from time to time, numbers of which are distributed to pertinent professional organizations. These volumes constitute important reference works on the topics with which they deal, and they are extensively cited by authorities throughout the United States and abroad. The papers presented at the meetings of The Academy are included in THE ANNALS.

Membership. Each member of The Academy receives THE ANNALS and may attend the meetings of The Academy. Membership is open only to individuals. Annual dues: $65.00 for the regular paperbound edition (clothbound, $100.00). For members outside the U.S.A., add $12.00 (surface mail) or $24.00 (air mail) for shipping of your subscription. Members may also purchase single issues of THE ANNALS for $20.00 each (clothbound, $30.00).

Subscriptions. THE ANNALS of the American Academy of Political and Social Science (ISSN 0002-7162) is published six times annually—in January, March, May, July, September, and November. Institutions may subscribe to THE ANNALS at the annual rate: $375.00 (clothbound, $425.00). Add $12.00 per year for subscriptions outside the U.S.A. Institutional rates for single issues: $70.00 each (clothbound, $75.00).

Periodicals postage paid at Thousand Oaks, California, and at additional mailing offices.

Single issues of THE ANNALS may be obtained by individuals who are not members of The Academy for $30.00 each (clothbound, $40.00). Single issues of THE ANNALS have proven to be excellent supplementary texts for classroom use. Direct inquiries regarding adoptions to THE ANNALS c/o Sage Publications (address below).

All correspondence concerning membership in The Academy, dues renewals, inquiries about membership status, and/or purchase of single issues of THE ANNALS should be sent to THE ANNALS c/o Sage Publications, 2455 Teller Road, Thousand Oaks, CA 91320. Telephone: (800) 818-SAGE (7243) and (805) 499-9774; FAX/Order line: (805) 375-1700. *Please note that orders under $30 must be prepaid.* Sage affiliates in London and India will assist institutional subscribers abroad with regard to orders, claims, and inquiries for both subscriptions and single issues.

Printed on recycled, acid-free paper

THE ANNALS

© 2001 *by* The American Academy *of* Political *and* Social Science

Editorial Office: Fels Center of Government, University of Pennsylvania, 3814 Walnut Street, Philadelphia, PA 19104-6197.

For information about membership* (individuals only) and subscriptions (institutions), address:

SAGE PUBLICATIONS
2455 Teller Road
Thousand Oaks, CA 91320

Sage Production Staff: MARIA NOTARANGELO, SCOTT SPRINGER, and ROSE TYLAK

From India and South Asia,		*From Europe, the Middle East,*
write to:		*and Africa, write to:*
SAGE PUBLICATIONS INDIA Pvt. Ltd		SAGE PUBLICATIONS LTD
P.O. Box 4215		6 Bonhill Street
New Delhi 110 048		London EC2A 4PU
INDIA		UNITED KINGDOM

*Please note that members of The Academy receive THE ANNALS with their membership.
International Standard Serial Number ISSN 0002-7162
International Standard Book Number ISBN 0-7619-2512-0 (Vol. 577, 2001 paper)
International Standard Book Number ISBN 0-7619-2511-2 (Vol. 577, 2001 cloth)
Manufactured in the United States of America. First printing, September 2001.

The articles appearing in THE ANNALS are abstracted or indexed in *Academic Abstracts, Academic Search, America: History and Life, Asia Pacific Database, Book Review Index, CAB Abstracts Database, Central Asia: Abstracts & Index, Communication Abstracts, Corporate ResourceNET, Criminal Justice Abstracts, Current Citations Express, Current Contents: Social & Behavioral Sciences, e-JEL, EconLit, Expanded Academic Index, Guide to Social Science & Religion in Periodical Literature, Health Business FullTEXT, HealthSTAR FullTEXT, Historical Abstracts, International Bibliography of the Social Sciences, International Political Science Abstracts, ISI Basic Social Sciences Index, Journal of Economic Literature on CD, LEXIS-NEXIS, MasterFILE FullTEXT, Middle East: Abstracts & Index, North Africa: Abstracts & Index, PAIS International, Periodical Abstracts, Political Science Abstracts, Sage Public Administration Abstracts, Social Science Source, Social Sciences Citation Index, Social Sciences Index Full Text, Social Services Abstracts, Social Work Abstracts, Sociological Abstracts, Southeast Asia: Abstracts & Index, Standard Periodical Directory (SPD), TOPICsearch, Wilson OmniFile V,* and *Wilson Social Sciences Index/Abstracts,* and are available on microfilm from University Microfilms, Ann Arbor, Michigan.

Information about membership rates, institutional subscriptions, and back issue prices may be found on the facing page.

Advertising. Current rates and specifications may be obtained by writing to THE ANNALS Advertising and Promotion Manager at the Thousand Oaks office (address above).

Claims. Claims for undelivered copies must be made no later than six months following month of publication. The publisher will supply missing copies when losses have been sustained in transit and when the reserve stock will permit.

Change of Address. Six weeks advance notice must be given when notifying of change of address to ensure proper identification. Please specify name of journal. **POSTMASTER:** Send address changes to: THE ANNALS of the American Academy of Political and Social Science, c/o Sage Publications, 2455 Teller Road, Thousand Oaks, CA 91320.

THE ANNALS

of The American Academy *of* Political *and* Social Science

ALAN W. HESTON, *Editor*
NEIL A. WEINER, *Assistant Editor*

FORTHCOMING

WHAT WORKS IN PREVENTING CRIME?
Special Editors: David Farrington
and Brandon C. Welsh

Volume 578   November 2001

DRUG POLICY
Special Editors: Peter Reuter
and Robert J. MacCoun

Volume 579   January 2002

FIXITY OF EXCHANGE RATES
Special Editors: Michael K. Ulan
and George Tavlas

Volume 580   March 2002

See page 2 for information on Academy membership and
purchase of single volumes of **The Annals.**

CONTENTS

BOOK DEPARTMENT CONTENTS

SOCIOLOGY

ECONOMICS

PREFACE

The centerpiece of welfare reform is the Personal Responsibility and Work Opportunity Reconciliation Act (PRWORA) of 1996. This piece of federal legislation was complemented by a wave of changes to welfare laws in the states. Although PRWORA was a watershed event, it could not have happened without 20 years of demonization and delegitimation of poor families on assistance, of the communities within which many of these families reside, and of the systems designed to serve them. Indeed, we see welfare reform as the result of a fusion of political, cultural, and ideological forces and policy presumptions that have ebbed, flowed, and regrouped over the past 50 years.

PURPOSE AND LIMITS OF THIS VOLUME

The overall purpose of this volume is to present welfare reform in the context of a bigger set of political, economic, and policy shifts and to examine how it forces us to reconceptualize poverty and antipoverty policies as well as to rethink the possibilities and limits of the U.S. welfare state. Since those most affected by welfare are single mothers, communities of color, and poor families, we also consider welfare changes in light of how they both mask and reveal gender, race, and class relations in the United States. In short, we think that the arguments here make the case for ending welfare reform as we know it. They provide part of a vision for a more dependable and responsive state, assuming that a democratic social movement must also be a part of ending the economic and political bases for poverty.

Before providing an overview of the issues this volume seeks to explore, however, it is instructive to set out what this collection is not.

This volume is not a compendium of what is happening now in the states nor a summary of all the amazingly well-funded research findings on the effects of reform. Some of our contributors, especially Sanford Schram, Joe Soss, and Linda Burnham, do provide some useful summarizing of these studies. However, we began this volume with the assumption that most such compendia and summaries are the "trees" of a welfare reform analysis. Instead, we want to look at the forest.

Nor is this volume a balanced assortment of the full spectrum of perspectives on this highly politicized topic. We have sought to neither cover nor critique all liberal or conservative points of view about what is wrong or possible. Instead, the perspective of the authors here is feminist, antiracist, and progressive. We selected our contributors because we see them as the scholars who are asking a range of critical questions about the meaning of welfare reform—questions not addressed in mainstream scholarship or journalism.

Also, this volume does not provide the sorely needed comparison of efforts to scale back or redirect antipoverty policies in Western nation-states. Rather,

8

several of our contributors, most carefully Frances Fox Piven, challenge the oft-heard notion that a globalization of the economy presumes a reduction in U.S. social provisions. Indeed, activist intellectuals Willie Baptist, Mary Bricker-Jenkins, and Burnham forcefully insist that a fully understood, internationally supported commitment to achieving economic and human rights offers an essential base for a radically expanded, and much more deeply democratic, social state.

Finally, we have not provided an inventory of all the strategies and tactics for welfare reform based on assessments of immediate political necessities. We believe that it is sometimes important to think politically and strategically without being bound by immediate electoral, congressional, or poll-generated realities. The end of welfare as we knew it did not happen overnight; the end of poverty will not be responded to overnight either.

GOING DEEPER: NECESSARY QUESTIONS
ABOUT WELFARE REFORM AS WE KNOW IT

This volume offers powerful critiques of welfare reform, but none of our contributors long for the welfare system we once knew. Each of us comes to the discussion with long-standing bona fide credentials as welfare critics. More than most mainstream welfare reformers and academic researchers, our authors share a history of viewing Aid to Families with Dependent Children (AFDC) as unsatisfactory: it never provided enough income for families to live even at the poverty level, so virtually everyone needed to break the rules to survive. As Linda Gordon argues, the accompanying programs never provided adequate service support, and they included disrespectful rules, which inherently demeaned both the workers who implemented the system and the poor women (for the most part) who dared to ask for help. The program was profoundly shaped by racist and ethnic presumptions, ultimately denying families of color the same lousy benefits and rules that applied to white families.

As Schram and Soss note, such deep political and moral critiques of AFDC were not reflected in the welfare reform that was created or in standards that now allow its bitterly worse successor to be deemed a success. Further, it is equally important, as Gordon and Gwendolyn Mink discuss, to acknowledge that welfare at least gave families the time they needed to pull their families together and to pull their own selves out of deepest poverty—which is exactly what the vast majority of families receiving welfare in the past have always done.

The first question that authors raise here is how best to convey the seismic changes in the way our nation deals with poor families and the consequent shake-up of the already fragile ground on which low-income families have always stood. We view welfare changes as failing to respect the ways in which poor families, particularly those headed by single mothers, have long coped with raising their families on and off welfare, usually in low-income communities, just as these changes simultaneously fail to acknowledge the patterns of behavior that both employers and fathers were able to exhibit (for ill and sometimes good) exactly because welfare was always present as a backup. We question whether the impact of welfare reform can be understand as the sum of its individual effects, even though this is how the vast majority of researchers are approaching it.

The second question, argued most fully by Schram and Soss, is to challenge why the media, politicians, and many researchers have dubbed the PRWORA a success, measured by declining caseloads and increased workforce participation. We cast doubt on the logic that welfare as we knew it was so bad, that anyone who leaves it, or never used it, must be better off. James Jennings and Ann Withorn extend this line of questioning by asking why whole communities and the network of service agencies within them are presumed to be improved if no one is no longer receiving welfare, as is the goal of so many local welfare-to-work campaigns, such as Project Zero in Michigan.

Another measure cited to prove the success of PRWORA is that about two-thirds of women leaving welfare seem to be employed. As Randy Albelda and Lucie White explain, this argument simply begs the question about the other third and ignores questions about the type of employment women are finding and about how many women left welfare for employment in the past. They especially ask us to wonder what fundamental changes to the low-wage labor market and child care system would be necessary for an employment-based strategy to really work.

Mink questions the mandate that poor women raising children mostly on their own must fend for themselves without dependable public assistance. Time limits and full family sanctions for bureaucratic infringements all but ensure that any individual family cannot rely on welfare benefits for very long. Promoting marriage as a substitute for welfare, Mink argues, serves to reassert patriarchal control, which erodes gender equality.

Burnham shows how more than welfare has been profoundly affected by welfare reform. Welfare reform has been accompanied by the erosion of the use and eligibility of the programs that were packaged with cash assistance. Programs such as Medicaid, food stamps, and WIC (Special Supplemental Nutrition Program for Women, Infants, and Children) have all plummeted even as poverty rates have remained high for a robust economy. Burnham, Jennings, and Withorn ask why any policy that leaves poor families and communities more isolated, with fewer supports and less respect for their real conditions than ever before, can be dubbed a success.

HOPES RAISED

The core messages embodied in welfare reform are ones that speak powerfully and frighteningly to who we are as a nation and what we think about women, people of color, and the poor and near-poor.

Taken together, our interconnecting questions imply that if society truly valued all the work of single moms, without denying that men were around, then it would have the best chance of taking care of all families and of both reducing economic inequality and recognizing the caregiving work that is, and must be, done for society to thrive. If we also acknowledge that poverty and welfare use are not evenly distributed but are concentrated in urban and rural low-income communities that are themselves highly segregated by race and ethnicity, then it will be obvious that the impact of welfare reform must also be examined in terms of its community impacts. Further, appreciation, as well as a critique, of the functions and practices of the U.S. welfare state, is essential if we are to move forward.

The questions raised about welfare reform by the authors in this volume demand serious rethinking about the nature of low-wage jobs and the necessary obligations of taking care of children. They insist that honestly taking into account the resource capacity of poor families and the lack of employment and employment discrimination in poor communities requires fundamentally different social responses than available through welfare reform. The authors here presume that real change can come only by acknowledging long-standing racial and ethnic divides, the barriers of domestic violence and the long-term effects of trauma, the imperatives of an international-integrated economic system that thrives on low-wage work, and the impossibility and even danger of attaining adequate income or court-mandated child support as a simple solution to family poverty.

The pitfalls of welfare reform are many and the results far from stellar. Still, embedded in the changes are opportunities. Welfare reform's employment imperative opens the door to legal and political arguments for sharing the costs of raising children, as White argues. Gordon, Albelda, and Mink stress that a new world of no mothers' entitlements leaves a gaping hole in the safety net that can potentially be filled by valuing the work of taking care of children.

Most important, the authors in this volume assume that only by building upon real traditions of activism, as Mimi Abramovitz reminds us, can poverty become unacceptable and real economic and human rights be achieved. And only through honest struggle among poor people and their allies, as Baptist and Bricker-Jenkins argue, can truly "winnable strategies" be envisioned.

For us, a full assessment of welfare reform serves to illuminate how the U.S. economic and political system is fundamentally unjust and how, as always, its current state defines the terms of both social struggle and civic discourse. In the end, by taking the time to compile this volume, we express our abiding hope that the American populace will eventually be able to see that the solutions offered by welfare reform are not solutions that provide income security and well-being for poor families.

RANDY ALBELDA
ANN WITHORN

Who Deserves Help?
Who Must Provide?

By LINDA GORDON

ABSTRACT: Human societies have always provided help for the needy, and this provision has frequently been calibrated according to notions of deservingness and obligation. These notions have been shaped by gendered double standards, including measures of sexual morality, personal demeanor, housekeeping, and self-sacrifice, that are applied to women but not to men. Most fundamental, the fact that women are the primary child raisers has given many of them, in modern societies, two jobs—working for wages and working without wages to raise children. The modern welfare system arose from campaigns to help mothers who try to perform these two jobs without male help. Focusing first on deserted women, then on widows, and more recently on never-married mothers, U.S. welfare policy in the twentieth century was self-defeating because it tried to provide for poor children while avoiding giving aid or encouragement to lone mothers.

Linda Gordon is professor of history at New York University. A historian of social policy, she has written Woman's Body, Woman's Right *(first published in 1976, revised edition 1990, 3rd edition forthcoming 2002), on the history of birth control;* Heroes of Their Own Lives *(1988), on the history of family violence policy; and* Pitied but Not Entitled: Single Mothers and the History of Welfare *(1994). Her most recent book is* The Great Arizona Orphan Abduction, *the story of how a group of white women organized a 1904 vigilante action against Mexican Americans.*

THE questions of deservingness and obligation regarding public assistance have been debated at least since the first moment that private or public groups began to organize, and thus depersonalize, care for the least fortunate. Oddly enough, the terms in which that question is discussed today are not much different from those of centuries ago, despite the fact that the context has been radically transformed.

The reasons people are needy in a contemporary society are not the same as those in traditional agrarian societies. There is, however, one paradoxical continuity: women and children have been more likely to be in need of help across the centuries and across many different cultures and economies, yet women and children have often found it harder to prove themselves deserving than have men.

This understanding, however fundamental, is relatively new. Only in the past few decades have scholars examined welfare states from a gendered perspective, demonstrating both the constraining assumptions about "proper" gender relations built into most welfare programs and how women's and children's disproportionate poverty derives from the gender structures of society (including women's responsibility for children, women's low wages and the predicament of mother-child families not supported by a male wage, male violence toward women, and discrimination against women in family, education, and the labor force).

These facts, easily ascertainable through research, have been until the last few decades veiled by an ideology that male breadwinning (the "family wage") and women's dependence on men not only are the desirable family order but accurately describe the way people actually live. In fact, there was never a time in U.S. history when the majority of men were able to support a wife and children single-handedly (Hughes 1925; Breckinridge 1928; Douglas 1920). Failure to scrutinize the family-wage myth has led many policymakers to assume that full employment and a decent minimum wage could eliminate poverty. This perspective, assuming male-headed households and family wages, ignores the fact that many women and children have no male wage earner to support them and that the demands of domestic labor make wage earning difficult for low wage earners with primary parenting responsibility. Today, this family-wage perspective explains lone-mother families in terms of the absence of marriageable men who can earn family-supporting wages, a perspective that considers women's marital status as but an artifact of men's earnings. Without a gendered understanding of intimate relationships and domestic labor, welfare scholarship cannot comprehend the degree to which lone motherhood is not reducible to male unemployment but derives from women's own aspirations, their aspirations for their children, and their rejection of male dominance. Equally problematic, this perspective assumes that women's dependence on male earnings remains a desirable social goal.

Without a gender analysis, it has been impossible to fully understand today's political struggle over welfare systems, conflicts about which programs are popular and which disdained and about which welfare recipients are entitled and which not. In the United States, much of the political argument has been about who deserves help and who is obligated to provide it. I offer here an analytic and historical perspective on this question by reviewing how the major U.S. program called welfare—aid to dependent children—defined those deserving of help. It will emerge that deservingness is a gendered concept that has been delineated on the basis of ideology and wishful thinking.

THE ETHICS AND STRUCTURES OF DESERVINGNESS

Most people in all cultures enjoy the feeling of helping others, and most cultures consider charity a community or religious duty or a measure of good character. But a distaste for freeloaders also characterizes many cultures. The violator may appear to not really need the help, or to use the help in a bad way, or to not work hard. The giver then feels taken in and may become hostile and resentful. But if the recipient is truly needy and unable to help himself or herself—a child, for example, or a handicapped person—the giver no longer feels exploited or concerned about freeloading. These mixed feelings about giving and sharing have surrounded aid to the needy for centuries in most cultures.

Human communities are, for better or for worse, moral communities. So helping others has often been conditional on approving their morals; a good moral reputation combined with genuine neediness creates deservingness. In the smaller communities that characterized most societies prior to a few centuries ago, people's need and morality were readily observable by others, and those who could help made their judgments with all the petty prejudices and partialities that characterize any community. When states developed large-scale welfare programs, they increasingly measured deservingness through formal supervision and bureaucratic tests, although not necessarily with more objectivity.

Responsibility for others has been imbedded in every human society, limited of course by an insider-outsider distinction. For whom are we responsible? The perimeter of the sphere of obligation varies, of course. We are usually expected to help family members, but the extent of that responsibility has drastically diminished in the past century: in the United States, for example, grown children are no longer legally responsible for their parents, or parents for their grown children, and siblings bear no legal responsibility for each other. A sense of obligation to help a neighbor is now the exception, not the rule, although many would help on the understanding that what they are doing is voluntary.

In the English colonies in North America, members of a township derived their entitlement to help from settlement, that is, continuing residence in a community. In the twentieth century, that community expanded so that residence in a state or nation is what matters. As governments developed programs such as public education, garbage collection, and water purification, it was settlement that created entitlement, while for other programs the standard was higher, and especially after migration became widespread, settlement was distinguished from citizenship. Many Europeans refer to entitlements to government programs promoting public welfare as "social citizenship." Benefits conceived in that way belong to the recipient as a right of citizenship. But in the United States, to a larger degree than elsewhere, some entitlements remain dependent on various tests of morality and neediness, that is, on deservingness.

Obligation, the other side of the exchange, can also derive from several positions: kinship, membership in a church, or membership in a fraternal order or a union. The obligation to help has shifted too in the last centuries, in some ways shrinking but in other ways expanding. Givers may ignore their neighbors' poverty but contribute generously to earthquake victims in Armenia or orphans in Rwanda. As states become democratized and citizens become increasingly unequal, demands for large-scale alleviation of poverty create state forms of provision, and these rely on taxation, an impersonal form of obligation. That form of obligation establishes no bond and engenders no joy of giving on the part of the taxpayer; the depersonalization of recipients deprives them of sympathy and makes them targets of resentment.

Two phenomena counteract this resentment. One is universal welfare programs, which are available to everyone. In the United States, for example, attending a public university (and thereby receiving valuable government assistance) is perfectly honorable, although some wealthier parents may choose to spend more on private schools. Discounts for the elderly are embarrassing only to those who wish to appear young. The second is the impression that poverty is not the poor person's fault. In agrarian societies, for example, poor harvests could be universal and were universally visible. Earthquakes, floods, and droughts remain in that category. The industrial equivalent of harvest failure—recessions, depressions, structural unemployment, deindustrialization—have been less perceptible because of market ideology. When nationwide catastrophes struck, for example, the Great Depression of the 1930s, poverty lost some of its stigma, and emergency federal government relief was popular and relatively uncontroversial. But in times that appear normal, work-ethic ideology, combined with ignorance about labor market opportunity, leads to blaming those who seek public assistance.

A major structural feature of the U.S. welfare state is that stratification in entitlement, justified by degrees of deservingness, creates public conceptions of deservingness and undeservingness. This is not an accidental but a conscious strategy. As one welfare administrator urged the Social Security Board in 1939, " 'denial of benefits to [some] would, by furnishing a convenient contrast, make those who are covered somewhat more aware of their benefits, and would thereby strengthen the

concept of a purchased right' "
(Gordon forthcoming). The most
expensive U.S. transfer programs,
like Social Security Old Age Insurance, were designed to appear to be
earned and based on worker contributions, although they were not.[1] The
Social Security Board operated a
large public relations campaign to
sell Old Age Insurance as a honored
entitlement. As sociologist Theda
Skocpol (1992) put it, "Through a
clever and widely disseminated public metaphor, Americans were told
that their 'contributions' insured
that each wage earner would be entitled in old age to collect benefits that
he or she had 'individually earned.'
Actually, benefits are paid out of a
common fund" (B1). By contrast, programs for the poor are stigmatized
in numerous ways: surveillance of
recipients for possible cheating
throws suspicion on all recipients;
surveillance of recipients for moral
standards throws suspicion on all
recipients; critics of welfare suggest
that paying for it raises taxes substantially. In fact, the word "welfare"
has metamorphosed in the last
half century to become a unique and
pejorative term for means-tested
programs.

THE GENDER OF
DESERVINGNESS

Most standards of deservingness
have been deeply gendered, expressing and reinforcing social norms
about appropriate male and female
behavior. Almost every category of
means-tested (and some non-means-
tested) benefits separates recipients
by gender and treats them differ-

ently. Old Age Insurance, for example, requires that the recipient has
been employed for 11 quarters in an
eligible job; when the program was
passed, the great majority of American women did not meet that condition because they were not employed,
they worked in "casual," uncovered
employment (hardly casual in the
case of maids or farmworkers), or
they worked for the government
(including tens of thousands of
schoolteachers). This gender difference was deliberate and explicit:
women's employment was, as welfare
designers ought to be, temporary
because most women married and
married women belonged at home.
As historian Alice Kessler-Harris
(1995) summed it up, the principles
of welfare were "the dignity of men
(defined as their capacity to provide)"
and "the virtue of women (their willingness to remain dependent on men
and to rear children" (95). But this
principle of women's domesticity was
always contradicted by a class double
standard. While prosperous mothers
were (and sometimes still are)
expected to devote full-time to home
and child care, poor and working
class mothers were not; public assistance was meager, and administrators expected recipients to supplement it with wages.

The most fundamental gendering
of social provision arises from the
fact that women do most of the child-
raising work, whether they have a
partner or not. If a man's wages could
rarely support a whole family, a
woman's wages (about 50 percent of a
man's in the early twentieth century)
surely could not do so. Mothers
without male support were often

forced to surrender their children to orphanages.

The program called "welfare" in the United States was designed to care for these mothers and children who lacked male support (Gordon 1994). Aid to Dependent Children (ADC)—Title IV of the Social Security Act—sailed through Congress in 1935, absolutely without controversy or opposition, in contrast to the unemployment compensation or old-age insurance titles that provoked strong opposition.[2] Partly, this is because ADC was cheap: cheap because the cost of institutionalizing children was much greater than paying their mothers to raise them, and cheap because the designers radically underestimated the number of lone-mother families. In 1930, there were approximately 10.5 million people living in female-headed households, accounting for 8.6 percent of the population. The ADC planners, by contrast, estimated that they would be serving 288,000 families, or 0.9 of 1 percent of the population (Gordon and McLanahan 1991; Coll 1988). Their estimate was even lower than the number of female-headed families already receiving public assistance in 1934—358,000 (Committee on Economic Security 1937, 241). ADC was also popular because at the time lone mothers and children seemed the quintessentially deserving recipients. By devoting themselves to mothering, the female recipients were performing what God, nature, and society intended women to do and doing so, moreover, under difficult circumstances. Children were by definition deserving. Mother-children families certainly seemed as deserving of public support as the elderly.

Yet lone mothers, 70 years later, have become the most reviled of all welfare recipients. To understand this radical shift, we need to examine changing definitions of deservingness and obligation. At each stage, we will see that sympathetic, pitying notions of lone mothers could not successfully counteract apprehension about supporting female-headed households and thereby rendering women less dependent on men. In other words, lone mothers could not stay in the "deserving" category despite the lingering ideology that they should devote full-time to their children.

When the first campaign for public assistance began, in the 1890s, deserted wives were envisaged as the primary recipients (Gordon 1994).[3] Progressive reformers blamed male irresponsibility: "The bread-winner shifts his burdens for bachelor freedom.... If he is at all clever, he can in most cases escape punishment" (Eliot 1900, 346). Social workers set up desertion bureaus to track down the absconders and, just as today, urged punitive action to get non-supporting fathers to provide child support, "making the deserter pay the piper" (Baldwin 1902; see also Zunser 1923). Reformers more conservative about gender provided justifications for deserting husbands. They described deserted wives as untidy, lazy, shiftless, neglectful of housework, intemperate, slovenly, having a "trying disposition," extravagant, and sexually immoral (Smith 1901, 41-42; Brandt 1905; Weyl 1908, 389). The premise here, of course, is that women who deviated from female virtue neither deserved help nor evoked any obligation among others. (Children were invisible in this discourse.)

Yet, in practice, woman-blaming analyses of the sources of desertion did not make things significantly worse for wives who seemed to behave badly. Even in the cases of wives deemed blameless, charity workers were reluctant to offer financial support for fear of encouraging desertion. They presumed that men who knew their families could receive support if they fled would lose their sense of responsibility (Gordon 1988). The result was that deserted wives themselves were made suspect by the stigma of the family form in which they functioned—single-mother families—no matter how blameless or blameworthy they were for landing in that situation.

Widows, who formed the majority of single mothers, came to dominate the discussion later, between 1910 and 1920. The shift did not result from an increase in widowhood; rather, welfare advocates redrew the picture of the single mother, erasing deserted wives and painting in widows, as a state-building strategy. By now they had stirred up enough public concern for unsupported mothers and children that they had a political chance to win public aid, but to do so, they believed, they needed to disarm those who charged that aid encouraged immorality. A chorus of sympathetic studies of the plight of widows emerged from among those who were campaigning for state and local mothers' aid laws (Commonwealth of Massachusetts 1913).

At first, the welfare advocates' new focus on quintessentially blameless widows seemed to succeed. The fervent sympathy widows engendered constituted an argument for public obligation. The widow had a "unique claim on the community" (New York State Commission 1914, 7). Between 1910 and 1920, 40 of the then 48 states instituted programs of public aid for widows. But the discursive strategy of the campaign produced contradictory consequences. Mothers' aid advocates praised widows' morality, forbearance, hard work, and good housekeeping. Of course, the same might have been said of deserted mothers and their children; the widow had become a synonym for the virtuous lone mother, while any woman whose marriage had come unstuck, whatever the circumstances, was suspect. Thus, the widow discourse worked to intensify the stigmatization of other lone mothers; the obvious implication of emphasis on the widow's innocence was, of course, the non-innocence of others.

But widows could not escape a stigma that spread to all lone-mother families. Even the staunchest supporters of public aid insisted on scrutinizing widows' domestic standards closely, examining their housekeeping, their children's cleanliness, whether they drank or had objectionable companions, and making sure they did not consort with men. Even widows were condemned if they did not actively seek employment, appeared inadequately grateful for their relief stipends, or appeared to take those stipends as an entitlement (Gordon 1994).

Unmarried mothers began to figure importantly in this discussion only in the 1920s, after the mothers' aid laws were passed. Progressive-era reformers avoided out-of-wedlock motherhood like a curse because they did not want to call attention to unchastity among potential beneficiaries. When public discussion of illegitimacy began, it was, of course, a moralistic discourse. Out-of-wedlock mothers in the nineteenth century were defined as "fallen women." Progressive-era feminists tried to make this moralistic discourse more sympathetic to the women: emphasizing their youth, positioning them as victims rather than sinners, and offering them opportunities for reform, for a new start. Conservatives were more likely to treat them as problem girls, delinquents (Lundberg and Lenroot 1921; Kunzel 1988). But both sides engaged in biologistic explanations, substituting "feeble-mindedness" where once there had been "hereditary depravity" (Lowe 1927, 793). Even the most sympathetic explanations of illegitimate motherhood were often inaccurate because many out-of-wedlock mothers were formerly married women or married women unable to be divorced, now living in out-of-wedlock partnerships. To understand the long-term impact of out-of-wedlock motherhood on the reputation of welfare, we need, however, to add race to our analysis.

THE RACE OF DESERVINGNESS

Moralism about out-of-wedlock childbirth was thoroughly racialized.

Until the 1940s, social workers tended to see unwed motherhood as arising from the inferior cultures and moral standards of Eastern- and Southern-European immigrants (Brush 1994). When African Americans with a civil rights consciousness began to insist on inclusion in welfare programs, in the 1950s and 1960s, social workers noticed high out-of-wedlock birth rates among blacks, which they interpreted similarly as an "accepted way of life" in an inferior culture. This analysis was often well intended, aimed to counteract stigmatizing individuals, but it also reflected ignorance about the complexity and variability of black family patterns and racist assumptions about black "simplicity." When prosperous whites gave birth out of wedlock, there arose a different explanation. In the 1940s and 1950s, psychiatric influences led social workers to diagnose unmarried pregnancy and childbirth as resulting from emotional disturbance. Black girls, by contrast, were not suspected of having individual motives for their sexual behavior—nor indeed were any signs of individual personality attributed to them; they were merely expressing the standard "low" culture and upbringing of their people. As white unwed mothers became increasingly individualized, medicalized, and interesting, black mothers remained a mass, objects not of medical but of sociological and anthropological investigation (Young 1954; National Council on Illegitimacy 1969; Weatherley 1987; Solinger 1992).

The U.S. system of public provision was also racialized, but its original racial label was "white." The designers of the Social Security Act had envisaged white male workers as characteristic beneficiaries, and race and sex discrimination was then made statutory through a series of congressional amendments excluding various occupational categories. First, amendments to the social insurance programs (Old Age Insurance, Unemployment Compensation) excluded agricultural and domestic workers—and thereby virtually all blacks, Latinos and Latinas, Asians, and American Indians. Amendments then eliminated most remaining women workers by excluding the small businesses, state and local governments, and temporary and part-time jobs in which women's employment was concentrated. Second, amendments to the public assistance programs, such as ADC, which were operated on the basis of joint federal-state funding, eliminated the federal oversight that might have prevented discrimination. State and local authorities were thus left free to determine eligibility, and they did so in grossly discriminatory ways. The southern states were the most notorious in excluding blacks and Latinos or in cutting off their stipends when cheap agricultural or domestic labor was needed. In a bitter irony, the federal government designated most mothers as unemployable when being employable might have allowed them to benefit from the public works jobs created by the New Deal; but the state governmen' s regularly designated women of color as employable when agricultural employers wanted pickers at harvest time, thereby depriving them of the relief

that unemployables were entitled to. The net result of these exclusions and discriminations was that in 1940, only 14 to 17 percent of ADC recipients were black, far below the proportion of their need; by another measure, two-thirds of eligible needy children were not covered by ADC, and those who were covered were disproportionately white—quite an irony in a program that most people imagine as overwhelmingly black today (Bell 1965; Mink 1995).

After World War II, bottom-up activism began to rewrite these definitions of deservingness. Voting with their feet, many poor mothers, especially African American mothers, many of them unmarried, began enrolling in welfare in large numbers. The ADC rolls increased by 17 percent in the 1950s and 107 percent in the 1960s. This has been primarily described as a bad omen. But it was also a sign that women of color were challenging their exclusion, insisting on citizenship rights by claiming welfare. The increase was greatest in cities, where communication about welfare availability was greatest and political assertiveness among the poor, particularly the African American poor, was highest.

Welfare claiming was a part of the civil rights movement. There is today a widespread but mistaken assumption that being on welfare is always a sign of dependency and despair. On the contrary, for many, especially women, going to the welfare office was a step toward citizenship, not only the first entrance into a relationship with the government but also a statement of self-esteem. Welfare claiming and then the 1960s welfare rights movement was also a women's movement. Claiming welfare was a strategy for upward mobility, especially for one's children, a means of keeping them out of the fields, where so many children of color labored, and in school.

STIGMATIZING WELFARE

But the very structure of ADC made its recipients seem undeserving. Local determination of eligibility resulted in inserting a "suitable home" requirement, which became the basis for a great deal of snooping into the private lives of welfare recipients: Did they have boyfriends? Were they buying clothes that were too "nice"? Was their housekeeping adequate? The humiliating and infantilizing surveillance not only forced recipients to be secretive but produced bad publicity that stigmatized welfare in general.

ADC was stigmatized not only by its means testing and morals checking but also by its contrast with programs defined as non-welfare, earned, and therefore free from surveillance. To this programmatic effect were added racist and misogynistic slurs, some coded and some explicit, that maligned welfare recipients as lazy, immoral, and dishonest. In the early 1960s, two nationally publicized welfare cutoffs—in Newburgh, New York, and in Louisiana—helped build antiwelfare sentiment by demonizing ADC recipients. Newburgh City manager Mitchell claimed that "trollops" and the "dregs of humanity" were migrating to his city from the South in order to collect welfare, and this discourse evoked widespread national support. In Louisiana, the legislature, at the request of the governor, expelled mothers of "illegitimate" children from the welfare rolls, thereby throwing 23,000 children, 95 percent of them black, off welfare. Both events featured rhetoric that vilified African American women in particular, and both events defined women as primary recipients in the public view, pushing children into the background (Levenstein 2000).

The repeal of Aid to Families with Dependent Children (AFDC, formerly ADC) in 1996, although promoted by a heavily funded conservative propaganda campaign against welfare, was conditioned on the structure of the welfare state itself. From the beginnings of public welfare programs in the United States, advocates sought political support through the manipulation of a presumably compassionate discourse about innocent, victimized, fragile, and morally pure women and children. That propaganda inadvertently rendered logical and acceptable the prototypical antiwelfare emphasis on immoral women and neglectful, self-centered mothers. In other words, both discourses shared the assumption not only that the state had the authority to hold women to an unrealistic, saintly standard of selflessness and submissiveness but also that the state should supervise and investigate to a degree that would not have been tolerated had the recipients been men. Both of these gendered discourses substituted for and contributed to preventing the grounding of entitlement in concepts of citizenship, collective responsibility, or even equal opportunity.

Moreover, the construction of deservingness emphasized the supposedly charitable nature of public assistance, thus distinguishing its recipients from taxpayers. Defining away the benefits that the welfare state provided to the nonpoor allowed taxpayers to think of themselves only as benefactors and not as beneficiaries, thus defining welfare recipients as parasites. Once deservingness had been the basis for assistance; now receipt of assistance itself became a marker of undeservingness.

True, the fundamental underpinning of antiwelfare sentiment is social structure rather than political structure. The deservingness and undeservingness of welfare recipients both rest on the fact that women raise children. Over time, the racialized nature of poverty in the United States radically escalated antiwelfare sentiment, associating the alleged immorality and parasitism of welfare recipients not only with their gender but also with their race. But the achievement of today's virtual consensus in the United States on the pejorative meanings of welfare dependency could not have been achieved without both the negative and the (allegedly) positive discourses about women and mothers that arose from political advocacy. The 1996 repeal of welfare could not have been achieved without this antidependency chorus, which has created even among decent and generous people the idea that reducing the welfare rolls by forcing women into independence—in reality, an independence characterized by dependence on low-wage labor and disappearance into a ghettoized poverty—represented an achievement.

The notions of deservingness and obligation that underlay the repeal of AFDC and its replacement by a nonmandatory, temporary aid program (Temporary Aid to Needy Families, or TANF) remain today structured by gender, race, and class ideologies so pervasive and hegemonic that they seem like realism or even common sense. Not only are they unsupported by evidence, but they actually defy widespread ethical values. The ethical premise for forcing poor mothers into independence, defined as reliance on wages, represents a repudiation of the value of the work most universally associated with women: parenting. More accurately, the new values represent a class double standard that esteems female parental labor among the prosperous but not among the poor, although the labor is far harder and requires more skill among the poor. Poor mothers who devote themselves to their children are now defined as undeserving.

This lack of deservingness ascribed to our poorest—women and children—serves simultaneously to negate a sense of public obligation to help those who do parenting labor or who lack the advantages to compete for living-wage jobs in the labor market. The denial rests on closely related and equally false ideologies: that there are living-wage jobs for all and that there is equal opportunity to gain the skills necessary for a living wage. As with earlier gendered notions, TANF's values represent in addition a specifically gendered ideology about the wage labor market, one that equally veils reality. The program requires poor mothers to shift their dependence to wage labor while ignoring the realities of women's lower wages and inferior jobs in relation to men, not to mention the realities of the demands of child raising, particularly among the poor.

Pointing out that these beliefs are ideological does not necessarily mean that wage labor is undesirable for poor mothers. Very few households—even those with two parents—can survive now without women's wages. Moreover, studies show repeatedly that most AFDC recipients *want* to support themselves with wages. Where ideology overcame realism is in the use of coercion to force mothers to take jobs rather than beginning by enabling those who wanted to do so to live and support children on these jobs. Not one state has enacted a program that realistically assesses what is needed to support even one mother and one child and then provided it.

Our welfare policy rests on a contradiction—an official honoring of motherhood combined with distrust, disdain, even contempt, for women who do it. As a result, those who were once quintessentially deserving, and to whom the whole society felt obligated—mothers—are often now prime examples of undeservingness, with very little sense of social obligation to aid them in their child-raising work. In fact, this contradiction extends to our overall policy toward working women and all poor women, whether they are lone mothers or not. The politicized family values of the last three decades often rest on denial of the actual difficulties of simultaneously earning for and caring for children, difficulties particularly great for low-wage-earning women.

Notes

1. When the Social Security Act was passed in 1935, the phrase "social security" was understood to refer to all types of programs of government provision, including aid to the elderly, the handicapped, the unemployed, the poor, and so on. Over three or four decades, the label migrated to refer specifically to old-age pensions, but in the 1930s and 1940s pensions were referred to by specific program titles, including Old Age Insurance and Old Age Assistance.

2. ADC became AFDC, Aid to Families with Dependent Children, in 1962 when coverage was extended to two-parent families, and AFDC-UP in 1961 when coverage was extended to two-parent families with unemployed fathers. In 1996, the program was repealed. It was replaced with Temporary Aid to Needy Families, which provides no guarantee of help and limits recipients to a certain number of years of aid.

3. Today, we would call these separated women. To understand the then common notion of desertion, we must recall the nineteenth-century Christian family and gender system that, in theory at any rate, considered marriage as an eternal sacrament and women as inevitably the weaker sex. Very few Americans at this time approved of breaking a marriage covenant. In such sinful behavior, there was a sinner and a sinned against; marital separation was rarely conceived of as mutual, a concept that expresses a greater acceptance (characteristic of the late twentieth century) of separation as an honorable alternative and of marriage as a human, not a divine, institution. Moreover, both feminists and antifeminists as well as most people in between agreed that women were usually the victims of marital breakup because of their economic dependence on men and their social and political subordination.

References

Baldwin, William. 1902. Making the Deserter Pay the Piper. *Survey* 23(20
Nov.):249-52.

Bell, Winifred. 1965. *Aid to Dependent
Children*. New York: Columbia University Press.

Brandt, Lilian. 1905. *Five Hundred and
Seventy-Four Deserters and Their
Families: A Descriptive Study of Their
Characteristics and Circumstances*. Com-
mittee on Social Research, no. 1. New
York: Charity Organization Society.

Breckinridge, Sophonisba P. 1928. The
Home Responsibilities of Women
Workers and the "Equal Wage." *Jour-
nal of Political Economy* 31.

Brush, Lisa, 1994. Worthy Widows, Welfare Cheats: Construing Single
Mothers, Constructing the U.S. Welfare State, 1900-1988. Ph.D. diss., Department of Sociology, University of
Wisconsin.

Coll, Blanche. 1988. Public Assistance:
Reviving the Original Comprehensive
Concept of Social Security. In *Social
Security: The First Half Century*, ed.
Gerald D. Nash, Noel H. Pugach, and
Richard F. Romasson. Albuquerque:
University of New Mexico Press.

Committee on Economic Security. 1937.
Social Security in America. Social Se-
curity Board, no. 20. Washington, DC:
Social Security Board.

Commonwealth of Massachusetts. 1913.
*Report of the Commission on the Sup-
port of Dependent Minor Children of
Widowed Mothers*. Boston: Wright &
Potter.

Douglas, Dorothy Wolf. 1920. The Cost of
Living for Working Women: A Criti-
cism of Current Theories. *Quarterly
Journal of Economics* 34:225-59.

Eliot, Ada. 1900. Deserted Wives. *Charities Review* 10(5):346-49.

Gordon, Colin. Forthcoming. *Dead on Ar-
rival*. Princeton, NJ: Princeton University Press.

Gordon, Linda. 1988. *Heroes of Their
Own Lives: The Politics and History of
Family Violence*. New York: Viking/
Penguin.

———. 1994. *Pitied but Not Entitled: Single Mothers and the History of Welfare*.
New York: Free Press.

Gordon, Linda and Sara McLanahan.
1991. Single Parenthood in 1900.
Journal of Family History 16(2):97-
116.

Hughes, Gwendolyn Salisbury. 1925.
*Mothers in Industry: Wage-Earning by
Mothers in Philadelphia*. New York:
New Republic.

Kessler-Harris, Alice. 1995. Designing
Women and Old Fools: The Construc-
tion of the Social Security Amend-
ments of 1939. In *U.S. History as
Women's History*, ed. Linda K. Kerber,
Alice Kessler-Harris, and Kathryn
Kish Sklar. Chapel Hill: University of
North Carolina Press.

Kunzel, Regina P. 1988. The Professionalization of Benevolence: Evan-
gelicals and Social Workers in the
Florence Crittenden Homes, 1915-
1945. *Journal of Social History*
22(1):21-44.

Levenstein, Lisa. 2000. From Innocent
Children to Unwanted Migrants and
Unwed Moms: Two Chapters in the
Public Discourse on Welfare in the
United States, 1960-61. *Journal of
Women's History* 11(Winter).

Lowe, Charlotte. 1927. The Intelligence
and Social Background of the Unmarried Mother. *Mental Hygiene* 11(4):
793.

Lundberg, Emma and Katharine F.
Lenroot. 1921. *Illegitimacy as a Child-
Welfare Problem*. U.S. Children's Bu-
reau, no. 75. Dependent, Defective,
and Delinquent Classes series, no. 10.
Washington, DC: U.S. Department of
Labor.

Mink, Gwendolyn. 1995. *The Wages of
Motherhood: Inequality in the Welfare*

State, 1917-1942. Ithaca, NY: Cornell University Press.

National Council on Illegitimacy. 1969. *The Double Jeopardy, the Triple Crisis—Illegitimacy Today*. New York: National Council on Illegitimacy.

New York State Commission on Relief for Widowed Mothers. 1914. Final Report. New York: New York State Commission on Relief for Widowed Mothers.

Skocpol, Theda. 1992. The Narrow Vision of Today's Experts on Social Policy. *Chronicle of Higher Education*, 15 Apr.

Smith, Zilpha. 1901. *Deserted Wives and Deserving Husbands: A Study of 234 Families*. Boston: Geo. H. Ellis.

Solinger, Rickie. 1992. *Wake Up Little Susie: Single Pregnancy and Race Before* Roe v. Wade. New York: Routledge.

Weatherley, Richard A. 1987. Teenage Pregnancy, Professional Agendas, and Problem Definitions. *Journal of Sociology and Social Welfare* 14(2):5-35.

Weyl, Walter E. 1908. The Deserter. *Charities and the Commons* 21(5 Dec.):389.

Young, Leontine. 1954. *Out of Wedlock*. New York: McGraw-Hill.

Zunser, Charles. 1923. The National Desertion Bureau. In *Proceedings*. New York: National Conference of Jewish Social Service.

ANNALS, *AAPSS*, **577**, September 2001

Globalization, American Politics, and Welfare Policy

By FRANCES FOX PIVEN

ABSTRACT: The welfare state is under attack in all of the rich countries where it flourished over the course of the twentieth century. Rollbacks are said to be imperative. The big argument for why this is so emphasizes globalization and technological change, which together have heightened international trade and investment competition. But rather than a widespread race to the bottom that these economic determinants would suggest, welfare state outcomes have been very different from country to country. These variations, and in particular the fact that the United States has been the rollback pioneer, argue that politics plays a large role in contemporary welfare state politics. American developments are best explained by paying attention to the political mobilization of business over the past two decades, on the one hand, and the uses of the politics of resentment and marginalization on the other hand.

Frances Fox Piven is on the faculty of the Graduate Center of the City University of New York. She is the author (with Richard Cloward) of Regulating the Poor, Poor Peoples' Movements, The Breaking of the American Social Compact, *and* Why Americans Still Don't Vote.

A T first glance, the pattern seems similar in most Western countries. All have income protection programs, won in response to the political mobilization of poor and working people over the course of the twentieth century. And efforts to roll back these programs—old-age pensions, disability allowances, unemployment insurance, social assistance or poor relief programs, and a range of other public services—are under way everywhere.

Moreover, in all of these countries, a similar argument is being made about the economic imperatives that are forcing changes in social policy. It goes like this. The social programs to which we have become accustomed made sense in an industrial era. But now we are in a new era. The economies of industrial countries have been transformed by globalization and by the electronic and transportation networks that make globalization possible. The capital mobility and accelerated trade that are the signposts of globalization mean that domestic producers, and entire domestic economies, confront intensified worldwide competition. Workers in the mother countries, whether Germany, France, or the United States, must compete with workers across the globe. And because globalization also means that capital races around the globe at the click of a mouse to take advantage of low wages and low taxes, governments themselves are pitted against each other in the contest to attract investors.

Under these conditions, the argument goes, the relatively generous social programs of the industrial era have become dysfunctional. Income support programs increase wage costs and interfere with competitiveness. They do this both because they require high taxes, whether payroll taxes or taxes on capital, and because they create a reservation wage, a floor below which wages cannot fall. The conclusion seems inescapable: generous social programs make domestic production uncompetitive and drive investment elsewhere.

The same argument is made in all of the rich democracies. But it is not equally successful everywhere. In continental Europe, actual program cuts have been modest, and this despite the vigor with which the Organization for Economic Cooperation and Development (OECD) has called for rollbacks in social programs to promote what is called "wage flexibility." The reason is simply that politicians do not dare! Popular resistance is too vigorous, rooted in political traditions that support an expanded public sector. Moreover, in many of these countries, unions have remained strong, and unions understand the role of generous social programs in undergirding wage levels (International Labor Organization 1997, tabs. 1.2 and 3.2). Consequently, wages in continental Europe have not fallen as they have in the United States over the past 25 years, and poverty levels have not risen (Gottschalk and Smeeding 1997). Still, the campaign to reform the European welfare state continues, and it is strident, insistent, and has powerful backers.

In that campaign, the United States is regularly pointed to as the exemplar, as the nation on which other rich democratic nations should model themselves. (Model USA was the title of a recent well-attended conference in Berlin.) First, the story is told of America's apparent economic success. We have lower unemployment levels, higher rates of economic growth, and extraordinary rates of growth in profits, all this in contrast to Western Europe. And why? The answer is because our wages are lower and more flexible. And wage flexibility in turn is traced to our different social policies. Not only did the United States enter the era of globalization with less generous social programs, but it has since made big cuts in these limited programs. And not unexpectedly, big cuts in social protections have been accompanied by declining wages. This of course is exactly what the OECD means by its call for wage flexibility. When public income supports that undergird wages are rolled back, workers are inevitably less secure, and it becomes easier for employers to roll back wages and restructure work. It's as simple as that.

The implications of this argument are chilling. For one thing, the logic of the argument means that workers everywhere must now accept wages driven down toward the level of the wages paid to the poorest workers in the world. The implications are especially chilling for democratic politics because the argument asserts that governments are helpless in the face of the threat of capital flight, and if governments are helpless, then so are citizens helpless. Indeed, citizenship loses much of its meaning if governments cannot act on matters crucial to the economic well-being of ordinary people. In this sense, democratic rights are rolled back along with the social programs.

But is it true that economic globalization is the force behind welfare rollbacks? Not according to the evidence. Although the argument that the welfare state impedes a global economy is louder and shriller in the United States, and although the United States has been the leader in actual social program cutbacks, the United States is far from a leader in economic globalization (Page, Simmons, and Greer 2000). Because imports and exports account for a smaller share of our gross domestic product, the American economy is in fact less exposed to international trade than are most European countries with export-oriented open economies.

Moreover, while U.S. multinationals are indeed leaders in overseas investments, most of their investments are in Western Europe (Tabb 1997). If competitive pressures were in fact the underlying reason for social program cutbacks, we would expect American investors to be seeking out locations with lower taxes and lower wages. In fact, when our big corporations invest abroad, it is mainly in Western countries with higher wages and higher tax levels.

What the American example actually suggests, I believe, is a model of a country adapting not to globalization but rather to the impact of politics, of class politics, and specifically, of a business class on a roll as it moves to use public policy to shore up private profits (Helleiner 1994, 1997). Of course, business is not the whole story. The path for a business political mobilization was smoothed by the weakness of popular opposition, especially during the past three decades. That weakness is partly owed to longstanding features of American politics: fragmented, weak political parties that privilege interest groups; the feebleness of organized labor; a political ideology with which the essentially mystical neoliberal argument about the necessary power and autonomy of markets, an updated version of laissez-faire, resonates easily; and a popular political culture deeply infused with racism and with sexual obsessions, as the debate over welfare showed once again.

THE POLITICS OF GREED

The logic of these changes in American social policy is not the anonymous logic of competitive global markets. Rather, it is the logic of unfettered greed.

Look at some of the evidence. The mobilization of the business community for an aggressive big grab began in the early 1970s. It unfolded first in the workplace, with a direct attack on unions, on wages and benefits, and on workplace protections. This campaign largely succeeded. New union organizing efforts were halted, and even established unions were rolled back, sometimes in unprecedented business campaigns for union decertification. With unions on the defensive, employers introduced two-tier employment, shifted from permanent to contingent workers, and implemented massive downsizings and speed-ups. No longer was a job at the auto plant a job for life and a job for your kids. The resulting pervasive insecurity among workers contributed to the success of persistent business efforts to reduce wages and benefits.

Business also mobilized to push for public policies that would shore up profits (Edsall 1984; Ferguson and Rogers 1986; Greider 1992; Judis 2000). By the late 1970s, it was able to halt most Carter administration regulatory or labor-oriented initiatives, and in the 1980 election, business threw its weight behind Ronald Reagan with his business agenda of tax cuts, a military buildup, and the rollback of regulatory controls and social program expenditures. The tax cuts of 1981 began a process that slashed the effective rate of taxation on the American rich from about 50 percent in 1980 to about 28 percent today. The military buildup was also a business grab, benefiting mainly our huge defense industry. Together, tax cuts and rising defense expenditures inevitably produced a large deficit and initiated the long period during which the growing deficit was regularly used as a club against social spending.

During the 1980s, this agenda met only mixed success. In particular, Congress resisted the cuts in social spending. But the business-Republican alliance persisted and persists. The last minimum wage bill was loaded with special interest tax cuts, as is the new minimum wage bill taking form in the Congress. The argument is incredible: if poor workers are insured a $5.15 minimum wage, the government has to make it up to businesses by reducing their taxes.

Huge tax cuts are again at the top of the agenda of the new Bush administration.

Meanwhile, government income support programs were steadily whittled back. Unemployment insurance benefits reached more than half of the unemployed during the 1970s and more than two-thirds during the mid-decade recession. By the 1980s, only a third of the unemployed were protected. The disability insurance rolls were also slashed in the early 1980s. And largely unnoticed, eligibility for social security was narrowed by raising the age at which seniors become entitled to full benefits to age 67, albeit so gradually, by one month a year, that the change was largely unnoticed and unopposed. And, of course, means-tested benefits were slashed (Piven 1997; Piven and Cloward 1993).

Public attention has mainly been focused on cuts in the programs that provide income supports to women and children and especially on the changes in welfare initiated by the Personal Responsibility and Work Opportunity Reconciliation Act (PRWORA) of 1996. In fact, the rollback of means-tested benefits began in the early 1970s and took the form of allowing inflation to erode the real value of benefits, by one-third between the early 1970s and the mid-1990s, while politicians began the assault on welfare mothers for their sexual and work behavior that culminated in the passage of the PRWORA, the capstone of this development. The PRWORA shifted to the states administrative authority over assistance to families headed by poor women; imposed time limits on assistance, including lifetime limits; required work as a condition for cash assistance, often by assigning women to work in private businesses or public agencies in exchange for their welfare grants; increased the behavioral monitoring of women as a condition for assistance; and reduced or eliminated in-kind food and medical assistance for many people as well.

The devolution of authority to the states in the PRWORA was important particularly because of the political advantages that state responsibility yields to the campaign against welfare. For one thing, many state capitols are now presided over by Republican governors. Even were that to change, there are other features of state politics that disadvantage the less powerful. For one thing, the politics of the state capitals are even murkier than the politics of Washington. There is less scrutiny from the press, for example. Even more important, state governments are inevitably more responsive to business, not only because they are shielded from public scrutiny but because state officials are acutely sensitive to the threat that mobile businesses will leave the state if they fail to win their demands from the state government. The new state-run welfare programs are, in other words, for structural reasons likely to be more responsive to the labor market interests of business and less responsive to the interests of the poor (Piven and Cloward 1985).

Given these developments, we should look a little more closely at the American economic success story. It is true that American unemployment levels are lower than those in West-

ern Europe (although unemployment is now declining in Europe).
And American profit levels are up, by
more than 100 percent since 1990.
CEOs' earnings are up much more,
by over 500 percent (Straus 2000;
Wolman and Colamosca 1997). And
of course, the stock market is boom-
ing. Overall, the top 1 percent of
Americans now controls 42 percent of
American wealth, a pattern familiar
in the so-called banana republics
(Wolff 1995). Sixty percent of all
gains in after-tax income have also
gone to the top 1 percent.

But viewed from the perspective of
the economic well-being of ordinary
people, the picture is quite different.
Average workers' wages are down by
about 10 percent since the 1970s,
despite the boom. Low-wage workers
are, to be sure, now seeing an increase in their take-home pay, but
the rise is still quite modest. Despite
the unprecedented length of the economic recovery, they have not fully
recovered from a two-decade pum-
meling that especially affected wages
among low earners (Bernstein and
Greenberg 2001). The real value of
the minimum wage is lower than it
was in the 1960s, when a family of
three with a minimum wage earner
was comfortably above the poverty
line. Today that family is below the
poverty line, and 20 percent of those
families have no employment-based
health or retirement benefits at all.
Western Europe presumably lags in
the social policy adjustments necessary for economic success in a global
world. But perhaps it is for just
that reason that Western Europe has
not experienced widening income in-

equality and stagnating wages comparable to the American pattern.

THE ARGUMENTS
AGAINST WELFARE

If so many people were harmed by
these new policies, why was there
so little political protest? Welfare
reform became the symbolic core of a
broad ideological campaign against
government income maintenance
programs. We all remember the deaf-
ening political roar generated by the
campaign against welfare. Arguments that had been bubbling on the
cookstoves of right-wing think tanks
for two decades burst onto the
talk shows, dominated the editorial
pages, were seized upon by state governors, and then blasted forth by
Congress and the president (Williams 1996).

We were told, again and again,
that while our so-generous welfare
system spoke well of the kindly spirit
of the American people, it was nevertheless bad for our society. Generosity had had perverse effects of two
kinds. First, a too generous welfare
system was leading people to become
slackers, to give up on work. (This
was actually the same argument that
the OECD has been making when it
says that generous European social
programs created wage inflexibility,
with deleterious consequences for
competitiveness.) Talk show guests
and politicians explained endlessly
that because these women were too
comfortable on welfare, they were
shunning work for wages.

The argument was made with a
good deal of animus, as evidenced by
the reiteration of the phrase "welfare

dependency," as if welfare were addictive. But if we leave this to one side, there was a certain logic in the view that there was a relationship between work and welfare (Danziger, Haveman, and Plotnick 1981). If women and their children could survive on welfare, they would not take low-wage work that did not improve their circumstances by providing a little more income and a little more respect. Quite logical. But note, the logic also makes room for a far more benign policy alternative than slashing welfare. If the concern was that welfare created a work disincentive, then the crusaders against welfare dependency could have proposed that we make work more rewarding, for example, by raising wages. Or that we provide health care to low-wage workers. Or that we guarantee reliable child care to ease the anxiety of poor working women about their children. These reforms can be justified by the same logic as the logic that justifies cutting welfare to enforce work. But of course nobody talked about the benign reform possibilities to which a concern with work might lead. Instead, the focus was on the "tough love" measures, benefit cuts, sanctions, forced work, and behavioral controls.

Even more excited and heated than the talk about the disincentive effects of welfare on work was the talk about the perverse effects of welfare on sexual and family morality. The availability of welfare to mothers, it was said, encouraged women, especially teenagers, to have out-of-wedlock babies. The argument seemed to dominate discussion in Congress and especially in the erstwhile more dignified Senate.

But the political talk ignored virtually all of the data that we have about out-of-wedlock births (Moffitt 1995). It ignored the fact that out-of-wedlock births have been increasing across the globe and in countries where women have no prospect of a welfare check. It ignored the fact that out-of-wedlock births were increasing among all income strata in the United States, not just among poor women who were, in a sense, at risk of welfare receipt. It also ignored the fact that out-of-wedlock births continued to increase even as welfare benefits fell, and fell sharply, in the 1970s and 1980s. It ignored the fact that there was no correlation between the rate of out-of-wedlock births and state welfare grant levels. And finally, it ignored comparative international evidence that shows no correlation whatsoever between rates of out-of-wedlock births and the generosity of welfare (or social assistance). In fact, in the United States, where benefit levels are very low, teenage out-of-wedlock birth rates are very high—two to six times higher than in the much more generous European welfare states. How, then, could the availability of generous benefits be to blame for out-of-wedlock births?

Opponents of welfare retrenchment tried to answer by showing that the facts being bruited about were wrong. But facts alone were a weak weapon in the face of a propaganda campaign tapping deep cultural antipathies and fueled by powerful economic and political interests.

THE NEW
WELFARE REGIME

Some of the consequences of the new social policy regime are now becoming apparent. The lower tiers of the labor market are already characterized by growing instability and insecurity as a result of job restructuring and growing reliance on contingent workers. To this mix we are now adding several million desperately poor women who have lost their welfare benefits and now compete with other low-wage workers for jobs that are already insecure (Gault and Um'rani 2000). As a consequence, despite low levels of unemployment, insecurity is increasing at the bottom of the labor market.

In some places, the welfare work programs are creating a virtually indentured labor force (Peck 2001). In Baltimore, for example, welfare recipients were used to break a strike of housekeepers in the Baltimore Omni Hotel. In New York City, some 45,000 welfare recipients are now cleaning the streets and the subways, doing jobs previously held by unionized public workers. In Mississippi, welfare recipients are assigned to chicken-processing and catfish plants, and one manager told the press cheerfully that he had been assured by welfare officials that women who did not work out at the plant would not be given welfare again.

Consider also the implications of the public spectacle created by the new welfare regime. Until it became clear that the practice was too outlandish, New York City workfare recipients were made to wear Day-Glo orange vests as they went about the streets and subways with their brooms and trash baskets. This public spectacle is important. Mickey Kaus (1986), writing in the *New Republic*, called for putting welfare recipients to work in the streets, scrubbing cobblestones for example. And the reason he gave for making Betsy M. get down on her knees with a scrub brush was not only to punish her but to give those who saw her a lesson in the degradation awaiting anyone who had an out-of-wedlock birth and did not work for wages.

The provisions barring legal immigrants from a range of benefits have similar work-enforcing effects. It is an especially ironic policy development. Very few immigrants, especially very few Latino immigrants, come into the country to go on welfare or Supplementary Security Income. They come for jobs. And the politicians cheering for welfare cutbacks, including cutbacks that single out legal immigrants, were generally in favor of relatively liberal immigration policies, as American business and its politician allies have been since the nineteenth century. A plentiful flow of immigrants means, after all, plenty of vulnerable people willing to take low-wage jobs. And by denying those people any recourse to government benefits, they are kept even more vulnerable, ensuring that their wages will remain low.

WHAT HAPPENED TO
DEMOCRATIC POLITICS?

The rise of business power was made easier by longstanding obstacles to the influence of ordinary Americans. This was no time more obvious than in the 1990s when both Republicans and Democrats actually ran on an agenda that promised to make conditions worse for a broad swath of the American people. When income supports were slashed not only did women on welfare suffer but so did the very large numbers of people whose wages and working conditions deteriorated as an indirect consequence. Even the direct con-sequences are substantial. The Public Policy Institute of California, for example, estimated that one-third of the families in California would lose income as a result of the new welfare regime. Yet there was overwhelming public support of PRWORA. How is this possible?

Public attitudes were influenced in part by the force of the argument that governments are helpless in the face of markets. These nineteenth-century laissez-faire themes gained new credibility because they were tied to globalization. Markets were now international markets, and government had to get out of the way because it had no power over international markets.

Furthermore, the Democratic Party did not resurrect popular economic issues as a campaign strategy. To be sure, Bill Clinton's slogan in 1992 was "It's the economy, stupid." But once in office, he did not follow through. Cowed by Alan Greenspan, head of the Federal Reserve, cowed by his investor-banker allies like Robert Rubin, cowed by his fat-cat contributors, Clinton allowed his very modest economic stimulus package to fail and proceeded to lead the Democratic Party with talk of family values and calls for v-chips and

school uniforms, even while he championed free trade and social program cutbacks. No wonder that the usual economic indicators failed to predict the outcome of the 2000 election.

But there was another political strategy at work to win votes. Everywhere in the world, when people are blocked from a politics that deals with the material problems of their daily life, that addresses the real substantive problems of their families and communities, they become susceptible to extremist and fundamentalist appeals. When institutional reforms seem impossible, people respond more readily to calls for individual moral rejuvenation, appeals based on resentment, and political arguments that blame vulnerable groups for society's troubles.

The arguments of the Right, of the new think tanks and the public intellectuals they support—people like Martin Andersen (1978), George Gilder (1981), Charles Murray (1984), or Lawrence Mead (1986)—are attempts to substitute calls for moral rejuvenation, coupled with castigation of the Other, for a politics that hinges on popular economic well-being. Hence we are told not only that government programs undermine our competitive position in the world economy but that they also undermine our moral fiber. Generous social policies cause worklessness, social disorganization, family breakdown, and so on. And it is not a coincidence that the arguments are heavily laced with racial allusions that take advantage of deep-seated racial resentments. Nor is it an accident that they are so steeped in the strange preoccupations with sexual behavior that characterize American culture and that were the basis for the alliance of the Christian Right with the business-led political mobilization of the past two decades.

Thus the campaign for welfare reform told a story, with pernicious effects for American politics. In a way, the story was about the nation's travails, about economic insecurity, about hard work and too much work,[1] about rising inequality. But the main actors in this story were not the corporations that dominate our economy and our politics. Rather, the main actors were poor women, especially poor women of color. In the story, these women were to blame for poverty, for social disorganization, for family breakdown, for the weakening of morality in America, and for all the economic anxieties Americans feel. It is a powerful story because it evokes the demons of our culturally informed imagination, the demons of poor people and dark-skinned people, and our insane preoccupation with the sexual license of women.

But this was not just a right-wing strategy. Even as Clinton was campaigning in 1992 on "It's the economy, stupid," he also raised the slogans of "End welfare as we know it" and "Two years and off to work." His pollsters told him the slogans struck a chord. Clinton had stumbled on the uses of the angry politics of resentment. The result was a contest between Republicans and Democrats, between national and state politicians, to own the welfare issue. And welfare reform is the consequence.

The welfare reform legislation is up for renewal in 2002. Is it possible to undo its most pernicious features, including time limits and work requirements, and the license it gives the states to refuse aid to poor women and to freely use sanctions to slash or terminate benefits to those already on the rolls? At first glance, the prospects seem grim. Politicians and the media seem never to tire of applauding the new welfare regime's success at lowering the numbers of women and children who receive aid (see Schram and Soss's article in this volume). By contrast, the hardships that result receive little or no attention. The new Bush administration and the cabal of businessmen it will elevate to power is surely unlikely to propose any reversals of the new practices (Vulliamy 2000; Palast 2000). Tommy Thompson, governor of Wisconsin and renowned as a pioneer of state-level welfare reform, is secretary of the Department of Health and Human Services. Thompson is applauded for the dramatic decline in Wisconsin's welfare rolls. There is less attention to the increase in extreme poverty in Wisconsin that has accompanied that decline.

In the short term, the prospects for a kinder welfare policy seem unlikely. But we should remember that all this is unfolding in the realm of politics, and it is not a politics predetermined by immutable and exogenous economic developments. The propelling force behind the campaign against welfare arises not from some quasi-mystical economic globalization but from business politics and from the political ideas and political strategies conceived by business and the political Right.

They are not likely to dominate the political stage forever. After all, even the Malthusian-inspired poor law that the PRWORA so much resembles, a law promoted by the rising English manufacturing class in 1834, was ultimately defeated by popular opposition. As the consequences of the new regime unfold, and especially as the business cycle turns, ordinary people and especially poor people are likely to regain their footing and their common sense. They will begin to penetrate ruling-class propaganda and develop their own assessments of their situation. This capacity for a measure of independence, of invention, of defiance, and the protest movements that result, has always been the real source of reform in American politics.

In the meantime, it is important to keep alive and to nourish the understandings about a gentler and more protective society that undergirded the development of social programs, however flawed particular programs might have been. To destroy these programs and leave so little in their stead is to allow life to become a jungle for our most vulnerable people.

Note

1. According to the U.S. Bureau of Labor Statistics, between 1976 and 1993 the average employed man added 100 hours of work per year, while the average employed woman increased her working time by 233 hours (*Left Business Observer* 1997).

References

Andersen, Martin. 1978. *Welfare: The Political Economy of Welfare Reform in the United States*. Stanford, CA: Hoover Institution.

Bernstein, Jared and Mark Greenberg. 2001. Reforming Welfare Reform. *American Prospect* 12(1):10-17.

Danziger, Sheldon, Robert Haveman, and Robert Plotnick. 1981. How Income Transfer Programs Affect Work, Savings, and the Income Distribution: A Critical Review. *Journal of Economic Literature* 19:975-1028.

Edsall, Thomas Byrne. 1984. *The New Politics of Inequality*. New York: Norton.

Ferguson, Thomas and Joel Rogers. 1986. *Right Turn: The Decline of the Democrats and the Future of American Politics*. New York: Hill and Wang.

Gault, Barbara and Annisah Um'rani. 2000. The Outcomes of Welfare Reform for Women. *Poverty & Race* 9(4):1-2, 6.

Gilder, George. 1981. *Wealth and Poverty*. New York: Basic Books.

Gottschalk, Peter and Timothy Smeeding. 1997. Cross-National Comparisons of Earnings and Income Inequality. *Journal of Economic Literature* 35: 633-88.

Greider, William. 1992. *Who Will Tell the People: The Betrayal of American Democracy*. New York: Simon & Schuster.

Helleiner, Eric. 1994. *States and the Reemergence of Global Finance: From Bretton Woods to the 1990s*. Ithaca, NY: Cornell University Press.

———. 1997. Markets, Politics and Globalization: Can the Global Economy Be Civilized? The 10th Raul Prebisch Lecture, Geneva, 11 Dec.

International Labor Organization. 1997. *World Labor Report 1997-98*. Geneva: International Labor Organization.

Judis, John B. 2000. *The Paradox of American Democracy*. New York: Pantheon.

Kaus, Mickey. 1986. The Work Ethic State. *New Republic*, 6 July.

Left Business Observer. 1997. No. 77, 14 May.

Mead, Lawrence. 1986. *Beyond Entitlement: The Social Obligations of Citizenship.* New York: Free Press.

Moffitt, Robert A. 1995. The Effect of the Welfare System on Nonmarital Fertility. In *A Report to Congress on Out-of-Wedlock Childbearing.* Washington, DC: U.S. Department of Health and Human Services, National Center of Health Statistics.

Murray, Charles. 1984. *Losing Ground: American Social Policy, 1950-1980.* New York: Basic Books.

Page, Benjamin I., James R. Simmons, and Scott Greer. 2000. What Government Can Do About Poverty and Inequality: Global Constraints. Paper presented at the annual meeting of the American Political Science Association, Washington, DC, 31 Aug.-3 Sept.

Palast, Gregory. 2000. Best Democracy Money Can Buy. *The Guardian,* 25 Nov.

Peck, Jamie. 2001. *Workfare States.* New York: Guilford.

Piven, Frances Fox. 1997. The New Reserve Army of Labor. In *Audacious Democracy*, ed. Steven Fraser and Joshua B. Freeman. New York: Houghton Mifflin.

Piven, Frances Fox and Richard A. Cloward. 1985. *The New Class War.* New York: Pantheon.

———. 1993. *Regulating the Poor.* New York: Pantheon.

Tabb, William. 1997. Globalization Is *an* Issue, the Power of Capital Is *the* Issue. *Monthly Review,* June.

Straus, Tamara. 2000. Study Finds Dangerous Rise in Corporate Power. Available at http://www.alternet.org/beta/story.html?StoryID=10184. Accessed 7 Dec.

Vulliamy, Ed. 2000. Ed Vulliamy in Washington. *The Observer,* 3 Dec. Available at http://www.observor.co.uk/print/O,3858,4099753,00.htm.

Williams, Lucy A. 1996. The Right's Attack on Aid to Families with Dependent Children. *Public Eye* 10(3-4):1-18.

Wolff, Edward N. 1995. How the Pie Is Sliced: America's Growing Concentration of Wealth. *American Prospect* (Summer):58-64.

Wolman, William and Anne Colamosca. 1997. *The Judas Economy: The Triumph of Capital and the Betrayal of Work.* Reading, MA: Addison-Wesley.

ANNALS, *AAPSS*, **577**, September 2001

Welfare Reform, Family Hardship, and Women of Color

By LINDA BURNHAM

ABSTRACT: Welfare reform has increased the hardships faced by many women leaving welfare for work. Their movement into low-wage jobs, or to no work, exposes them to higher levels of housing insecurity, homelessness, food insecurity, and hunger. Women of color, overrepresented on the welfare rolls, are especially vulnerable to the negative impacts of welfare reform.

Linda Burnham is cofounder and executive director of the Women of Color Resource Center, a nonprofit education, community action, and resource center committed to developing a strong, institutional foundation for social change activism by and on behalf of women of color. Her most recent publications include Women's Education in the Global Economy, *a workbook on the impact of the global economy on women coauthored with Miriam Louie, and* Working Hard, Staying Poor, *coauthored with Kaaryn Gustafson, a study of the impact of welfare reform on poor women and their families.*

NOTE: This article is based on *Working Hard, Staying Poor: Women and Children in the Wake of Welfare Reform*, coauthored with Kaaryn Gustafson, published in June 2000 by the Women of Color Resource Center. The full report may be ordered at www.coloredgirls.org.

S IX years ago, tens of thousands of women's and human rights activists gathered at the United Nations Fourth World Conference on Women, held in Beijing, China, to focus their attention on improving the condition and status of women worldwide. Working through cultural, religious, political, economic, and regional differences, women from the nations of the world produced a comprehensive document, the Beijing Platform for Action, that detailed actions to be taken by governments, nongovernmental organizations, and multilateral financial and developmental institutions to improve women's conditions. The platform for action called on governments to take action to relieve "the persistent and increasing burden of poverty on women" and address gender "inequality in economic structures and policies, in all forms of productive activities and in access to resources" (United Nations 1995).

Yet, in the six years since Beijing, in a time of unparalleled national prosperity, policies contradictory to the spirit and intent of the platform for action were promulgated in the United States, targeting the most vulnerable citizens and, rather than assisting women onto the path of economic security, driving many deeper into poverty. While U.S. officials pledged in international forums to uphold women's human rights, those rights were substantially undermined by the 1996 passage of the Personal Responsibility and Work Opportunities Reconciliation Act (PRWORA).

INCREASING FAMILY HARDSHIP

There are many studies that document how much worse off women are due to welfare reform. Those who remain in the welfare system, those who leave for employment, and those who might have used Aid to Families with Dependent Children (AFDC) are in worse shape, with less support, than the woefully inadequate earlier system provided. Only a few highlights of the growing grief will be highlighted here, before turning to the particular problems facing immigrants and women of color, and then briefly returning to place them in the context of international human rights.

The stated intent of welfare reform was at least twofold: to reduce the welfare rolls and to move women toward economic self-sufficiency. The first objective has been achieved; welfare rolls have declined dramatically since 1996. Welfare reform has stripped single mothers of any sense that they are entitled to government support during the years when they are raising their children.

Despite the "success" of welfare reform, research has repeatedly found that many women who move from welfare to work do not achieve economic independence. Instead, most find only low-paid, insecure jobs that do not lift their families above the poverty line. They end up worse off economically than they were on welfare: they work hard and remain poor. Others are pushed off welfare and find no employment. They have no reported source of income.

Women in transition from welfare to work—or to no work—face particular difficulties and crises related to housing insecurity and homelessness and food insecurity and hunger.

Low-income people in the United States faced a housing crisis long before the passage of the PRWORA. In most states, the median fair-market cost of housing for a family of three is considerably higher than total income from a Temporary Aid to Needy Families (TANF) grant (Dolbeare 1999). Further, as a consequence of two decades of declining federal support for public and subsidized housing, the great majority of both current and former TANF recipients are at the mercy of an unforgiving private housing market.

The withdrawal of the federal government's commitment to need-based income support adds a powerful destabilizing element to already tenuous conditions. The evidence that welfare reform is contributing to rising levels of housing insecurity and homelessness is piling up. The author of one recent study noted, "Young children are without homes in the largest numbers since the Great Depression. Welfare reform has made things much worse. Shelters are overflowing and gridlocked" (Griffin 1999, 4A).

Utility payment problems are another important indicator of housing insecurity because they reveal that many families, while they may have a roof over them, spend at least some time without heat and light. And utility problems are often a prelude to inability to pay the rent. A 1998 survey of social service clients who had left welfare within the previous six months found that 25 percent had had their heat cut off (Sherman et al. 1998, 13). A recent Illinois study found that 61 percent of TANF recipients who were not working could not pay their utility bills. But former recipients who were working were also struggling with their budgets, and 48 percent were unable to meet their utility payments (Work, Welfare and Families 2000, 25).

Confronting the absurd and agonizing decision of whether to feed their children or house them, most mothers will use the rent money to buy food and then struggle to deal with the consequences. In one national study, 23 percent of former welfare recipients moved because they could not pay the rent (Sherman et al. 1998, 13). A New Jersey survey found that 15.8 percent of respondents who had had their benefits reduced or terminated in the previous 12 months had lost their housing (Work, Poverty and Welfare Evaluation Project 1999, 53). Furthermore, in Illinois, 12 percent of former recipients who were not working and 5 percent of former recipients who were working experienced an eviction (Work, Welfare and Families 2000, 25).

Welfare reform has also put severe pressures on an already strained shelter system. The U.S. Conference of Mayors reported that requests for emergency shelter increased by 12 percent between 1998 and 1999 in the 26 cities surveyed and were at their highest levels since 1994 (U.S. Conference of Mayors 1999, 94). "When I started here three years ago, we had plenty of family space. Since welfare reform, I don't have a bed," said a social service worker in a Salvation Army Shelter in New Orleans (Cobb 1999, 1).

According to a survey conducted by social service agencies in six states, 8 percent of the single parents who had stopped getting welfare in the previous six months had to turn to homeless shelters to house their families (Sherman et al. 1998, 16). In an Illinois study, 7 percent of former recipients who were not working became homeless. Prospects were not much better for former recipients who were working, of whom 5 percent became homeless (Work, Welfare and Families 2000, 25).

Although the PRWORA was trumpeted as a step toward strengthening families, increased housing insecurity and homelessness have led to families being split apart. Most family shelters do not take men, so the fathers of two-parent families that become homeless must either go to a single men's shelter or make other housing arrangements. Many shelters also do not accommodate adolescent boys or older male teens. Family breakup may be required for a shelter stay.

The housing instability of poor women and their children has profound consequences, both for them and for society as a whole. Homelessness compromises the emotional and physical health of women and children, disrupts schooling, and creates a substantial barrier to employment. It widens the chasm between those who are prospering in a strong economy and those who fall ever further behind. In the six years since the United States made its Beijing commitments to improving women's lives, welfare policy, rather than widening poor women's access to safe and affordable housing, has created higher levels of housing instability and homelessness.

Like homelessness, the problems of food insecurity predate welfare reform. Low-income workers and welfare recipients alike have struggled for years to provide adequate food for themselves and their families. The robust economy of the late 1990s did not fundamentally alter this reality. Of families headed by single women, 1 in 3 experience food insecurity and 1 in 10 experience hunger (Work, Welfare and Families 2000, 25).

Welfare reform has made women's struggles to obtain food for themselves and their families more difficult. Several studies document that former recipients cannot pay for sufficient food and that their families skip meals, go hungry, and/or use food pantries or other emergency food assistance.

The figures are astoundingly high. In New Jersey, 50.3 percent of former recipients who were not working reported an inability to sufficiently feed themselves or their children. Former recipients who were working were no better off: 49.7 percent reported the very same problem (Work, Poverty and Welfare Evaluation Project 1999, 58). The situation conveyed by an Illinois study is even more disturbing. Here, the population reporting the most difficulty with food insecurity was former recipients who were participating in the labor force. Sixty-three percent of them said that there was a time when they could not buy the food they needed, a significantly higher proportion than either former recipients who were not working or current recipients. (Work, Welfare and Families 2000, 25). In other words, the higher costs associated with participating in the labor force, combined with reduction or elimination of the food stamp allotment, meant women's access to adequate food became more precarious rather than less so as they moved from welfare to work. Entering the workforce came at a very high price.

The Food Stamp Program is intended to ensure that no family goes hungry, but many families do not receive the food stamps to which they are entitled. Even before welfare reform, the rate of participation in the Food Stamp Program was declining more rapidly than the poverty rate. The number of people receiving food stamps dropped even more steeply later, from 25.5 million average monthly recipients in 1996 to 18.5 million in the first half of 1999 (U.S. General Accounting Office 1999, 46). The rate of participation is the lowest it has been in two decades, with a growing gap between the need for food assistance and families' use of food stamps.

Welfare reform has itself contributed to the underutilization of food stamps. Many families that leave the welfare system do not know that as long as their income remains below a certain level, they are still eligible for food stamps. Believing that termination of TANF benefits disqualifies them for food stamps as well, they fail to apply or to reconfirm eligibility. Confusion and misinformation on the part of eligibility workers, or their withholding of information, are also factors in the low participation of former recipients. Additional contributing factors include the lack of bilingual staff and burdensome application and recertification processes (Venner, Sullivan, and Seavey 2000, 17). Among families who had left welfare, only 42 percent of those who were eligible for food stamps were receiving them (Zedlewski and Brauner 1999, 1-6).

Not surprisingly, demands for food from other sources are increasing. As the welfare rolls shrink, requests for food from charities rise. Catholic Charities reported a 38 percent rise in demand for emergency food assistance in 1998. "For many low-income people, the 'emergency' need for food assistance has become 'chronic'—a basic component of their efforts to survive" (U.S. Conference of Mayors 1999, 20). The U.S. Conference of Mayors's study showed that 85 percent of the cities surveyed experienced increased demand for emergency food and that requests for emergency food assistance increased by an average of 18 percent between 1998 and 1999 (U.S. Conference of Mayors 1999, 94). In many cases, the demand for food goes unmet. As one report states, "The bottom line is that . . . for millions of households, work force participation has been accompanied by hunger" (Venner, Sullivan, and Seavey 2000, 16).

WOMEN OF COLOR
AND IMMIGRANT WOMEN

Welfare reform is a nominally race-neutral policy suffused with racial bias, both in the politics surrounding its promulgation and in its impact. It may not have been the intent to racially target women of color for particular punishment, yet women of color and immigrant women have nonetheless been particularly hard hit in ways that were highly predictable.

Feminist theory has for some time recognized that the social and economic circumstances women of color must negotiate are shaped by the intersection of distinct axes of power—in this case primarily race, class, and gender. The relationships of subordination and privilege that define these axes generate multiple social dynamics that influence, shape, and transform each other, creating, for women of color, multiple vulnerabilities and intensified experiences of discrimination.

Welfare reform might legitimately be regarded as a class-based policy intended to radically transform the social contract with the poor. Poverty in the United States, however, is powerfully structured by racial and gender inequities. It is not possible, therefore, to institute poverty policy of any depth that does not also reconfigure other relations, either augmenting or diminishing race and gender inequalities. By weakening the social safety net for the poor, PRWORA necessarily has its greatest effect on those communities that are disproportionately represented among the poor. Communities of color and immigrant communities, already characterized by significantly higher levels of minimum wage work, homelessness, hunger, and poor health, are further jeop-

ardized by the discriminatory impact of welfare reform.

As a consequence of the historical legacy and current practices of, among other things, educational inequity and labor market disadvantage, patterns of income and wealth in the United States are strongly skewed along racial lines, for example, the disproportionate burden of poverty is carried by people of color. While the white, non-Hispanic population constituted 72.3 percent of the total population in 1998, they made up only 45.8 percent of the population living below the poverty line. In stark contrast, blacks made up just over 12 percent of the general population, but 26.4 percent of the U.S. population in poverty. People of Hispanic origin, of all races, comprise 23.4 percent of the people below the poverty line, while making up 11.2 percent of the total population. While 8.2 percent of the white, non-Hispanic population lives in poverty, 12.5 percent of Asian and Pacific Islanders do (U.S. Census Bureau 1999, 2000).[1]

Economic vulnerabilities due to race and ethnicity may be further compounded by disadvantages based on gender and immigration/citizenship status. Thus, for households headed by single women, the poverty rates are also stark. Over 21 percent of such white, non-Hispanic households were below the poverty line in 1998, as compared to over 46 percent of black and 48 percent of Hispanic female-headed households (U.S. Census Bureau 1999). Immigrants, too, are disproportionately poor, with 18 percent below the poverty line as compared to 12 percent of the native born (U.S. Census Bureau

1999). Given the disproportionate share of poverty experienced by people of color, and the significant poverty of single-mother households, it is no surprise that the welfare rolls are racially unbalanced, with women of color substantially overrepresented (see Table 1).

This racial imbalance has been cynically used for decades in the ideological campaign to undermine support for welfare—a crude but ultimately effective interweaving of race, class, gender, and anti-immigrant biases that prepared the consensus to "end welfare as we know it." Having been maligned as lazy welfare cheats and something-for-nothing immigrants, Latinas, African American women, and Asian women of particular nationality groups are now absorbing a punishing share of welfare reform's negative impacts.

Much of the data on welfare reform are not disaggregated by race. We will not know the full impact of welfare reform on women of color until we have countywide, statewide, and national studies of women transitioning from welfare to work that consistently include race as a variable. However, to the extent that communities of color experience some of the most devastating effects of poverty at exceptionally high rates, and to the extent that welfare reform has rendered these communities more rather than less vulnerable, we may expect that the policy will deepen already entrenched inequalities.

For example, African American women are massively overrepresented in the urban homeless population. Their particular vulnerability

TABLE 1

TANF RECIPIENTS BY RACE,
1998 (in percentages)

White	32.7
Black	39.0
Hispanic	22.2
Native	1.5
Asian	3.4
Other	0.6
Unknown	0.7

SOURCE: U.S. Department of Health and Human Services 1999.

to homelessness has been shaped by, among many factors, high rates of reliance on welfare in a period in which the value of the welfare grant plummeted and housing costs climbed steeply; low marriage rates and, therefore, lack of access to a male wage; overconcentration on the bottom rungs of the wage ladder; and high unemployment rates, especially for young women with less than a high school education.

Beyond intensified impact due to disproportionate representation in the affected population, additional factors compound the disadvantages of women of color and immigrant women. One Virginia study found noteworthy differences in how caseworkers interact with black and white welfare recipients. A substantial 41 percent of white recipients were encouraged to go to school to earn their high school diplomas, while no black recipients were. A much higher proportion of whites than blacks found their caseworkers to be helpful in providing information about potential jobs (Gooden 1997). Other studies showed that blacks were removed from welfare for noncompliance with program rules at considerably higher rates than white recipients, while a higher proportion of the cases of white recipients were closed because their earnings rose too much to qualify for welfare (Savner 2000).

Further, while welfare use is declining among all races, white recipients are leaving the welfare rolls at a much more rapid rate than blacks or Latinos. In New York City, for example, the number of whites on welfare declined by 57 percent between 1995 and 1998, while the rate of decline for blacks was 30 percent and that of Latinos, 7 percent. White recipients have also been leaving the rolls at faster rates than minorities in states such as Illinois, Pennsylvania, Michigan, and Ohio. And nationally, the decline has been 25 percent for whites but only 17 percent for African Americans and 9 percent for Latinos (DeParle 1998, A1).

The causes of this phenomenon have been insufficiently studied, but some of the factors may include higher average educational levels among white recipients, greater concentrations of recipients of color in job-poor inner cities, racial discrimination in employment and housing, and discriminatory referral policies on the part of welfare-to-work caseworkers. Whatever the combination of contributing factors, it appears that white recipients are making a more rapid transition into the labor force.

Some of the most punitive provisions of PRWORA are directed at immigrants. The 1996 legislation banned certain categories of legal immigrants from a wide array of federal assistance programs, including TANF, food stamps, Supplementary Security Income, and Medicaid. In the year following passage, 940,000 legal immigrants lost their food stamp eligibility. Strong advocacy restored some of the cuts and removed some restrictions, but legal immigrants arriving in the United States after the 22 August 1996 legislation passed are ineligible for benefits for five years. States have the discretion of barring pre-enactment legal immigrants from TANF and nonemergency Medicaid as well (National Immigration Law Center 1999).

These restrictions have had profound effects on immigrant communities. First of all, many immigrant women who are on welfare face significant barriers to meeting TANF work requirements. Perhaps the most formidable obstacles are limited English proficiency and low educational levels. A study of immigrant recipients in California found that 87 percent of the Vietnamese women had limited or no proficiency in English, as did 48 percent of the Mexican American women. Many of these women were also not literate in their native languages, with the Mexican Americans averaging 6.5 years in school and the Vietnamese 8.7 years (Equal Rights Advocates 1999, 7). A study of Hmong women found 90 percent with little or no English proficiency, 70 percent with no literacy in the Hmong language, and 62 percent with no formal education whatsoever (Moore and Selkowe 1999).

Limited English, lack of education, and limited job skills severely restrict immigrant women's options in the job market, making it very difficult for them to comply with welfare-to-work requirements. Language problems also impede their ability to negotiate the welfare bureaucracy, which provides very limited or no translation services. These women lack information about programs to which they are entitled, and they worry about notices that come to them in English. When immigrant women recipients are able to find work, it is most often in minimum wage or low-wage jobs without stability or benefits (Center for Urban Research and Learning 1999, 5; Equal Rights Advocates 1999, 31).

It should come as no surprise that immigrant women report high levels of hardship. In a study of Santa Clara County, California, 50 percent of the Mexican American recipients had experienced food shortages, as had 26 percent of the Vietnamese women (Equal Rights Advocates 1999, 32). One out of three Hmong women recipients in Wisconsin reported running out of food in the six months prior to the survey, and 51.8 percent said they had less food on the state's W-2 program than they had had on AFDC (Moore and Selkowe 1999, 4). Of 630 Latino and Asian households surveyed in California, Texas, and Illinois, 79 percent faced food insecurity, and 8.5 percent reported experiencing severe hunger. A study of Los Angeles and San Francisco immigrant households whose food stamps had been cut found that 33 percent of the children in the San Francisco households were experiencing moderate to severe hunger (Venner, Sullivan, and Seavey 2000, 21).

Immigrant women recipients are also likely to experience severe overcrowding and to devote a huge portion of their income to housing. They share housing with relatives or with unrelated adults; live in garages or other makeshift, substandard dwellings; and worry constantly about paying the rent.

A more hidden, but still pernicious, impact of welfare reform has been the decline in applications for aid from immigrants who would be eligible to receive it. One report documents PRWORA's "chilling effect on immigrants" who mistakenly believe they are no longer eligible for any benefits. Reporting on the numbers of TANF applications approved each month, this study showed a huge drop—71 percent—in the number of legal immigrant applicants approved for TANF and MediCal between January 1996 and January 1998. That number fell from 1545 applicants in January 1996 to only 450 in January 1998 (Zimmerman and Fix 1998, 5). The intensive anti-immigrant propaganda that accompanied the passage of PRWORA and statewide anti-immigrant initiatives appears to have discouraged those who need and are entitled to aid from applying for it, surely undermining the health and welfare of immigrant women and their families.

WELFARE REFORM IS
INCOMPATIBLE WITH
WOMEN'S HUMAN RIGHTS

One of the chief accomplishments of the Beijing conference and the Platform for Action was to position women's issues squarely within the context of human rights. Building on the foundational work of activists worldwide, Beijing became the first U.N. women's conference in which "women's rights are human rights" was articulated not as a platitude but as a strategic assertion. Indeed, the phrase was taken up by former First Lady Hillary Rodham Clinton who, in her 5 September 1995 speech to the conference, asserted that "women will never gain full dignity until their human rights are respected and protected."

PRWORA is wholly incompatible with the strategic objectives of the Beijing Platform for Action and profoundly compromises the exercise of women's human rights. Rather than improving the status of poor women, the legislation has deepened the misery of tens of thousands of women and their children. By undermining women's access to a stable livelihood, welfare reform constructs barriers to their exercise of political, civil, cultural, and social rights.

Undoing the damage of welfare reform—and bringing U.S. policy in line with its stated commitments to the world community—will require the promulgation and implementation of policies that restore and strengthen the social safety net for women and children while funding programs that support women along the path to economic self-sufficiency. In the absence of the political will for such a comprehensive reworking of U.S. social welfare policy, advocates for poor women and families face an extended, defensive battle to ameliorate the cruelest and most discriminatory effects of this radically regressive policy.

Note

1. In citing Census Bureau statistics, I use their terminology. Elsewhere, I use the term "Latino" to refer to immigrants from Mexico, Central and South America, and the Spanish-speaking Caribbean and their descendants in the United States.

References

Center for Urban Research and Learning. 1999. *Cracks in the System: Conversations with People Surviving Welfare Reform*. Chicago: Center for Urban Research and Learning, Loyola University, Howard Area Community Center, Organization of the NorthEast.

Clinton, Hillary. 1995. Remarks by First Lady Hillary Rodham Clinton for the United Nations Fourth World Conference on Women, 5 Sept.

Cobb, Kim. 1999. Homeless Kids Problem Worst in Louisiana; Welfare Reform, Housing Crunch Are Among Reasons. *Houston Chronicle*, 15 Aug.

DeParle, Jason. 1998. Shrinking Welfare Rolls Leave Record High Share of Minorities. *New York Times*, 24 July.

Dolbeare, Cushing. 1999. *Out of Reach: The Gap Between Housing Costs and Income of Poor People in the United States*. Washington, DC: National Low-Income Housing Coalition.

Equal Rights Advocates. 1999. *From War on Poverty to War on Welfare: The Impact of Welfare Reform on the Lives of Immigrant Women*. San Francisco: Equal Rights Advocates.

Gooden, Susan. 1997. Examining Racial Differences in Employment Status Among Welfare Recipients. In *Race and Welfare Report*. Oakland, CA: Grass Roots Innovative Policy Program.

Griffin, Laura. 1999. Welfare Cuts Leaving More Families Homeless, Study Finds. *Dallas Morning News*, 1 July.

Moore, Thomas and Vicky Selkowe. 1999. *The Impact of Welfare Reform on Wisconsin's Hmong Aid Recipients.* Milwaukee: Institute for Wisconsin's Future.

National Immigration Law Center. 1999. *Immigrant Eligibility for Public Benefits.* Washington, DC: National Immigration Law Center.

Savner, Steve. 2000. Welfare Reform and Racial/Ethnic Minorities: The Questions to Ask. *Poverty & Race* 9(4):3-5.

Sherman, Arloc, Cheryl Amey, Barbara Duffield, Nancy Ebb, and Deborah Weinstein. 1998. *Welfare to What: Early Findings on Family Hardship and Well-Being.* Washington, DC: Children's Defense Fund and National Coalition for the Homeless.

United Nations. 1995. *Fourth World Conference on Women Platform for Action.* Geneva, Switzerland: United Nations.

U.S. Census Bureau. 1999. *Poverty Thresholds in 1998 by Size of Family and Number of Related Children Under 18 Years.* Washington, DC: U.S. Census Bureau.

———. 2000. *Resident Population Estimates of the United States by Sex, Race, and Hispanic Origin.* Washington, DC: U.S. Census Bureau.

U.S. Conference of Mayors. 1999. *A Status Report on Hunger and Homelessness in America's Cities.* Washington, DC: U.S. Conference of Mayors.

U.S. Department of Health and Human Services. 1999. *Characteristics and Financial Circumstances of TANF Recipients.* Washington, DC: U.S. Department of Health and Human Services, Administration for Children and Families.

U.S. General Accounting Office. 1999. *Food Stamp Program: Various Factors Have Led to Declining Participation.* Washington, DC: U.S. General Accounting Office.

Venner, Sandra H., Ashley F. Sullivan, and Dorie Seavey. 2000. *Paradox of Our Times: Hunger in a Strong Economy.* Medford, MA: Tufts University, Center on Hunger and Poverty.

Work, Poverty and Welfare Evaluation Project. 1999. Assessing Work First: What Happens After Welfare? Report for the Study Group on Work, Poverty and Welfare. Legal Services of New Jersey, New Jersey Poverty Research Institute, Edison, NJ.

Work, Welfare and Families. 2000. *Living with Welfare Reform: A Survey of Low Income Families in Illinois.* Chicago: Chicago Urban League and UIC Center for Urban Economic Development.

Zedlewski, Sheila R. and Sarah Brauner. 1999. *Are the Steep Declines in Food Stamp Participation Linked to Falling Welfare Caseloads?* Washington, DC: Urban Institute.

Zimmerman, Wendy and Michael Fix. 1998. *Declining Immigrant Applications for MediCal and Welfare Benefits in Los Angeles County.* Washington, DC: Urban Institute.

ANNALS, *AAPSS*, **577**, September 2001

Success Stories:
Welfare Reform, Policy Discourse,
and the Politics of Research

By SANFORD F. SCHRAM and JOE SOSS

ABSTRACT: Welfare reform is now widely hailed as a success. In this article, the authors analyze this public verdict as a political construction. During the 1980s and 1990s, welfare discourse shifted to emphasize concerns over program dependency. This shift not only promoted policy retrenchment, it also defined the terms on which retrenchment would be judged. Specifically, it established caseload levels and studies of program "leavers" as a common frame of reference for judging welfare reform. This article presents evidence that a majority of media stories on welfare reform from 1998 to 2000 offered positive assessments. The authors then show that perceptions of reform as a policy success depend chiefly on the diversion of attention away from standards of evaluation and interpretations of evidence that might suggest failure. They conclude by discussing how the construction of policy success is likely to affect upcoming debates over the renewal of welfare reform.

Sanford F. Schram is visiting professor in the Graduate School of Social Work and Social Research at Bryn Mawr College and author of After Welfare: The Culture of Postindustrial Social Policy *(2000) and* Words of Welfare: The Poverty of Social Science and the Social Science of Poverty *(1995), which won the Michael Harrington Award from the American Political Science Association.*

Joe Soss is associate professor of government at American University and author of Unwanted Claims: The Politics of Participation in the U.S. Welfare System *(2000). His research has also appeared in* American Political Science Review, American Journal of Political Science, Political Research Quarterly, Public Opinion Quarterly, Political Communication, *and* Politics & Society.

NOTE: We wish to thank Frances Fox Piven, Fred Block, Joan Davitt, Kira Dahlk, Randy Albelda, Ann Withorn, Cynthia Peters, and Leslie Alexander for helpful comments on earlier drafts. We also thank Margaret Berman for superb research assistance.

We live in a forest of symbols on the edge of a jungle of fact.
—Joseph Gusfield (1981, 51)

Our understanding of real situations is always mediated by ideas; those ideas in turn are created, changed, and fought over in politics.
—Deborah Stone (1997, 282)

Welfare reform is a success! Or so one might think based on a majority of evaluations coming from leading public officials and media sources. After four years under the new policy regime, initial anxieties have given way to a rough consensus that welfare reform, up to this point, has succeeded. As the architects of Temporary Assistance for Needy Families (TANF) had hoped, the welfare rolls have dropped precipitously from 12.24 million recipients in August 1996 to 6.28 million recipients in June 2000, a decline of 53 percent (Administration for Children and Families 2001). In addition, a number of studies have suggested that many people leaving welfare are faring well (Assistant Secretary for Planning and Evaluation [ASPE] 2000). To many observers, these facts suggest that the success of welfare reform is self-evident, indisputable among reasonable people.

Our goal in this article is to question the prevailing consensus on welfare reform by showing how TANF's status as a policy success may be viewed as a political construction (M. Edelman 1988). Evaluations of public policy inevitably require political choices regarding which facts will be valued as indicators of success and which interpretations of facts will serve as a basis for judgment (Stone

1997; Cobb and Ross 1997). Welfare reform is now widely viewed as a success not because of the facts uncovered by researchers (which paint a murky picture) but because of a political climate that privileges some facts and interpretations over others.

Judgments of policy success and failure are built on the backs of what Joseph Gusfield (1981) once called "public facts"—statements "about an aggregate of events which we do not and cannot experience personally" (51). Although any one of us may have personal experience with poverty or welfare, it is impossible to draw from such experience a conclusion about whether welfare reform in general is working or whether poor people in general are faring well. To arrive at such judgments, we must rely heavily on what media stories, public officials, and experts report about general states of affairs. Such reports serve to establish the success or failure of government policy as an authentic fact for the public.

The popular belief that welfare reform has succeeded can be traced chiefly to positive interpretations of two public facts: declining caseloads and outcomes for program "leavers." In what follows, we explore the politics that surround these two facts. We argue that the meanings of caseload decline and leaver outcomes remain far from clear, and we ask how alternative criteria might point to less sanguine evaluations of reform.

WELFARE REFORM AS A SUCCESS STORY

That the new welfare policies have succeeded where earlier, more liberal efforts failed is now taken by many to be an irrefutable fact. Writing in the *Washington Post*, Michael Kelly (2000) stated, "In all arguments of policy and politics, there comes sooner or later the inevitable moment when it becomes simply undeniable that one side of the argument is true, or mostly so, and the other is false, or mostly so." "The inevitable moment," Kelly wrote, "arrived for liberals on . . . welfare reform" (A31). As early as the summer of 1997, President Clinton was ready to conclude, "The debate is over. We now know that welfare reform works" (Miller 1998, 28). Three years later, the debate really did seem to be over. The 2000 presidential campaign included almost no significant disagreement over issues of poverty and welfare, as the Democratic and Republican nominees both touted the achievements of reform and pledged to build on its successes.

Media stories on welfare reform have been more measured in their tone but have largely bolstered the image of success. Because welfare reform has produced so many new policies and outcomes in such a diversity of places, it has been a difficult story for the news media to cover. Some journalists have made great efforts to meet these challenges. Jason DeParle's (1999) yearlong series in the *New York Times*, for example, was an admirable piece of journalism. In the main, however, media stories have tended to forgo investigative journalism and critical inquiry in favor of presentations that rely heavily on statistics and interpretations proffered by government. Such stories are typically written in a traditional journalistic idiom that emphasizes balance, impartiality, and presentation (rather than critical interrogation) of facts; however, in a majority of cases, these stories portray new TANF policies as a success.

Between January 1998 and September 2000, the top 50 newspapers in the United States ran 250 stories on welfare reform and caseload decline.[1] Examining these stories, we found that only 28.4 percent offered an unmitigated positive or negative view of reform; most assessments came with some counterpoints. Over half the articles in our sample were either wholly positive (19.6 percent) or generally positive with caveats (32 percent). By contrast, only about a quarter were wholly negative (8.8 percent) or generally negative with caveats (15.6 percent). Twenty-four percent gave equal weight to the pros and cons of reform.[2] The modal story on welfare reform raised concerns about families leaving the TANF program and about what might happen if the economy sours; with these caveats in place, it went on to suggest that welfare reform so far has had remarkably positive results (see Figure 1).

Media stories on welfare reform have tended to be framed in terms that establish and dramatize the success of new TANF policies. By this claim, we do not mean that journalists have disseminated incorrect facts, exhibited overt bias, or colluded with those who have a stake in welfare reform's success. Rather, our argument is that media coverage has been shaped by policy makers' concerns with the problem of depen-

FIGURE 1
MEDIA COVERAGE OF WELFARE REFORM, 1998-2000

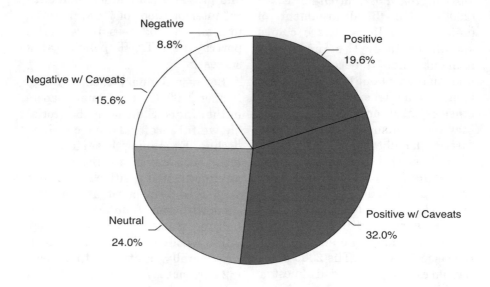

NOTE: Based on an analysis of welfare reform stories that ran in the top 50 newspapers in the United States between 1 January 1998 and 1 September 2000. Number of stories = 250.

dence and, hence, has focused on a set of facts and interpretations that support a verdict of policy success. The roots of this focus, we argue, lie in an antiwelfare discourse that not only produced policy retrenchment in the 1990s but also defined the terms on which this retrenchment would be judged. As we describe below, the current framing of welfare evaluation in terms of caseload levels and leaver outcomes is far from natural or neutral. The "inevitable moment" described by Michael Kelly was not inevitable; it was and is an outcome of political battles fought on the contested terrain of public discourse.

CONSTRUCTING
THE STANDARDS OF
POLICY SUCCESS

Constructivist political analyses suggest that any object or event, however real, can take on diverse meanings, and it is these meanings rather than brute facts alone that form the basis of political thought and action (Schram 1995). Political information is inherently ambiguous; the public that receives this information is typically ambivalent. Thus, when citizens evaluate a complex political object such as welfare policy, they are likely to hold a variety of conflicting, potentially relevant considerations. A major way in which political actors shape public responses is by advancing issue frames that highlight some of these considerations while obscuring others. When consensus emerges on an issue such as welfare reform, it suggests that some political group has succeeded in constructing what Dennis Chong (1995) called "a common frame of reference"—a frame pervasive and powerful enough to focus diverse publics on a shared set of considerations.

The TANF program is now perceived as a success in large part because caseloads and leavers have become a shared frame of reference for evaluating reform. Some well-known characteristics of mass media arguably have contributed to the construction of this common frame. Social networks, organizational routines, and shared work pressures invite a kind of pack journalism in which reporters focus on the same top stories (Fishman 1980). Norms of objectivity encourage reporters to build these stories out of information provided by a small stock of "credible" government officials and experts (Sigal 1973, 119-30). Narrative conventions push reporters to dramatize and then normalize these stories in similar ways. Concentrated ownership and the use of wire stories increase the likelihood that a small number of reports will run repeatedly in different media outlets.

Perhaps most important, the diversity of frames presented by mass media on a given policy issue usually depends on the extent to which public officials generate competing flows of information (Zaller 1992; Hallin 1984). In recent years, leaders of both major political parties have been committed to new welfare policies, and activists have generally failed to disrupt this harmony with pressures from below. In such a bipartisan context, elite consensus usually gives rise to large numbers of media stories that paint a relatively consistent portrait of reality.

The implicit frame of reference for most recent reporting on welfare reform can be traced to a discourse of dependency that grew influential in the 1980s and 1990s. Dependency discourse identifies reliance on public assistance as an important social problem and defines transitions from welfare to low-wage work as steps, however perilous, toward self-sufficiency. Within this paradigm, champions of welfare reform point to roll decline as clear evidence of policy success, while critics use evidence from leaver studies to suggest that former recipients are not actually achieving self-sufficiency. Only marginal voices seem to raise the possibility that the TANF program might be better evaluated by other criteria. To explain how welfare reform got labeled a policy success, one must investigate how this discourse came to prevail and how it obscures evaluative criteria that might cast reform in a different light.

Beginning in the 1970s, conservatives waged a disparate but effective campaign to change the terms of debate on welfare. Moral conservatives entered the fray as part of a broader countermovement against changes in gender and race relations, consumption patterns, and sexual and familial norms that they saw as evidence of moral decline (Ehrenreich 1987). Business interests had more material goals: by pushing the poor out of welfare and into low-wage work, employers hoped to lighten their tax burden and, more important, prevent tight labor markets from enhancing the bargaining position of labor or pushing wages upward (see Frances Fox Piven's article in this volume).

Throughout the 1980s and 1990s, foundations with funds supplied by corporate interests and moral conservatives promoted a string of influential critics whose books charged that welfare encouraged perverse behavioral choices, flouted the obligations of citizenship, and undermined the voluntarism of civil society (Stefancic, Delgado, and Tushnet 1996). Soon, such critics were joined by government officials who saw political capital to be made in attacking federal welfare programs and shifting control over welfare resources down to the state level. Liberal and left advocates, suddenly forced to defend an unpopular program that they perceived as inadequate, failed to establish a positive alternative to dependence and devolution as grounds for debating the future shape of welfare policy.

The achievements of the political campaign against welfare are easy to miss if one accepts the one-sided myth that Americans are selfish individualists who oppose government assistance on principle. Most Americans do place a high value on personal responsibility and the work ethic, but these commitments are balanced by a belief that government has an obligation to help those in need (Feldman and Zaller 1992). Seventy to 90 percent of Americans say they support government assistance targeted at the poor and believe the government has a responsibility to guarantee every citizen food to eat and a place to sleep (Gilens 1999, 37).

The campaign against welfare did not persuade the public that aid to the poor was undesirable; it simply reframed welfare in terms that highlighted alternative considerations. Dependence and personal responsibility were central to the new frame, but there were other elements as well. Critics evoked antistatist and antielitist sentiments in the public by attacking welfare as a self-serving creation of liberals in government and the "intelligentsia" (Ehrenreich 1987, 165-73). Welfare, in this frame, was not a hard-won protection for poor workers and their families; it was a policy imposed against workers' values as well as their bank accounts. Second, welfare also got reframed in racial terms by coded political rhetoric and distortions in media coverage (Gilens 1999). In media stories and in the public mind, black people (especially black single mothers) became the most damnable and most frequent welfare recipients. As a result, racial resentments and old stereotypes of black laziness became fuel for hostility toward welfare.

All these frames contributed to the demise of the Aid to Families with Dependent Children (AFDC) program, but the effort to reframe welfare debates in terms of the issue of dependency arguably played the most crucial role in shaping later evaluations of welfare reform. Here, it is important to recall that in an earlier era liberals had framed "troubling" behaviors among the poor as products of poverty and used images of social disorganization as evidence for the necessity of extending aid (Scott 1997). The crucial move made by conservatives was to reframe these same behaviors as products of permissive social programs that failed to limit program usage, require work, and demand functional behavior. Long-term dependency became a key word in welfare debates, usually treated as part of a broader syndrome of underclass pathologies that included drug use, violence, crime, teen pregnancy, single motherhood, and even poverty itself. Gradually, permissiveness and dependency displaced poverty and structural barriers to advancement as the central problems drawing attention from those who designed welfare policy.

The discursive turn to dependency had important political consequences. First, welfare dependency and its effects on the poor set the agenda for poverty research in the 1980s and 1990s (Schram 1995). To distinguish myths from realities, researchers expended great effort in identifying the typical duration of participation spells and the individual-level correlates of long-term program usage (e.g., Bane and Ellwood 1994). Structural questions received less attention as defenders responded to critics in a debate that focused on work effort, program usage, and poor people's behaviors. Second, as dependency came to be seen as a cause of intergenerational

poverty, it became a kind of synecdoche—a single part used to represent the whole tangle of problems associated with the poor. To fight dependency was, in essence, to fight a kind of substance abuse that led to unrestrained sexuality, drug problems, violent crime, civic irresponsibility, and even poverty itself.

As a synecdoche for diverse social ills, dependency became the basis for a powerful crisis narrative in the 1980s and 1990s. Critics spoke of a "crisis of dependency," often in conjunction with fellow travelers such as the "teen pregnancy crisis" and the "underclass crisis" (Luker 1996). As M. Edelman (1977, chap. 3) explained, such crisis language evokes perceptions of threat, conveys the need for immediate and extraordinary action, and suggests that "now is not the time" to air dissent or seek deliberation.[3] Claims about the prevalence of long-term program usage were often overblown, and images of wholesale social disintegration depended on highly selective readings of poor people's attitudes and behaviors (Rank 1994). But by applying the label of crisis, critics turned ambiguous trends among the poor (many of which also existed in the rest of society) into a fearsome threat to the values of middle America.

Just as the so-called drug crisis seemed to require a tough, incarceration-minded war on drugs, the crisis of dependency called for nothing short of an assault on permissiveness. In this environment, poverty advocates who tried to direct attention toward issues other than dependency were seen as fiddling while Rome burned. Long-term program usage was a major social problem requiring a bold solution; it called for extraordinary measures, not tepid liberal palliatives. The only suitable response was to attack dependency at its root by imposing a new regime of welfare rules designed to dissuade and limit program usage, enforce work, and curb unwanted behaviors. In 1996, that is exactly what welfare reform did.

The key point for our purposes is that when advocates established dependency as a synecdoche for underclass pathology and as the central target for reform, they simultaneously highlighted caseload decline and employment among leavers as preeminent standards for judging the success of reform. One point to note about these standards is that they are not very demanding. Compared to improving material conditions in poor communities, it is relatively easy to pare the welfare rolls and push the poor into low-wage work. When these outcomes are treated as ipso facto evidence of policy success, they make it easier for the architects of TANF to deflect criticism for current hardships, gain standing to make future policy decisions, and claim credit in front of their constituencies.

The second point to note about these standards is that they direct attention away from criteria that might suggest policy failure. One such criterion, of course, is poverty reduction. Antipoverty effectiveness served as a primary measure of success for public assistance programs through most of the twentieth century (Danziger and Weinberg 1994). Yet the TANF program does not offer

benefits sufficient to lift recipients out of poverty, and (despite a strong economy) the majority of families who have moved off the TANF rolls have remained in poverty (ASPE 2000). Consideration of another traditional economic goal, reduction of inequality, only makes matters worse. Welfare reform has coincided with massive growth in income and wealth disparities; it has done little to slow the expansion of inequality and may have actually accelerated the trend (Collins, Leondar-Wright, Sklar 1999). Has welfare reform created job opportunities for the poor? Has it promoted wages that allow low-wage workers to escape poverty? In all these areas, the economic story remains the same: we have little evidence that reform has produced achievements that warrant the label of success.

Introduction of less market-centered criteria creates even more uncertainty about the success of reform. For at least a century, liberals have hoped that welfare programs might ease the social marginality of the poor and, thereby, enhance the solidarity of the national community. Participatory welfare programs have also been viewed as opportunities to build political efficacy, engagement, and leadership in poor communities (Soss 2000). With TANF recipients now being hassled, fingerprinted, forced to work in public settings wearing distinguishing clothing, and otherwise made into objects of public scorn, it is difficult to see how welfare reform has been successful in relation to these criteria (Schram 2000, 73-84). Alternatively, consider the long-standing goal of providing aid in a manner that is equitable across categories of race and gender. Welfare reform has applied a profusion of new rules to poor women that are not applied to men in any sector of the welfare state (see Gwendolyn Mink's article in this volume); the toughest TANF rules have been disproportionately implemented in states where people of color make up higher proportions of the caseloads (Soss et al. 2001). A more inclusive society, a deeper democracy, a more just and humane system of provision—we have little evidence that reform is meeting any of these standards of success.

A narrow focus on caseload reduction and leaver outcomes obscures not only liberal measures of welfare success but also traditional conservative tests. Before 1996, conservatives routinely cited waste, fraud, and incompetence in the administration of welfare funds as evidence of policy failure. Such a standard of evaluation has rarely been applied to welfare reform despite well-documented cases in which clients have been unable to gain access to remaining entitlements (Dion and Pavetti 2000; Bell and Strege-Flora 2000) and corporate welfare providers have used public funds for profit-enhancing purposes (Schultze 2000; Hilzenrath 2000). Likewise, the old permissive welfare was deemed a failure because it did little to end social problems in poor communities, but there are good reasons to believe that such problems have not waned under the new welfare (DeParle 1999). Proponents touted TANF as a form of moral tutoring, a way to instill responsibility and other

desirable values in the poor; however, client studies under TANF report that "paternalist reform seems to be a lesson about power, not responsibility" (Wilson, Stoker, and McGrath 1999, 485).

This list of alternative criteria could go on indefinitely, but our point by now should be clear. The success of welfare reform has seemed indisputable primarily because of how the TANF program's achievements have been evaluated. What must be underscored is that the public does not necessarily view alternative criteria as less important than caseload reduction. Rather, these criteria have been obscured by a discourse that focuses attention narrowly on the contrast of dependency and self-sufficiency.

FROM POSSIBLE
INTERPRETATIONS TO
AUTHENTIC FACTS

Thus far, we have made two arguments about the current focus on caseloads and leaver studies. First, it is chiefly a political outcome: a victory for those who sought to frame the goals of welfare policy in terms of dependency and a loss for those who valued other objectives. Second, it renders welfare reform a success by obscuring evaluative criteria that would otherwise complicate or perhaps reverse public assessment. In this section, we make a third point. Even if one ignores other criteria, the belief that caseload decline and leaver studies demonstrate the success of welfare reform depends on a particular framing of the evidence. Roll decline and leaver outcomes are facts and fictions (Gusfield 1981).

The facts are that caseloads have dropped, leavers have experienced outcomes, and researchers have produced measures of each. The fictions are that such measures offer an unambiguous rendering of reality and that they do so in a way that establishes the truth of welfare reform's success.

Consider the fact of caseload decline. As Wendell Primus, former deputy assistant secretary of Health and Human Services, observed in August 1999, "The conventional wisdom here in Washington is that welfare reform is an unqualified success because caseload reductions have been so dramatic" (Associated Press 1999, C10). Welfare rolls have declined by about 53 percent since 1996 (Administration for Children and Families 2001). With concern over dependency as a backdrop, observers have tended to interpret this figure as evidence that TANF policies are motivating and assisting program users to leave the rolls. Such an interpretation, however, can be maintained only by isolating one possible meaning of roll decline and minimizing the play of alternative readings (M. Edelman 1997).

Mainstream media stories typically recite a list of important but limited questions regarding the meaning of caseload decline. Most point out that a significant portion of the 53 percent drop can be attributed to an unusually strong economy (Wallace and Blank 1999). A small number do even better, noting the impact of policies that augment the earnings of low-wage workers, such as the earned income tax credit (EITC). Most stories highlight the need to evaluate roll decline by studying leavers, and many suggest that caseloads could rise again if the economy takes a dive. What these reports rarely do, however, is question the underlying premise that the TANF program's contribution to lower caseloads has consisted primarily of encouraging and helping dependent recipients to leave welfare for work.

Such an interpretation may seem self-evident, but a closer look at the evidence reveals that it is based on faulty assumptions about the sources of continuity and change in welfare caseloads. Before the 1996 reforms, large numbers of recipients left the welfare rolls each year; continuity was maintained because these recipients were replaced with new cohorts (Bane and Ellwood 1994). Of the people who entered the old AFDC program each year, 56 percent left within a year (averaging 5.3 months), and only 18 percent stayed on continuously for more than five years (Pavetti 1993). Even among long-term clients who accumulated in the annual caseload, significant numbers would leave each year to enter jobs or relationships or because children became too old to qualify for benefits. Caseload levels were maintained through a process of cohort replacement: new and former recipients would enter AFDC, taking the places of those who left.

Thus, over the five years since 1996, we would have expected a large number of program exits even if the "permissive" AFDC program had remained in place. Given the imposition of tough new TANF rules, roll decline since 1996 undoubtedly reflects some increase in program exits, but a significant portion of the decline may also be traced to a decline in the number of replacements entering the rolls. Our ability to distinguish between these processes is hampered by the fact that, under TANF, states have not had to report exit and entry figures.[4] Several observations, however, suggest that a significant portion of TANF's impact on caseloads can be linked to a decline in new cases rather than movement of long-term recipients into work.

First, although we do not have good TANF data, we do know that roll decline under AFDC between 1994 and 1997 was based more on a drop in new and recent cases than on a decline among long-term recipients (Falk 2000). The nationwide roll decline of 28 percent from 1994 to 1997 cannot be accounted for by the 2.5 percent increase in the number of long-term recipients during this period; it is far more plausibly tied to the 37 percent decline in new cases (Falk 2000).[5] Second, under TANF, a majority of states have added new diversion policies that deflect claimants toward job searches or private assistance rather than adding them to the rolls (Maloy et al. 1998). Third, although evidence is sparse, many observers suggest that the cultural and administrative climates that have accompanied welfare reform have functioned to deter eligible families from claiming benefits (Bell and Strege-Flora 2000). Fourth, recent data on the remaining TANF caseload suggest that long-term recipients with barriers to work make up a disproportionate number of clients who are not exiting TANF (Loprest and Zedlewski 1999).

Despite these facts, public discourse on caseload decline focuses primarily on leavers, paying little attention to those who do not or cannot gain entry to public aid. Of the 250 media stories we analyzed (see notes 1 and 2), only 7 mentioned diversion as a possible source of roll decline; 114 discussed people leaving welfare in conjunction with roll decline. The fact that prevailing interpretations of roll decline emphasize leavers and exit rates rather than diversion and entry rates has major political implications. Moving long-term recipients out of welfare and into jobs that raise them out of poverty would be widely hailed by the public as a major policy achievement (Gilens 1999). By contrast, we suspect that paring the rolls by shutting the gates on needy families would be viewed by many as a small and ignoble feat.

Beyond the issue of take-up rates, there is an additional reason to question the use of caseload statistics as symbols of policy success. If roll decline primarily resulted from TANF policies' helping recipients to move toward self-sufficiency, one would expect to find the largest declines in states that have the strongest work promotion, training, and opportunity-producing policies. This is simply not the case. The welfare rolls have dropped the most in states that impose immediate, full-family sanctions—that is, states that punish a client's first failure to comply with a program rule by eliminating aid for an entire family (Rector and Youssef 1999). From 1997 through 1999, an estimated 540,000 families lost their entire TANF check due to a full-family sanction (Goldberg and Schott 2000), yet only 24 of our sample of 250 media stories raised questions about the impact of sanctions policy.

Our purpose here is not to suggest that caseload decline should be interpreted solely as bad news. Rather, it is to recover the lost frames of reference that could and should make observers uncertain about what roll decline really means. Some of the decline can be traced to a strong economy, some is due to wage supplements such as the EITC, a portion can be traced to diversion and deterrence of income-eligible families, and some percentage can be attributed to sanctions that simply cut families off the rolls. How much of the remaining portion really reflects successful movement of clients from long-term dependence to self-sufficiency? Our best answer is that no one really knows, and too few people are asking. Instead, caseload decline is assumed to be about people trading in welfare checks for paychecks and, hence, is evaluated primarily in terms of leaver outcomes.

Since TANF was implemented in 1997, a welter of studies have attempted to track families who have left the TANF rolls (for example, ASPE 2000; U.S. General Accounting Office 1999; Loprest 1999). The mass media has given heavy coverage to these studies and has treated them as key arbiters of claims that welfare reform is succeeding. Leaver studies provide important information on a particular set of outcomes for poor families. But like reports on caseload decline, these studies supply ambiguous evidence that must be framed in particular ways to support claims of policy success.

The key leaver outcomes cited as evidence that welfare reform is working are that 50 to 60 percent of former recipients have employment one quarter after exiting the program, that such former recipients generally experience a modest increase in income, and that they tend to make wages equivalent to those of low-income women (ASPE 2000; Loprest 1999). Do these statistics suggest success? It depends on what one uses as a baseline for judgment. That 40 to 50 percent of first-quarter leavers are trying to survive without a job and without cash assistance hardly seems like good news—especially since this percentage rises over later quarters, and eventually, almost a third of leavers have to return to TANF (Loprest 1999). The evidence of success becomes even less convincing if one uses outcomes under the old "permissive" welfare as a baseline for comparison: about 46 percent of AFDC recipients left the welfare rolls because of employment earnings (Pavetti 1993). This is a lower percentage than one finds under TANF, but given that unemployment rates have been at historic lows and that TANF workers have been promoting employment of almost any sort, the shift hardly suggests a stunning policy achievement.

Turning to the evidence on income increases, one finds the same story. The baseline most frequently used to frame leaver incomes is previous income as a TANF recipient. By this standard, leaver earnings are almost guaranteed to suggest success. To encourage work, welfare benefits have always been set well below the lowest wages in the labor market (Piven and Cloward 1993). Moreover, the real value of welfare benefits has declined by about half since 1970 and is currently too low to cover basic family necessities, let alone lift families out of poverty. Thus, TANF income provides a very low bar for gauging leaver success.

A comparison of leaver earnings to those of low-income women poses an equally lax test. In 1998, the poverty threshold for an adult and two children was $1095 per month; the median earnings for TANF leavers in a study of 11 states ranged from only $665 to $1083 per month (ASPE 2000). In fact, leavers have incomes so low that 49 percent report that often or sometimes food does not last until the end of the month and that they do not have money to buy more; 39 percent report a time in the last year when they were unable to pay rent, mortgage, or utility bills (Loprest 1999). Whether leaver earnings indicate positive program outcomes depends, critically, on how much hardship one sees as acceptable for disadvantaged families to endure.

Finally, the claim that welfare reform is a success rests, to a significant degree, on the idea that leavers are now being provided a stronger system of support to smooth the transition to self-sufficiency. As in other areas, there is a grain of truth here. Public assistance prior to 1996 provided clients with limited resources to facilitate a lasting transition into work and out of poverty.[6] TANF policies have arguably expanded these resources. But while many forms of transitional assistance are now on the books, survey-based leaver studies show that large numbers of former recipients are not actually receiving benefits. Despite widespread need, 53 percent of children in leaver families are not receiving Medicaid assistance, 66 percent of adult leavers do not receive Medicaid coverage, and 69 percent of leaver families do not receive food stamps (Loprest 1999). Among those making the initial transition to work (in the first three months), 81 percent do not receive child care assistance, 89 percent do not receive any help with expenses, and 85 percent do not receive help finding or training for a job (Loprest 1999).

None of these figures should be taken as unambiguous evidence that welfare reform, as a whole, is a failure. There is some nontrivial number of former welfare recipients who have been well served by new TANF policies—who have been encouraged and assisted to find jobs that lift them out of poverty and who are now doing well enough not to need transitional or ongoing assistance. The problem is that recent leaver statistics have been framed to misleadingly suggest that such experiences (1) rarely occurred under the old AFDC program, (2) characterize a majority of TANF leaver outcomes, and (3) account for the bulk of caseload decline.

CONCLUSION

It is official: the reform of the welfare
system is a great triumph of social
policy.
—Michael Kelly (1999, A21)

Although one can find significant
dissenting voices in the government,
the press, and advocacy organizations, welfare reform is now widely
viewed as a policy success. The backdrop for this assessment is a causal
story suggesting that permissive
welfare policies from the 1960s to the
1990s produced a crisis of long-term
dependency that, in turn, bred
behavioral pathologies and intergenerational poverty. Over a 25-year
period, promotion of this story
turned the size of welfare caseloads
into a key indicator of policy performance and established transitions
off the rolls as a central policy goal.
Accordingly, in the current era of welfare reform, caseloads and leaver
outcomes have become the most
salient measures of policy success—
even for many who doubt that cash
assistance was ever the root cause of
poor people's problems. The secret of
success for welfare reform has been a
frame of reference that suggests positive interpretations of roll decline
and leaver outcomes while simultaneously obscuring alternative criteria that might produce more critical
assessments.

The discursive processes that we
have highlighted in this article merit
close attention because judgments of
policy success and failure are more
than just political outcomes; they are
also political forces. Beliefs about
which policies are known failures
and which have been shown to

succeed set the parameters for reasonable debate over the shape of
future legislation. Reputations for
developing successful ideas confer
authority, giving some advocates
greater access and influence in the
legislative process. Public officials
who are able to claim credit for policy
success hold a political resource that
bestows advantages in both electoral
and legislative contests. For all these
reasons, politically constructed
beliefs about the successes and failures of welfare policy can be expected
to play a key role in determining the
fate of TANF reauthorization in the
107th Congress. Such beliefs, and the
political actions that sustain them,
constitute major influences on the
shape of social provision in America.

Notes

1. We used a two-step process to identify
relevant stories. First, we searched Lexis-
Nexis to find all stories with at least one sentence that included both "welfare" and "reform" and at least one sentence that included
one of four combinations: "roll" and "decline,"
"roll" and "drop," "caseload" and "decline," and
"caseload" and "drop." This procedure yielded a
preliminary sample of 358 stories. Second, to
limit our analysis to relevant media portray-
als, we identified and removed all letters to the
editors and news stories that were either irrel-
evant or made only passing reference to welfare. This procedure resulted in a loss of 108
cases, producing a final sample of 250 relevant
stories.

2. The sample of 250 stories and
prototypical articles representing each of the
five coding categories are available from the
authors on request. Coding reliability was
evaluated by having two individuals independently code a random subsample of 50 stories. Applying the five categories described in
the text, the two coders agreed on 82 percent of
the cases in this subsample, a rate of agreement that meets conventional standards for

interrater reliability (see Rubin and Babbie 2000, 192-93).

3. In the 1960s, liberals used such crisis language in tandem with the militaristic metaphor of a war on poverty—a construction that cued anxieties about the costs of inaction while also suggesting the state's capacity to use its arsenal of weapons to achieve victory (Stone 1997).

4. Congressional action in 2000 restored some efforts to collect data on welfare entry and exit. It will be some time, however, before enough data will be available to support trend analyses of caseload dynamics under TANF.

5. Long-term recipients were defined in this analysis as those receiving welfare for 60 or more months; new recipients were defined as those who had been on the rolls for 3 months or less.

6. During the last decade of the AFDC program, the nominal transition benefits for exiting families included ongoing access to food stamps for those who qualified, one year of Medicaid coverage for those who qualified, and one year of child care for those leaving AFDC for a job.

References

Administration for Children and Families. 2001. *Temporary Assistance for Needy Families (TANF), 1936-2000*. Washington, DC: U.S. Department of Health and Human Services. Available at http://www.acf.dhhs.gov/news/stats/3697.htm.

Assistant Secretary for Planning and Evaluation. 2000. *Leavers and Diversion Studies: Summary of Research on Welfare Outcomes Funded by ASPE*. Washington, DC: U.S. Department of Health and Human Services.

Associated Press. 1999. Welfare Reform Fails Poorest: Many Who Are Eligible Don't Get Food Stamps. *Chicago Tribune*, 22 Aug.

Bane, Mary Jo and David T. Ellwood. 1994. *Welfare Realities: From Rhetoric to Reform*. Cambridge, MA: Harvard University Press.

Bell, Lissa and Carson Strege-Flora. 2000. *Access Denied: Federal Neglect Gives Rise to State Lawlessness*. Seattle, WA: Northwest Federation of Community Organizations.

Chong, Dennis. 1995. Creating Common Frames of Reference on Political Issues. In *Political Persuasion and Attitude Change*, ed. D. C. Mutz, P. M. Sniderman, and R. A. Brody. Ann Arbor: University of Michigan Press.

Cobb, Roger W. and Marc Howard Ross, eds. 1997. *Cultural Strategies of Agenda Denial: Avoidance, Attack, and Redefinition*. Lawrence: University Press of Kansas.

Collins, Chuck, Betsy Leondar-Wright, and Holly Sklar. 1999. *Shifting Fortunes: The Perils of the Growing American Wealth Gap*. Washington, DC: United for a Fair Economy.

Danziger, Sheldon H. and Daniel H. Weinberg. 1994. The Historical Record: Trends in Family Income, Inequality, and Poverty. In *Confronting Poverty: Prescriptions for Change*, ed. S. H. Danziger, G. D. Sandefur, and D. H. Weinberg. Cambridge, MA: Harvard University Press.

DeParle, Jason. 1999. *The Welfare Dilemma: A Collection of Articles by Jason DeParle*. New York: New York Times. Available at http://www.nytimes.com/library/national/deparle-index.html.

Dion, M. Robin and LaDonna Pavetti. 2000. *Access to and Participation in Medicaid and the Food Stamp Program: A Review of the Recent Literature*. Washington, DC: Mathematica Policy Research.

Edelman, Murray. 1977. *Political Language: Words that Succeed and Policies that Fail*. New York: Academic Press.

———. 1988. *Constructing the Political Spectacle*. Chicago: University of Chicago Press.

Edelman, Peter. 1997. The Worst Thing Bill Clinton Has Done. *Atlantic Monthly* Mar.:43-58.

Ehrenreich, Barbara. 1987. The New Right Attack on Social Welfare. In Frances Fox Piven, Richard A. Cloward, Barbara Ehrenreich, and Fred Block, *The Mean Season: The Attack on the Welfare State.* New York: Pantheon.

Falk, Gene. 2000. *Welfare Reform: Trends in the Number of Families Receiving AFDC and TANF.* Washington, DC: Congressional Research Service, Domestic Social Policy Division.

Feldman, Stanley and John Zaller. 1992. The Political Culture of Ambivalence: Ideological Responses to the Welfare State. *American Journal of Political Science* 36(1):268-307.

Fishman, Mark. 1980. *Manufacturing the News.* Austin: University of Texas Press.

Gilens, Martin. 1999. *Why Americans Hate Welfare.* Chicago: University of Chicago Press.

Goldberg, Heidi and Liz Schott. 2000. *A Compliance-Oriented Approach to Sanctions in State and County TANF Programs.* Washington, DC: Center on Budget and Policy Priorities.

Gusfield, Joseph. 1981. *The Culture of Public Problems.* Chicago: University of Chicago Press.

Hallin, Daniel C. 1984. The Media, the War in Vietnam, and Political Support: A Critique of the Thesis of an Oppositional Media. *Journal of Politics* 46:2-224.

Hilzenrath, David S. 2000. N.Y. Judge Shelves Welfare Contracts Won by Maximus; Procurement Process Ruled "Corrupted." *Washington Post,* 22 Aug.

Kelly, Michael. 1999. Assessing Welfare Reform. *Washington Post,* 4 Aug.

———. 2000. Doves' Day of Reckoning. *Washington Post,* 11 Oct.

Loprest, Pamela. 1999. *Families Who Left Welfare and How They Are Doing.* Washington, DC: Urban Institute.

Loprest, Pamela J. and Sheila R. Zedlewski. 1999. *Current and Former Welfare Recipients: How Do They Differ?* Washington, DC: Urban Institute.

Luker, Kristin. 1996. *Dubious Conceptions: The Politics of Teenage Pregnancy.* Cambridge, MA: Harvard University Press.

Maloy, Kathleen A., LaDonna A. Pavetti, Peter Shin, Julie Darnell, and Lea Scarpulla-Nolan. 1998. Description and Assessment of State Approaches to Diversion Programs and Activities Under Welfare Reform. Available at http://aspe.os.dhhs.gov/hsp/isp/diverzn/.

Miller, William H. 1998. Surprise! Welfare Reform Is Working. *Industry Week,* 16 Mar.

Pavetti, LaDonna. 1993. The Dynamics of Welfare and Work: Exploring the Process by Which Women Work Their Way off Welfare. Ph.D. diss., Harvard University.

Piven, Frances Fox, and Richard A. Cloward. 1993. *Regulating the Poor: The Functions of Public Welfare.* New York: Vintage.

Rank, Mark R. 1994. *Living on the Edge: The Realities of Welfare in America.* New York: Columbia University Press.

Rector, Robert E. and Sarah E. Youssef. 1999. *The Determinants of Welfare Caseload Decline.* Report no. 99-04. Washington, DC: Heritage Center for Data Analysis, Heritage Foundation.

Rubin, Allen and Earl Babbie. 2000. *Research Methods for Social Work.* 4th ed. Belmont, CA: Wadsworth.

Schram, Sanford F. 1995. *Words of Welfare: The Poverty of Social Science and the Social Science of Poverty.* Minneapolis: University of Minnesota Press.

———. 2000. *After Welfare: The Culture of Postindustrial Social Policy*. New York: New York University Press.

Schultze, Steve. 2000. Lawmakers Want Maximus Fired: Six Legislators say W-2 Contractor Has Broken Faith. *Milwaukee Journal Sentinel*, 27 Oct.

Scott, Daryl Michael. 1997. *Contempt & Pity: Social Policy and the Image of the Damaged Black Psyche, 1880-1996*. Chapel Hill: University of North Carolina Press.

Sigal, Leon V. 1973. *Reporters and Officials: The Organization and Politics of Newsmaking*. Lexington, MA: D.C. Heath.

Soss, Joe. 2000. *Unwanted Claims: The Politics of Participation in the U.S. Welfare System*. Ann Arbor: University of Michigan Press.

Soss, Joe, Sanford F. Schram, Thomas P. Vartanian, and Erin O'Brien. 2001. Setting the Terms of Relief: Explaining State Policy Choices in the Devolution Revolution. *American Journal of Political Science* 45(2):378-95.

Stefancic, Jean, Richard Delgado, and Mark Tushnet. 1996. *No Mercy: How Conservative Think Tanks and Foundations Changed America's Social Agenda*. Philadelphia: Temple University Press.

Stone, Deborah A. 1997. *Policy Paradox: The Art of Political Decision Making*. New York: Norton.

U.S. General Accounting Office. 1999. *Welfare Reform: Information on Former Recipients' Status*. Washington, DC: U.S. General Accounting Office.

Wallace, Geoffrey and Rebecca Blank. 1999. *What Goes Up Must Come Down? Explaining Recent Changes in Public Assistance Caseloads*. Chicago: Northwestern University.

Wilson, Laura A., Robert P. Stoker, and Dennis McGrath. 1999. Welfare Bureaus as Moral Tutors: What Do Clients Learn from Paternalistic Welfare Reforms? *Social Science Quarterly* 80(3):473-86.

Zaller, John. 1992. *The Nature and Origins of Mass Opinion*. New York: Cambridge University Press.

ANNALS, *AAPSS*, **577**, September 2001

Fallacies of
Welfare-to-Work Policies

By RANDY ALBELDA

ABSTRACT: One main effort of welfare reform is to replace public assistance with earnings. To date, politicians and welfare reform advocates have applauded the efforts and claimed success. However, lurking at the surface of welfare-to-work policies are serious problems and structural impediments. Lack of jobs, low pay, job-readiness, and difficulties in securing ancillary supports like transportation and child care are obvious problems that are not easily resolved. However, a deeper and usually unaddressed problem is that the jobs low-income women take (or need) are not mother ready. Full-time low-wage work does not provide enough income to support families, nor does it accommodate the demands that full-time parents have. These problems plague welfare-to-work efforts and make life very difficult for poor, single-mother families. At the same time, they create an opportunity to consider the value of caregiving work and to reform the nature of low-wage work.

Randy Albelda, a professor of economics at the University of Massachusetts Boston, is the author of Economics and Feminism: Disturbances in the Field *and coauthor of* The War on the Poor: A Defense Manual *and* Glass Ceilings and Bottomless Pits: Women's Work, Women's Poverty. *She often contributes to state and local groups' legislative and educational efforts to improve welfare and employment policies affecting low-income women and their families.*

WITH the draconian changes to welfare at the state and federal levels, a great many scholars are cashing in on the waves of foundation and government money attached to studying the impacts of welfare reform. A hefty share of these researchers are examining how adults leaving welfare are faring, with an emphasis on their earnings and employment situations. What is astonishing about the results from these "leaver" studies is how similar they are, despite the supposed diversity of programs adopted by the states. Between two-thirds and three-quarters of adults are employed most often for about 35 hours a week, earning an average hourly wage of about $7.50 in jobs that as often as not do not have health care benefits and rarely provide any sick days and little or no vacation time.[1] Evidence is mounting that many leavers do not stay employed for very long, reproducing a pattern well established before welfare reform of cycling in and out of the labor market. Soon, however, some will not cycle back onto welfare because time limits preclude that.

Average income levels of the families leaving welfare are still at or near poverty levels. Families in the bottom 20 percent of the income distribution—most of whom are poor—have more earnings-related income (wages and the earned income tax credit [EITC]) but a lot less government income associated with being poor (welfare and food stamps). Overall, the loss of public assistance swamps increases in earnings and tax credits, leaving families with about the same, or even less, income, despite the high levels of employment generated since welfare reform.

These not-so-spectacular results occurred during the best economic expansion in 40 years and before most states hit time limits on welfare receipt. In short, these are the best results we can expect from welfare reform. Still, politicians are thrilled with the results. Almost universally they tout declines in caseloads as evidence of the resounding success of welfare reform (see the article by Sanford F. Schram and Joe Soss in this volume). Researchers argue that most of those who were once on welfare are now employed and see this as a positive result.[2]

The effort to place former welfare mothers in jobs is not costless or effortless. States, nonprofit organizations, and advocates are spending enormous amounts of resources trying to make welfare-to-work policies work. Researchers are busily documenting the types of supports women need to make a successful transition into the low-wage labor market. Despite claims of success, lurking at the surface are problems and structural impediments. Problems such as whether there are enough jobs and if the jobs former welfare recipients get pay living wages are being raised and sometimes get play in the press (and other outlets). Some of these problems are being addressed head-on, like the issue of whether mothers are job ready. However, there are other problems, ones that are much more structural and symbolic, that are not being raised. These problems revolve around the nature of the low-wage labor market and the overriding reality that poor mothers are primary caretakers. It is not only that the jobs pay far too little—even with financial incentives—but that they are not mother ready.

Most accept the general strategy of replacing public assistance with earnings but do not dare address the dramatic changes needed in low-wage labor markets or the implementation of adequate caregiving policies that must accompany this strategy. As currently implemented, the welfare-to-work solution is a match made in hell. It joins together poor mothers with few resources whose family responsibilities require employment flexibility with jobs in the low-wage labor market that often are the most inflexible, have the least family-necessary benefits (vacation time, health care, sick days), and provide levels of pay that often are insufficient to support a single person, let alone a family. This mismatch will not be resolved by providing the types of supports that are currently being discussed and provided: short-term job training, work vans, poor-quality child care, or refundable earned income tax credits.

The welfare-to-work mismatch is more than an individual problem to be resolved by sympathetic counseling and financial incentives. It is a political, social, and economic problem that must be addressed in our policies as well as in our national psyche. It starts with valuing the work that families do. Raising children—with or without two adults in a family—is absolutely vital and deserving work to our individual and collective well-being.

Overlooking or not counting unpaid work conceptually and empirically overestimates the "success" of welfare reform and undermines women's progress for economic equality. Promoting more family-based benefits for low-income workers will help immensely. But we will not be able to totally eliminate public income support for low-income parents who are taking care of families. The ideological base for providing employment-based benefits are well established in the United States, but the base for appreciating the value of care is not. We will need to make more progress by engaging in a new kind of family values debate, one that argues that the work families do is valuable and worth supporting, even—or especially—if the family is poor.

WELFARE TO WHAT?

Before addressing the welfare-to-work strategy, it is instructive to think about the other ways in which poor women leave welfare. This is important because time limits and full-family sanctions virtually assure that the majority of families who receive welfare will be cut off, at least from federal funding. Not having access to welfare poses some historically familiar alternatives for women. First, instead of being dependent on the state, women can be dependent on family members—a much more acceptable form of dependency. Single mothers can get their income or in-kind support from parents, sisters, boyfriends, or former husbands. Efforts to crack down on deadbeat dads and fatherhood initiatives are a modern corollary to family dependency (see the article by Gwendolyn Mink in this volume). Getting married and staying married was of course the fond hope and major inspiration for conservatives who sponsored the 1996 welfare reform federal legislation.[3]

A second way families without public assistance or income from other family members support themselves is to give up their children—by choice or by force. Newt Gingrich was lambasted for floating the idea of orphanages in the mid-1990s, but it seems totally plausible that the states will be seriously discussing this option soon. Newspaper accounts across the country often report on overloaded child protection agencies, increasingly removing children from families for poverty-related reasons. Preliminary data are consistent with this scenario: the percentage of child-only cases on the welfare rolls has increased steeply in a short period of time, from 17 percent in 1994 to 29 percent in 1999 (U.S. Department of Health and Human Services 1999, exhibit 1).

Promoting marriages and discussing ways to snatch children, while important ways to end welfare, are not usually the main focus. Instead, most states, as well as the ancillary not-for-profit agencies and for-profit companies that get lucrative welfare-to-work-related contracts, are putting their energies into getting adult welfare recipients to work. In this case, work is always intended to mean paid employment or unpaid community or public service placements (that is, workfare).

Welfare-to-work policies embody a wide range of methods for promoting paid work instead of welfare. These include the punitive work-first strategies pursued by over half the states to the more liberal strategies that include a generous package of training and education options, financial incentives, day care, transportation, and health care. And despite its current popularity, the notion of putting welfare mothers to work is hardly new. Gwendolyn Mink (1998) traces the history of work requirements in the Aid to Families with Dependent Children (AFDC) program since the legislation's inception and argues that by the late 1960s work requirements were seen as an important way to get women, particularly black women, off the welfare rolls. It was only in the early 1990s, however, that paid work was viewed as the main alternative in light of time-limit benefits.

Most researchers, politicians, agency heads, and advocates assume that work is good and that people on public assistance, if physically possible, should be working. It is easy to see why they, as well as liberals and progressives, find work appealing. Employment breaks welfare recipients' presumed (although not empirically validated) cycle of dependency. Further, when adult recipients work, even if they receive hefty supplements, they are not perceived as receiving handouts and hence are deserving. It would seem, then, putting welfare mothers to work solves the welfare problem of growing welfare rolls and plays into American values that will help restore safety nets for the poor. There are other reasons to want to see women employed as well, such as the ability to be economically independent. This allows for a much larger range of choices and less control by men or by the state.

THE WORK DEBATE

These are clearly important and laudable reasons to want to see low-income mothers employed, but there should be considerable unease with current efforts to put welfare mothers to work.

One issue is whether there are jobs at all and what happens to the low-wage labor market when millions of welfare mothers look for paid employment. Outside of exceptional expansions, the macroeconomic structure makes jobs for workers with low educational attainment and few marketable skills difficult if not impossible to get and keep (see, for example, Hoynes 2000; Smith and Woodbury 2000). Further, wage pressures caused by the increased ranks of the low-wage labor market caused by welfare-to-work policies could serve to reduce wages for all workers at the bottom (Burtless 2000; Bartik 2000). With black adults facing unemployment rates twice that of whites, the availability of jobs and the persistence of labor market discrimination cannot be dismissed.

The economic expansion of the 1990s has both accompanied and accommodated welfare-to-work policies. The economy has almost seamlessly absorbed close to 1 million new workers from welfare, but come the downturn, many who did get jobs will lose them and caseloads

will creep back up. Smith and Woodbury (2000) estimate that in the last recession over 1 million low-wage jobs were lost. The long expansion has allowed states to be slack, if not entirely unimaginative, in their training and education efforts, relying on the economic expansion to reduce rolls.

Another problem with welfare-to-work policy is the low pay women get. Without having to do much academic heavy lifting, Nobel prizewinner Robert Solow (1998a, 1998b) conjures up basic macroeconomic theory on labor markets, results on experiments with the previous welfare program—AFDC—some common sense, and compassion to make a forceful case that welfare reform is both wishful thinking and pure folly. Current policy will turn those who are already poor and receiving cash assistance into the working poor, at the same time making some of the non-welfare-receiving poor worse off. For Solow, the economics of the problem are quite simple. Society cannot expect single mothers to enter low-wage labor markets and exit poverty. Recent examinations of the low-wage labor force come to similar conclusions (Bernstein and Hartmann 2000). The obvious solutions are to improve low-wage jobs and improve the supplements to workers with low-wage jobs.

There have been important efforts toward supplementing earnings. The federal government has expanded the EITC, which serves to both boost low wages and provide financial incentives to employment. Several states have established or expanded their own EITC programs as well.

Generous financial incentives—like high earnings disregards and the EITC—seem to work not only in encouraging employment but in reducing poverty (Miller et al. 2000; Blank, Card, and Robins 2000). However, most states are not implementing generous financial incentives, and at least one state that did—Minnesota—saw welfare use increase because in order to truly support families when employed requires sustained commitment to providing cash benefits. Instead, most states use time-limited financial incentives that have low-income thresholds of eligibility (including the EITC). This is precisely why women leaving welfare for earnings or packaging welfare and earnings are still poor (see, for example, Danziger 2000). As a result, current wage supplements are not proving an antidote for welfare reduction. Despite the fact that more families rely on earnings rather than on public aid, the income of the bottom quintile of single mothers has declined (Porter and Primus 1999; Primus et al. 1999). There is little doubt that carrots—financial incentives like EITC and higher earnings disregards—are better than sticks like sanctions and time limits, both in terms of outcomes and welfare policy gestalt. However, they have yet be very successful in taking most poor families off the poverty track for long.

A third problem with welfare-to-work policies is the issue of the job readiness of welfare mothers. Research confirms that many welfare mothers have low educational attainment and lack recent job experience (although the vast majority

have been employed at some point). Both of these characteristics impede entry into the labor market and, once there, all but assure low wages. Recent research is uncovering another set of barriers to work that have little to do with individual motivation, human capital investments, or self-help. These barriers include women's learning disabilities, severe bouts of depression, and experiences with domestic violence.

There is growing evidence that states, especially those that promote work-first strategies, are finding that the easy-to-place recipients have left the welfare system, but those who require much more training to get paid employment remain (see, for example, Danziger 2000). Ironically, or perhaps cynically, welfare is becoming more and more like it was portrayed for years—a system that serves very-low-functioning women with many children who need assistance for many years. Women with barriers to employment will need time and long-term training to move up and out, something welfare reform is discouraging or prohibiting.

Finding a job, earning enough to support a family, removing barriers to employment, and skill development are problems faced by any poor adult in the United States. However, what distinguishes welfare recipients from other poor people is that the vast majority are children being raised, most often, by a mother on her own. Not surprisingly, a fourth concern or critique with welfare-to-work policy revolves around the set of ancillary supports that mothers need to get to work. While there are several needs, such as transportation and health care coverage, by far the biggest and most expensive is child care. While states are using the money from the Temporary Assistance for Needy Families (TANF) program to purchase child care, there still is not enough. There already is a child care crisis without welfare mothers boosting demand. The cost of quality care is typically far beyond the reach of many low-income parents. Very little attention has been paid to the quality of child care that women leaving welfare are finding. Who knows what is happening to children, including school-age children, when mothers are employed? These are problems that have not been solved and will have enormous implications for both the sustainability of welfare-to-work policies and the well-being of families now and in the future.

THE PROBLEMS
NOT DISCUSSED

As pressing as these concerns are, they are by now relatively well established. Solving them will be necessary in constructing any decent system of welfare but will not be sufficient to crafting policies that work.

What is almost always ignored or conveniently forgotten in critiques of welfare-to-work policies is that the U.S. labor market has always failed women who have little formal education and sporadic job experiences. Women have a very hard time supporting themselves, let alone supporting families. Low-income women are still segregated into low-paying occupations, despite the vast improvements for college-educated women. In 1998, 54 percent of all women worked in sales, service, or administrative support occupations (U.S. Bureau of Labor Statistics 2000, 176). Over one-third (35.3 percent) of all women in 1997 earned too little to pull themselves up to the poverty level for a family of four, even if they worked 52 weeks a years, 40 hours a week (Bernstein and Hartmann 2000, 20). For former welfare recipients, the likelihood of being in low-paying work is remarkably high. One study found that between 1984 and 1990 two out of every three women moving off welfare worked in sales, service, or clerical jobs (Spalter-Roth et al. 1995). Recent leaver studies indicate little change in these results. Even though the new solution to welfare is immediate employment, there are still the same old problems that single mothers have always faced: a low-wage labor market, coping with family demands, overcoming barriers to employment, and the need for ancillary supports.

Jobs that pay family-sustaining wages are not mother ready, nor are the jobs that low-income mothers are finding, even when they get training, find work, have child care arrangements, and receive wage supplements. The needs jobs cannot meet include remarkably mundane events such as sick children, school and medical appointments, school vacations, and early-release school days. Employers, especially those who employ low-wage workers, will not tolerate workers who come in late because a school bus did not show up, miss days because there was no child care or a kid was sick, or worry about their children at 3 p.m. instead of doing their work.

The work of taking care of families is often inconsistent with the demands of being a family breadwinner. Yet, this work-family dilemma is overlooked in welfare reform research and policy. For example, the work of taking care of children is not seen as work or as an important family and economic input in the welfare-to-work strategy; rather, it is seen as a cost of going to work and only recognized as important when women get jobs.

What much of the welfare-to-work debate fails to confront is the complex nature of paid and unpaid work for all families, particularly those with children, and particularly for poor families. Adults responsible for children many times cannot (and probably should not) put their jobs—especially low-wage ones—before the needs (mundane or profound) of their children. Instead of trying to reform poor mothers to become working-poor mothers, we need to take a closer look at job structures and what it will take to make work possible for mothers who support families.

THE VALUE DEBATES

The obsession with employment for poor mothers is the culmination of a major value shift in thinking about women and public assistance. The Social Security Act of 1935 entitled poor single mothers to receive AFDC, although the levels received were far lower than in the other two major programs (Social Security and Unemployment Insurance) included

in that historic legislation. Further, the value set governing aid for single mothers was in direct contrast to that guiding both the benefit levels and the allocation of Social Security and Unemployment Insurance. The latter are employment-based cash assistance doled out to those who have long-term, continuous employment participation. In the 1930s, paid work became the entry door to entitlements, and the benefits were not based on need—although they were initially based on type of employment, which effectively excluded black and female workers. In 1935, single mothers in the industrial North were not expected to do paid labor—indeed, white women were discouraged from it in the 1930s. However, the benefits were kept intentionally low so as not to discourage marriage (Gordon 1994). Widows were seen as deserving, whereas divorced, separated, and never-married mothers were not. Benefit levels reinforce these values. Widows and their children received much more generous funds from Social Security than did nonwidowed single mothers receiving AFDC (and now TANF).

Today, what makes a single mother entitled and deserving has changed. It is no longer sufficient to be a parent raising children on one's own. Indeed, the most salient factor in determining the level and length of support one might receive is if one is engaged in paid labor. This sentiment is only possible in an age where most women are in the paid labor market and when the moral repugnance of women without men has dissipated. Making the demand that single mothers work because other mothers do is politically, although not necessarily economically, feasible. Few seem to notice that the majority of married mothers do not work in year-round, full-time jobs, yet for single mothers to move from welfare to work to self-sufficiency would require being employed more than 40 hours a week every week of the year.[4] In order to deserve the generosity of American taxpayers, single mothers need to give back something in return. Importantly, this goes beyond doing the work of raising children. In the words of Mary Jo Bane (1997), "The public, rightly, wanted welfare reform that expected work and parental responsibility" (47).

The positive value of employment has been accompanied by the negative value placed on receiving welfare. Led by Ronald Reagan and Charles Murray in the 1980s, women on welfare were given the title of welfare queen. Women on welfare were presumed to have loads of children and then pass down the legacy of welfare receipt to their children. Receiving welfare, in these accounts, constituted dysfunctional behavior. Liberal poverty researchers carried this banner as well. Notably, William Julius Wilson (1987) and Christopher Jencks (1991), as well as their left detractors, such as William Darity and Samuel Myers (1994), discuss welfare receipt as a pathology—one of the many "bad" behaviors that helps reproduce poverty. Jencks (1991, 83) even refers to women receiving welfare as the "reproductive underclass." In this debate, paid work is good, and welfare receipt is bad. Therefore, to make progress, poor mothers need to be in the labor force and off welfare.

I am not arguing that paid work is bad. Indeed, earnings can and do buy economic security and some independence from men, especially from abusive relationships. In a society that values paid work, employment can build one's self-esteem as well. There is no doubt that women's ability to earn wages has the potential to set them free. However, welfare-to-work policies are a set up. The types of jobs many poor mothers get and keep do not provide much dignity or sufficient wages. Working enough hours at low wages to support a family is often untenable. Women fail too often. This is not only demoralizing; it is economically debilitating. For many, welfare-to-work policies are a cruel hoax that makes legislators feel better about themselves, but leaves poor families in the lurch.

Ironically, for different reasons, many conservatives and some progressives are not so comfortable with the new welfare values of putting mothers to work—at least as they apply to middle- and upper-income mothers. Many would prefer to see all mothers in heterosexual marriages rather than on welfare or working. But conservatives are having a very hard time mandating marriage for anyone. Instead, they will settle for bullying welfare mothers, making sure gays and lesbians cannot get married, and providing hefty tax breaks for married stay-at-home moms.

The antifeminist version of this argument is that feminists have played a cruel hoax on the American people by insisting that women can do it all—have fulfilling careers and be terrific mothers. For example, Danielle Crittenden (1999) argues that feminism is unnatural because women need to raise their own children and not be in the labor force full-time and hiring nannies. Women should stay home and let their husbands support them.

While the analysis and solution is faulty, the problem of having it all is real. Even assuming, as these authors typically do, that everyone is white and college educated, what may be at fault is not women wanting to be employed but, rather, what it means for both men and women to be in full-time jobs that pay living wages. Our current job structure is built on the assumption that unpaid labor is free and plentiful, while family-supporting jobs (with high pay and benefits) preclude the actual work of taking care of families. For families without the benefit of college education or ones that have historically and currently faced barriers to employment, men's falling wages and families' need for women's income means that all parents must be employed in order to have enough income to make ends meet.

For progressives, the sole focus on making employment a deserving behavior without also reevaluating the nature of care work is both practically and politically problematic. Rather than be preoccupied with the value of paid work in building a safety net, more progress for all might be made by focusing on the value of the economic work performed in the home and what constitutes a family.

WHAT WE NEED

A national discussion about the value of women's work in the home and the nature of low-wage work for women with children might redirect our nation's priorities. Rather than tax breaks, we might consider an infusion of public funds to help raise and take care of family members. Such a discussion might promote employers and the government to construct policies that revamp paid work to accommodate unpaid work, rather than the other way around.

At a minimum, we need universal early education programs, extended school day programs, and child allowances. We should consider a shorter work week or at least income supplements to low-income workers who take part-time jobs so that families can still pay for basic needs like housing, health insurance, child care, food, and clothing. Paid family and medical leave and expanding unemployment insurance to cover less continuous and low-paying part-time work must also be in place. Pay equity would help, since women's wages are lower than men's in jobs that require comparable skills and effort. Enforcement of antidiscrimination laws and affirmative action would help low-income women of color.

If we as a nation recognized the value of women's work, we would not have welfare reform that substitutes public assistance with the earnings of mothers in low-wage jobs and a shallow set of supports that vanish quickly. Seeing the work of raising children as a benefit to families and society, not merely as a cost of going to work, would mean developing a welfare-to-work regime that truly supports part-time waged work. Further, it might makes us more cognizant that for some families at some points in their lives, having the sole adult in the labor force is not possible or desirable. Public income supports for poor single mothers will always need to exist precisely because we value the work of mothers taking care of their children. Arbitrary time limits, meager benefits, and a fractured system of welfare defined by individual states (and sometimes counties) all work against a real safety net.

If there is an opportunity in welfare-to-work welfare reform, it is in recognizing that jobs, especially at the low end of the pay scale, do not pay enough to support families and do not provide the flexibility that parents need. It is only an opportunity, however, if we can get past the welfare-to-work mentality.

Notes

1. There are many leaver studies, too many to mention. A catalog of them can be found at http://www.researchforum.org/. For an excellent list of studies, go to http://www.welfareinfo.org/trackingstudies.htm. In addition, Appendix L to the 2000 congressional *Green Book* includes findings from leaver studies (U.S. House of Representatives 2000).

2. For example, the introduction of a recent edited volume on employment and welfare reform by highly respected and relatively liberal labor economists concludes, "So far, the evidence suggests that welfare reform is proceeding as well as or better than most analysts had expected. In terms of declining caseloads and increasing work effort among single mothers, welfare reform has been an astonishing success. . . . The research in this book suggests we are on the right track with many policy efforts" (Blank and Card 2000, 17-18).

3. This is made very clear in the findings section (101) of the 1996 Personal Responsibility and Work Opportunity Reconciliation Act (H.R. 3734), which leads with these two findings: "1) Marriage is the foundation of a successful society; and 2) Marriage is an essential institution of a successful society which promotes the interests of children" (Public Law 104-193).

4. For a notable exception, see Cohen and Bianchi 1999.

References

Bane, Mary Jo. 1997. Welfare As We Might Know It. *American Prospect* 30(Jan./Feb.):47-53.

Bartik, Timothy J. 2000. Displacement and Wage Effects of Welfare Reform. In *Finding Jobs: Work and Welfare Reform*, ed. Rebecca Blank and David Card. New York: Russell Sage Foundation.

Bernstein, Jared and Heidi Hartmann. 2000. Defining and Characterizing the Low-Wage Labor Market. In *The Low-Wage Labor Market: Challenges and Opportunities for Economic Self-Sufficiency*, ed. Kelleen Kaye and Demetra Smith Nightingale. Washington, DC: U.S. Department of Health and Human Services.

Blank, Rebecca and David Card. 2000. Introduction: The Labor Market and Welfare Reform. In *Finding Jobs: Work and Welfare Reform*, ed. Rebecca Blank and David Card. New York: Russell Sage Foundation.

Blank, Rebecca M., David E. Card, and Phillip K. Robins. 2000. Financial Incentives for Increasing Work and Income Among Low-Income Families. In *Finding Jobs: Work and Welfare Reform*, ed. Rebecca Blank and David Card. New York: Russell Sage Foundation.

Burtless, Gary. 2000. Can the Labor Market Absorb Three Million Welfare Recipients? In *The Low-Wage Labor Market: Challenges and Opportunities* for Economic Self-Sufficiency, ed. Kelleen Kaye and Demetra Smith Nightingale. Washington, DC: U.S. Department of Health and Human Services.

Cohen, Philip N. and Suzanne M. Bianchi. 1999. Marriage, Children and Women's Employment: What Do We Know? Monthly Labor Review 122(12):22-31.

Crittenden, Danielle. 1999. What Our Mothers Didn't Tell Us: Why Happiness Eludes the Modern Woman. New York: Simon and Schuster.

Danziger, Sheldon. 2000. Approaching the Limit: Early Lessons from Welfare Reform. Paper prepared at Rural Dimensions of Welfare Reform, sponsored by the Joint Center for Poverty Research, Northwestern University/University of Chicago, May. Available at http://www.jcpr.org/wp/WPprofile.cfm?ID=203.

Darity, William A. Jr. and Samuel Myers Jr., with Emmett D. Carson and William Sabol. 1994. The Black Underclass: Critical Essays on Race and Unwantedness. New York: Garland Press.

Gordon, Linda. 1994. Pitied but Not Entitled: Single Mothers and the History of Welfare. New York: Free Press.

Hoynes, Hilary W. 2000. The Employment, Earnings, and Income of Less Skilled Workers over the Business Cycle. In Finding Jobs: Work and Welfare Reform, ed. Rebecca Blank and David Card. New York: Russell Sage Foundation.

Jencks, Christopher. 1991. Is the American Underclass Growing? In The Urban Underclass, ed. Christopher Jencks and Paul E. Peterson. Washington, DC: Brookings Institution.

Miller, Cynthia, Virginia Knox, Lisa A. Gennetian, Martey Dodoo, Jo Anna Hunter, and Cindy Redcross. 2000. Reforming Welfare and Rewarding Work: Final Report on the Minnesota Family Investment Program. Vol. 1: Effects on Adults. New York: Manpower Demonstration Research Corporation.

Mink, Gwendolyn. 1998. Welfare's End. Ithaca, NY: Cornell University Press.

Porter, Kathryn and Wendell Primus. 1999. Changes Since 1995 in the Safety Net's Impact on Child Poverty. Washington, DC: Center on Budget and Policy Priorities.

Primus, Wendell, Lynette Rawlings, Kathy Larin, and Kathryn Porter. 1999. The Initial Impact of Welfare Reform on the Incomes of Single-Mother Families. Washington, DC: Center on Budget and Policy Priorities.

Smith, David M. and Stephen A. Woodbury. 2000. Low-Wage Labor Markets: Changes over the Business Cycle and Differences Across Region and Location. In The Low-Wage Labor Market: Challenges and Opportunities for Economic Self-Sufficiency, ed. Kelleen Kaye and Demetra Smith Nightingale. Washington, DC: U.S. Department of Health and Human Services.

Spalter-Roth, Roberta, Beverly Burr, Heidi Hartmann, and Lois Shaw. 1995. Welfare That Works: The Working Lives of AFDC Recipients. Washington, DC: Institute for Women's Policy Research.

Solow, Robert. 1998a. Lecture I: Guess Who Likes Workfare? In Work and Welfare, ed. Amy Gutmann. Princeton, NJ: Princeton University Press.

———. 1998b. Lecture II: Guess Who Pays for Workfare? In Work and Welfare, ed. Amy Gutmann. Princeton, NJ: Princeton University Press.

U.S. Bureau of Labor Statistics. 2000. Employment and Earnings. Washington, DC: Government Printing Office.

U.S. Department of Health and Human Services. 1999. Administration for Children and Families. Office of Planning, Research and Evaluation. Characteristics and Financial Cir-

cumstances of TANF Recipients, July-September 1999. Available at http://www.acf.dhhs.gov/programs/opre/characteristics/fy99/analysis.htm.

U.S. House of Representatives. 2000. Committee on Ways and Means. *2000 Green Book: Background Material and Data on Programs Within the Juris-* *diction of the Committee on Ways and Means*. Washington, DC: Government Printing Office.

Wilson, William Julius. 1987. *The Truly Disadvantaged: The Inner City, The Underclass, and Public Policy*. Chicago: University of Chicago Press.

ANNALS, *AAPSS*, **577**, September 2001

Violating Women:
Rights Abuses in the
Welfare Police State

By GWENDOLYN MINK

ABSTRACT: The Temporary Assistance for Needy Families (TANF) program subordinates recipients to a series of requirements, sanctions, and stacked incentives aimed at rectifying their personal choices and family practices. In exchange for welfare, TANF recipients must surrender or compromise their vocational freedom, sexual privacy, and reproductive choice, as well as the right to make intimate decisions about how to be and raise a family. As TANF's foremost objective is to restore the patriarchal family, numerous provisions promote marriage and paternal headship while frustrating childbearing and child-raising rights outside of marriage. Implementation decisions and a new wave of welfare reform underscore the centrality of marriage in welfare policy. The current thrust of welfare policy encourages poor mothers to be dependent on men, punishes them for independence, and withholds the material recognition necessary to sustain independence.

Gwendolyn Mink is author of Hostile Environment *(2000),* Welfare's End *(1998),* The Wages of Motherhood *(1995), and* Old Labor and New Immigrants in American Political Development *(1986). She also is editor of* Whose Welfare? *(1999) and coeditor of* The Readers' Companion to U.S. Women's History *(1998). From 1995 to 1997, she cochaired the Women's Committee of 100, a feminist mobilization against punitive welfare reform; currently, she is working on the Women's Committee's efforts to change welfare policy.*

WHEN the 1996 Personal Responsibility and Work Opportunity Reconciliation Act (PRWORA) repealed the old welfare system, it set up a harsh new system that subordinates recipients to a series of requirements, sanctions, and stacked incentives aimed at rectifying their personal choices and family practices. The Temporary Assistance for Needy Families (TANF) program, the welfare system established in 1996, disciplines recipients by either stealing or impairing their basic civil rights. In exchange for welfare, TANF recipients must surrender vocational freedom, sexual privacy, and reproductive choice, as well as the right to make intimate decisions about how to be and raise a family. Ordinarily, these rights are strongly guarded by constitutional doctrine, as they form the core of the Supreme Court's jurisprudence of (heterosexual) personhood and family. Not so for a mother who needs welfare.

The most talked-about aspect of TANF is its dramaturgy of work (cf. Piven and Cloward 1993, 346, 381, 395), but TANF's foremost objective is to restore the patriarchal family. Accordingly, numerous TANF provisions promote marriage and paternal headship while frustrating childbearing and child-raising rights outside of marriage. TANF's impositions on poor mothers' rights to form and sustain their own families—as well as to avoid or exit from untenable relationships with men—proceed from stiff paternity establishment and child support enforcement rules. According to the *2000 Green Book*, TANF's "exceptionally strong paternity establishment requirements" compose its most direct attack on nonmarital childbearing, while mandatory maternal cooperation in establishing and enforcing child support orders impairs nonmarital child raising (U.S. House 2000c, 1530). If mothers do not obey these rules, they lose part or all of their families' benefits.

TANF's patriarchal solutions to welfare mothers' poverty have enjoyed bipartisan support. Democrats and Republicans did fight over some of the meaner provisions of the 1996 TANF legislation, but both agreed that poor women with children should at least be financially tied to their children's biological fathers or, better yet, be married to them. Endangering poor single women's independent childbearing decisions by condemning their decision to raise children independently, both parties agreed that poverty policy should make father-mother family formation its cardinal principle.

The 1996 PRWORA, which created TANF, spelled out policy makers' belief in the social importance of father-mother families in a preamble that recited correlations between single-mother families and such dangers as crime, poor school performance, and intergenerational single motherhood. Declaring that "marriage is the foundation of a successful society," the act went on to establish that the purpose of welfare must be not only to provide assistance to needy families but also to "end the dependence of needy parents on government benefits by promoting job preparation, work, and marriage," "prevent and reduce the incidence of out-of-wedlock pregnancies," and "encourage the formation and maintenance of two-parent families" (U.S. Public Law 104-193, Title I). Subsequent legislation and administrative regulations have strengthened TANF's founding goals through fatherhood programs that "strengthen [fathers'] ability to support a family" and that promote marriage (U.S. House 2000a).[1]

The TANF welfare regime backs up these interventions into poor single mothers' intimate relationships by sanctioning mothers with mandatory work outside the home if they remain single. Mothers who are married do not have to work outside the home, even though they receive welfare, for labor market work by only one parent in a two-parent family satisfies TANF's work requirement (U.S. Public Law 104-193, Title I, sec. 407(c)(1)(B); U.S. House 2000c, 357).[2] Notwithstanding a decade of rhetoric about moving from welfare to work, the TANF regime treats wage work as the alternative to marriage, not to welfare—as punishment for mothers' independence.

Far from "ending dependency," the TANF regime actually fosters poor mothers' dependence on individual men. Provisions that mandate father-mother family relations assume that fathers are the best substitute for welfare. The TANF regime's refusal to invest in mothers' employment opportunities and earning power enforces this assumption, for the combination of skills hierarchies and discrimination in the labor market keeps poor mothers too poor to sustain their families unassisted (see, for example, Acs et al. 1998; Moffitt and Roff 2000; Wider

Opportunities for Women 2000). Moreover, the TANF regime's inattention to social supports such as transportation and child care ensures that single mothers' full-time employment will be an unaffordably expensive proposition indeed.

More than a cruel punishment for their persistent independence, the TANF work requirement is an injury to poor mothers' liberty as both mothers and workers. Obliging recipients to work outside the home 30 hours each week, the work requirement forecloses TANF mothers' choice to work as caregivers for their own children. It also interferes with their independent caregiving decisions, as absences due to lack of child care, for example, can lead to loss of employment—a failure to satisfy the work requirement. Further, the work requirement constrains TANF mothers' choices as labor market workers, such as the choice to prepare for the labor market through education or the choice to leave a hostile workplace (for key provisions see U.S. Public Law 104-193, Title I, sec. 407 (a)(1), 407(c)(2)(B), 407(e)(1)).

These injuries of welfare reform are born of poverty but lived through race. About two-thirds of recipients today are African American, Asian American, Latina, and Native American. From the 1960s to the present day, 35 to 40 percent of recipients have been African American; in 1998, 37.1 percent of TANF recipients were black. Latina and Asian American participation has increased over this period, as the Latino and Asian American populations as a whole have increased. Latina participation in 1998 was 20 percent, Asian American participation was 4.6 percent, and Native American participation was 1.6 percent (U.S. Department of Health and Human Services [DHHS] 1999, tab. 12; U.S. House 2000c, 438).

Steeper racial disparities in welfare participation may be in store, as white recipients are leaving the rolls more rapidly than are women of color or are not entering the rolls at all. In New York City, for example, the number of whites on welfare declined by 57 percent between 1995 and 1998, while the number of blacks declined by 30 percent and the number of Latinas by only 7 percent (DeParle 1998). Nationwide, whites' welfare participation has declined by 25 percent, while African Americans' participation has declined by 17 percent and Latinas' by 9 percent. As a result, women of color have increased as a percentage of TANF adults. In 24 states, women of color compose more than two-thirds of adult TANF enrollments; in 18 of those states, they compose three-quarters or more of enrollments (U.S. House 2000c, 439, tab. 7-29).

This racial distribution of welfare is the logical consequence of the racial distribution of poverty. Women of color have been and still are poorer than everyone else, single mothers of color even more so. In 1999, when 25.4 percent of (non-Hispanic) white single-mother families lived below the poverty line, 46.1 percent of African American and 46.6 percent of Latina single-mother families did so (U.S. Census Bureau 2000, tab. B-3). The racial distribution of poverty is enforced by racism and discrimination in most walks of life. In the labor market, for example, African American women who are employed full-time earn only 64 cents to the white male dollar and 84 cents to a white woman's. The wage gap for Latinas is even larger: 55 cents and 72 cents, respectively (U.S. Bureau of Labor Statistics 2000, chart 2, 3).

If the TANF regime's assault on poor mothers' rights wields an unmistakably disparate racial impact, it does so by imposing unmistakable constraints on poor mothers' gender practices. TANF's paternity establishment, child support enforcement, and work requirements primarily or exclusively target mothers who are not married—because they are not married. Although the total number of nonmarital births is highest among white women, the rate of nonmarital births per 1000 unmarried women has been highest among women of color: 73.4 for non-Hispanic black women and 91.4 for Latinas, as compared to 27 for non-Hispanic, white women (U.S. House 2000c, 1238, 1521). Furthermore, although the total number of single-parent families is highest among whites, the percentage of single-parent families among black families (62.3 percent) is more than twice that among whites (26.6 percent). Moreover, the percentage of black families sustained by never-married mothers (36.5 percent) is exponentially greater than the percentage of white families (6.6 percent) (U.S. House 2000c, 1239, tab. G-4). Finally, according to the *2000 Green Book*, the poverty rate is highest among "independent families" (57.7 percent) and "cohabiting families" (58 percent) sustained by never-married mothers, among whom women of color figure disproportionately (U.S. House 2000c, 1246, tab. G-11).

Given the racial distribution of poverty, the presence of nonmarital mothers of color on TANF rolls is disproportionately high. TANF's gendered provisions are therefore racialized in their effects. These effects are not unplanned, for sounding the alarm against "fatherless childrearing," the TANF regime stakes itself to "the perspicacity of Moynihan's vision" that "black Americans [are] held back economically and socially in large part because their family structure [is] deteriorating" (U.S. House 2000c, 1519). And so the TANF regime exploits women-of-color poverty to suffocate single mothers' independence.

WOMEN'S RIGHTS UNDER TANF

The rights imperiled by TANF policies range from basic expectations of autonomy and privacy among civilized and respectful people to liberty guarantees that have been deemed fundamental to constitutional citizenship. Diminishing or withholding liberty guarantees from poor single mothers who receive welfare, the TANF regime creates a welfare caste to whom constitutional principles do not apply.

One of the engines behind the 1996 welfare reform was the idea that constitutional protections won by recipients during the 1960s and early 1970s had undermined recipients' responsibility and increased their dependency. The 1996 law accordingly aimed to substitute

welfare discipline for welfare rights. This involved inventing or refining program requirements to minimize participants' decisional autonomy, personal privacy, and independent personhood. Program rules not only require states to injure recipients' rights but also require recipients to explicitly acquiesce to injury in personal responsibility contracts that they must sign either to apply for or to participate in TANF (State Policy Documentation Project 1999b).

The most visible rights abuse of the TANF regime is its impairment of recipients' vocational liberty. Mandatory work requirements obligate recipients to perform labor market work even if they are not paid for that work. Work requirements compel recipients entering the paid labor force to take the first job they are offered, even if they will not be paid a fair wage or supplied with tolerable working conditions. Moreover, work requirements prohibit recipients from performing family work except after hours, while these requirements permit them to perform the same work (that is, child care) for other people's families. By compelling a particular kind and location of work, TANF indentures recipients to the dramaturgy of work and so dictates their vocational choices (Mink 1998, chap. 4).

Family freedom is another right impaired by TANF program requirements, incentives, and preferences. TANF provisions tell recipients who gets to be part of their families. Paternity establishment and child support rules require mothers to associate at least financially with biological fathers. States may excuse a mother from complying for "good cause," if it is "in the best interest of the child" (U.S. House 2000c, 470). In general, however, a mother must reveal the identity of her child's father and must pursue a child support order against him, whether or not she wants him financially involved in her family's life. Seventeen states require mothers to cooperate with paternity establishment and child support enforcement while their TANF applications are pending—before they receive even a dime in cash assistance (State Policy Documentation Project 1999a). Once a mother receives TANF benefits, her failure to cooperate results in an automatic 25 percent reduction in cash assistance to her family; states are permitted to terminate welfare eligibility altogether (Public Law 104-193, Title I, sec. 408(a)(2)).

In addition to requiring mothers to associate financially with fathers through child support, if not through marriage, TANF pressures mothers to yield parental rights to biological fathers. Access and visitation provisions authorize states to require mothers to open their families to biological fathers. Until 1996, the federal government historically had separated fathers' rights from their obligations, treating visitation and child support as legally separate issues. Under TANF, however, these issues are explicitly connected because policy makers believe that "it [is] more likely for noncustodial parents to make payments of child support if they [have] either joint custody or visitation rights" (U.S. House 2000c, 469).

As TANF's implementing agency at the federal level, the DHHS not only enforces TANF provisions but enhances enforcement with additional regulations and programs. One program, the Clinton administration's Fatherhood Initiative, aggressively works to improve paternity establishment rates. It claims to have contributed to the tripling of established paternities from 512,000 in fiscal year 1992 to 1.5 million in fiscal year 1998 (U.S. DHHS 2000c).

The DHHS administers TANF's provisions for access and visitation programs for fathers through a $10 million annual block grant to states to promote such programs. States may use their funds for mandatory mediation services, for visitation enforcement, and to develop guidelines for alternative custody arrangements (U.S. DHHS 2000c). Access and visitation funds may also be used for programs to encourage or require separating or divorcing parents to reconsider their decision, such as Iowa's mandatory education program on the impact of divorce on children (Bernard 1998, 9-10).

To further promote fathers' involvement in families, Clinton's DHHS awarded grants and waivers to states in support of governmental, faith-based, and nonprofit initiatives such as Parents' Fair Share and Partners for Fragile Families, which aim to engage fathers in the legal, emotional, and financial aspects of parenthood (U.S. DHHS 2000b). DHHS complements its strategy toward fathers with suggestions about how TANF funds can be used to promote marriage among mothers. Department guidelines point out that TANF block grants are "extraordinarily flexible" and allow states to *"change eligibility rules to provide incentives for single parents to marry or for two-parent families to stay together"* (U.S. DHHS 2000d, 3, 19; italics added). Eligibility rules for parents who need TANF—mostly single mothers—can include mandatory enrollment in marriage classes and couples counseling; incentives can include cash payments to TANF mothers who marry.

Asserting an inexorable connection between family structure, economic well-being, and child welfare, these sorts of initiatives override mothers' judgment of their own and their children's best interests. A condition of receiving welfare, these initiatives force poor single mothers to compromise their independence and even to put their rights to their children at risk.

TANF's insistence on biological fathers' responsibility for welfare mothers' children also invades recipients' sexual privacy. Although only consensual heterosexual sex between adults is shielded by privacy under reigning jurisprudence, even that partial right is withheld from unmarried mothers who seek welfare. Mandatory paternity establishment and child support provisions require a mother to identify her child's biological father in order to be eligible for welfare. These provisions single out nonmarital mothers for scrutiny and punishment, as paternity is automatically established at birth if a mother is married. A mother who is not married, who does not know who her child's biological father is, or who does not want

anything to do with him must nevertheless provide welfare officials with information about him.

Even under TANF's predecessor, the Aid to Families with Dependent Children program, paternity establishment rules compromised recipients' privacy. To get the needed information, welfare officials and courts have required independent mothers to answer such questions as, "How many sexual partners have you had? . . . whom did you have sex with before you got pregnant? . . . how often did you have sex? . . . where did you have sex? . . . when did you have sex?" (Kelly 1994, 303-4). TANF encourages more aggressive and systematic intrusion into recipients' sex lives because states are required to punish noncooperating mothers with benefits cuts, because mothers must sign child support income over to the state as a condition of receiving welfare, and because the federal government offers states incentives and services to boost paternity establishment rates.

Sexual privacy is an aspect of reproductive freedom. TANF injures other reproductive rights when it interferes in women's childbearing decisions. For example, the TANF regime let stand state-level policies withholding benefits from children born to mothers who are enrolled on welfare. Beginning in the early 1990s, many states had promulgated these "family cap" policies after securing waivers from federal welfare standards from the Bush (I) and Clinton administrations. The family cap impairs reproductive rights because it punishes and deters a recipient's choice to complete a pregnancy.

TANF further injures reproductive rights through something called "illegitimacy bonuses" (Public Law 104-193, Title I, sec. 403(a)(2)). The bonus is paid to the five states that most successfully reduce the number of nonmarital births without raising the abortion rate. This gives states incentive to discourage conception by unmarried women—by offering cash awards to women who use Norplant, for example.

Sending a further message against having children outside marriage, the TANF regime funds states that offer abstinence education programs. The abstinence education program is required to teach women not to have sex, let alone babies, until they are "economically self-sufficient." States may devolve these programs to private grantees, including church-based groups that teach that abstinence is a matter of "values" and "sexual morality" (Toussaint n.d.). As a corollary to abstinence education, TANF calls for invigorated statutory rape prosecutions—underscoring the abstinence message with the threat of criminal sanctions where teenagers are involved (Public Law 104-193, Title I, sec. 402(a)(1)(v)). As a poor minor woman's nonmarital pregnancy is proof of sex before economic self-sufficiency, the threatened prosecution of nonmarital sex involving welfare recipients is another intrusion on poor single mothers' independence, including their reproductive autonomy. When threats fail in their desired effect of preventing sex and pregnancy, TANF's prohibition on assistance to unmarried teenage

mothers delivers unambiguous punishment.

The TANF regime's various injuries to recipients' reproductive rights ultimately assail poor single women's right to be mothers. The final blow to this right is delivered by child welfare and adoption provisions that speed and ease terminating poor mothers' custody of children. Although the TANF legislation repealed the income entitlement that had belonged to poor mothers and their children, it continued children's entitlement to be removed from unfit parents and their placement in foster care. I have no quarrel with children's entitlement to protective services. However, the discretion delegated to child welfare workers permits them to deploy children's entitlement to foster care as a weapon of welfare discipline against their mothers. A mother who does not comply with work requirements might be deemed an unfit provider, for example. A mother who leaves her child alone to go to a job interview because she cannot find child care might be deemed an unfit caregiver. If she is sanctioned off welfare, has to take a low-wage job, or exhausts her eligibility, a mother may not be able to pay the rent or feed her children. These kinds of circumstances can lead to a finding that she is neglectful. A "neglectful" mother may lose custody of her child, or she may come under intensive supervision by government.

Indeed, DHHS TANF guidelines specifically encourage states to sustain scrutiny of sanctioned recipients for possible unfit parenting. The TANF regime mandates sanctions against recipients who do not meet work requirements, do not cooperate in establishing paternity, or do not cooperate in enforcing child support orders. Sanction penalties vary among states and range from a reduction in an individual mother's benefit the first time she fails to meet her work requirement, to the federally mandated reduction in a family's benefit when a mother fails to cooperate with paternity establishment and child support enforcement, to termination of a family's TANF assistance altogether (see State Policy Documentation Project 1999c). As a practical matter, sanctioned families frequently also lose their Medicaid, even though they remain entitled to receive it. Accordingly, TANF penalties not only breed material vulnerability but also medically endanger families (Dion and Pavetti 2000, 15-17).

DHHS guidelines stipulate that welfare monies may be used to "screen families who have been sanctioned under TANF" to determine whether children are at risk of child abuse or neglect. Mothers who do not want child support, or who do not want to identify biological fathers, or who cannot meet the 30-hour-weekly work requirement thus come under suspicion as abusive or neglectful parents. Mothers who exercise their rights and independent judgment are held to account for the consequences of TANF's brutal rules. If a mother's children are found to be at risk due to sanctions, TANF funds may be used to provide "case management services" to "cure" the mother's noncompliance with TANF rules (U.S. DHHS 2000d, 19).

TANF mothers who lose their benefits, like employed single mothers whose wages are too low to pay for housing, food, or medical care, may surrender their children to foster care. Occasionally, a mother might do so voluntarily until she can get back on her feet. Alternatively, child welfare workers might pressure a mother to do so. The 1997 Adoption and Safe Families Act threatens mothers who have lost their children to foster care with the permanent termination of their parental rights. Designed to accelerate and increase foster care adoptions, the act requires child welfare workers to consider terminating parental rights if a child has been in foster care for 15 out of the previous 22 months (U.S. House 1997; Public Law 105-89). In the four years since enactment of the adoption law, adoptions have increased significantly. According to DHHS, adoptions rose from 28,000 in 1996 to 46,000 in 1999 (U.S. DHHS 2000a). We do not yet have hard evidence directly linking the rise in adoptions with recipients' loss of children. However, with a time limit on parental rights shorter even than the federal time limit on welfare, the adoption law hovers within the TANF regime as the regime's final solution to independent motherhood.

ENSURING INDEPENDENCE

Time limited and disciplinary, the terms of cash assistance enforce poor single mothers' inequality. One measure of this inequality is the persistence of poverty even among mothers who have left welfare for the labor market. Three years after leaving welfare, the median income among employed former welfare recipients was only $10,924 in 1999—well below the poverty line of $14,150 for a family of three. In many former TANF families, income is so low or so tenuous that families must skip meals, go hungry, use food pantries, or apply for emergency food assistance (Women of Color Resource Center 2000; Study Group on Work, Poverty and Welfare 1999). The main reasons for the persistence of poverty among former TANF recipients is that they are moving primarily into low-wage and contingent jobs without benefits, losing access to food stamps and Medicaid, and surrendering as much as 25 percent of their paychecks to child care.

Recognizing that ending welfare did not end single mothers' poverty, many policy makers are eager to pursue a next step in welfare reform. Already under way, this next step has taken legislative form in bipartisan initiatives to promote marriage and to enhance paternal wages and the paternal role. Such proposals have been espoused in various ideological quarters: by both Al Gore and George Bush during the 2000 presidential campaign; by Republican congresswoman Nancy Johnson (R-Conn.) and Democratic senator Evan Bayh (D-Ind.); by the Heritage Foundation's Robert Rector and by House Democrat Jesse Jackson Jr. (D-Ill.). They reveal a consensus that what poor single mothers need is a father's income. A related consensus is that if welfare reform has fallen short it is because too few recipients have gotten married.[3]

The most extreme calls for marriage promotion and fatherhood enhancement come, not surprisingly, from Robert Rector and others at the Heritage Foundation and from Wade Horn, a founder of the National Fatherhood Initiative whom the second George Bush picked to become assistant secretary of DHHS for welfare and related issues. In the Heritage Foundation's *Priorities for the President*, published to greet the new Bush (II) presidency in January 2001, Rector proposed substituting the current financial incentives to states that increase their marriage rates with financial punishments to states that fail to do so. In addition, he urged policymakers to set aside $1 billion in TANF funds annually for marriage promotion activities; to offer incentives and rewards to parents who marry; and to create an affirmative action program in public housing for married couples. Many of Wade Horn's proposals closely track Rector's. In fact, he has endorsed Rector's suggestion that women "at high risk of bearing a child out of wedlock" be paid $1000 annually for five years if they bear their first child within marriage and stay married (Horn 2001). In addition, Horn would further ratchet up the pressure on poor mothers to marry by limiting social programs—such as Head Start, public housing, and welfare—to married parents, allowing participation by single mothers only if funds are left over (Bush and Horn 1997).

Although the most strident calls to condition social benefits on poor mothers' family formation decisions come from conservatives, the idea that social policy should encourage marriage and promote fatherhood enjoys favor in both political parties. Some Democrats and liberal policy wonks—Evan Bayh and Wendell Primus, for example—have argued for Wade Horn's confirmation (Pear 2001). Meanwhile, four bipartisan fatherhood bills had been introduced into the 107th Congress by May 2001 (H.R. 1300; H.R. 1471; S. 653; S. 685).

The first major fatherhood bill to surface in Congress was the Fathers Count Act, which sailed through the House of Representatives in fall 1999. During the final months of the 106th Congress in 2000, Representative Nancy Johnson shepherded similar fatherhood legislation though the House. Part of the Child Support Distribution Act of 2000, Johnson's bill included a $140 million matching-grant program for local projects that promote marital family formation among poor single mothers and a $5 million award to a national fatherhood organization with "extensive experience in *using married couples* to deliver their program in the inner city" (U.S. House 2000a, Title V, Subtitle B, sec. 511 (c)(2)(c); italics added). The committee report accompanying the bill explained that "increasing the number and percentage of American children living in two-parent families is vital if the nation is to make serious and permanent progress against poverty" (U.S. House 2000b, 17).

Measures like the Johnson bill explicitly give fathers incentives to enter poor mothers' families. For example, the Johnson bill offered funds to projects that teach fathers about their visitation and access rights (U.S. House 2000b, 42);

promoted forgiveness of child support arrearages owed by men who become residential fathers; enhanced fathers' earning power through job training and "career-advancing education"; and tracked nonmarital fathers into various social services that encourage marriage (U.S. House 2000a, Title V, Subtitle A, sec. 501(a) and 501(b)). These incentives to fathers impose substantial pressures on mothers, for it is mothers, not fathers, who must obey TANF rules and suffer the consequences of time limits. Fathers get the "carrots," to borrow from Charles Murray, while mothers get the "sticks."

Jesse Jackson Jr.'s Responsible Fatherhood bill duplicated the Johnson bill in many respects. Perhaps more astounding, much of the race-coded, anti-single-mother rhetoric that introduced the Republicans' 1996 PRWORA was repeated in the preamble to the Jackson bill. For example, Jackson's bill asserted that "violent criminals are overwhelmingly males who grew up without fathers and the best predictor of crime in a community is the percentage of absent father households." The preamble concluded, "States should be encouraged, not restricted, from implementing programs that provide support for responsible fatherhood, promote marriage, and increase the incidence of marriage" (U.S. House 2000d).

Bipartisan marriage and fatherhood initiatives assume that poor mothers' intimate decisions about family forms and relationships cause their poverty. They also assume that it is appropriate for government to interfere in the intimate associational life of poor mothers. Even as government scales back its affirmative role in mitigating poverty, it is intensifying its coercive reach into the lives of the poor. Now squarely at the center of poverty policy, marriage promotion and fatherhood initiatives seek to compel mothers to follow the government's moral prescriptions and to accept economic dependence on men.

It is true that a family with a male income generally is better off than a family without one. While some moralistic welfare strategists believe that married fatherhood per se is an important governmental objective, more pragmatic policy strategists reason syllogistically that if men's families are better off economically than women's, then poverty can be cured by the presence of a male income in families. This kind of thinking short circuits equality, foreclosing the question of improving women's own income. If we look at the various measures of women's and mothers' poverty—women's income as compared to men's, for example—it is clear that single mothers are poor because women's work is not valued. This is true of women's labor market work, where a racialized gender gap in wages reflects the devaluation of the work women do. And it is true of women's nonmarket caregiving work, which garners no income at all.

The interconnectedness between poverty, caregiving, and inequality never has received wide or focused attention in the United States. While there have been policies that have provided income assistance to family caregivers, either those policies have been stingy and marginal or their beneficiaries have been relatively few. In addition, to the extent that welfare and other policies have assisted family caregivers, they have done so primarily to protect children's interests rather than to compensate mothers' work or to promote mothers' equality.

Most U.S. feminists have been leery of taking up the cause of women's caregiving work, preferring to promote women's equality as labor market workers than to risk a return to compulsory domesticity. In response to the TANF regime, however, some feminists have begun not only to resist welfare's moral discipline but also to reconceive welfare as caregivers' income (Women's Committee of One Hundred 2000). The idea is that what caregivers—usually mothers—do for their families is work. Moreover, it is work that is indispensable not only to a mother's own family but to her community, the economy, and the polity as well.

Far from a sign of dependence on government, a caregivers' income would provide mothers with economic means in their own right. This would promote equality in father-mother relations both because it would unmask the economic value of mothers' side of the sexual division of labor and because it would enable mothers to exit unhappy, subordinating, or violent relations with the fathers of their children. It also would nurture equality among citizens by establishing that it is not only market work that should earn a living wage but also the caring work upon which the market depends for workers. In turn, a caregivers' income would promote equality among women—between middle-class married caregivers who enjoy social and political support when they choose to work in the home raising children and poor unmarried caregivers whom welfare policy now compels to choose wages over children.

Improved economic rewards and social supports for women's work outside the home are necessary companions to a social wage for their work inside the home. Women must not be pressured into giving care by the low returns of their labor market participation. Just as important, they must not be pressured to forsake care work by the threat of destitution. In combination with labor market reforms, a caregivers' income would indemnify women's—and even men's—vocational choices. "Making work pay" both in the home and in the labor market would combat persistent poverty among single-mother families without pinning family security to fathers' responsibility.

Rethinking welfare as an income owed to caregivers would mitigate severe material vulnerabilities endured by single mothers. Further, it would exhume the rights suffocated by both poverty and the current welfare system. Once it is understood that welfare mothers are poor because their family caregiving work is unremunerated, not because they do not work or are not married, the focus of welfare prescriptions can shift from how to reform poor caregivers to how to ensure their economic and constitutional equality.

Notes

1. The 1999 welfare-to-work amendments loosened rules governing noncustodial parents' eligibility for services. Noncustodial fathers of children enrolled in TANF are eligible for welfare-to-work services, for example, if they are unemployed, underemployed, or having difficulty paying child support obligations. Eligibility for welfare-to-work services is not an entitlement—that is, it is not guaranteed to all who meet the program's criteria. Hence, fathers' increased access to services takes services away from mothers on the brink of reaching welfare time limits. (U.S. Department of Labor 1999).

2. A two-parent family is required to work 35 hours weekly (as compared to the 30-hours-per-week requirement for single parents), unless the family receives federally funded child care. A two-parent family that sends its child or children to federally funded child care must perform 55 hours of labor market work weekly, which permits married mothers to work part-time.

3. Only 0.4 percent of TANF cases closed between October 1997 and September 1998 were closed due to marriage (U.S. DHHS 1999, tab. 31).

References

Acs, Gregory, Norma Coe, Keith Watson, and Robert I. Lerman. 1998. *Does Work Pay? An Analysis of the Work Incentives Under TANF*. Washington, DC: Urban Institute.

Bernard, Stanley. 1998. Responsible Fatherhood and Welfare: How States Can Use the New Law to Help Children. In *Children and Welfare Reform*. Issue Brief no. 4. New York: Columbia University, National Center for Children in Poverty.

Bush, Andrew and Wade Horn. 1997. Fathers, Marriage and Welfare Reform. Available at http://www.welfare reformer.org/articles/father.htm.

DeParle, Jason. 1998. Shrinking Welfare Rolls Leave Record High Share of Minorities. *New York Times*, 24 July.

Dion, Robin M. and LaDonna Pavetti. 2000. *Access to and Participation in Medicaid and the Food Stamp Program*. Washington, DC: Mathmatica Policy Research.

Heritage Foundation. 2001. *Priorities for the President*. Alexandria, VA: Heritage Foundation.

Horn, Wade. 2001. Wedding Bell Blues: Marriage and Welfare Reform. *Brookings Review* 19(3):39-42.

Kelly, Lisa. 1994. If Anybody Asks Who I Am: An Outsider's Story of the Duty to Establish Paternity. *Yale Journal of Law and Feminism* 6:303-4.

Mink, Gwendolyn. 1998. *Welfare's End*. Ithaca, NY: Cornell University Press.

Moffitt, Robert and Jennifer Roff. 2000. The Diversity of Welfare Leavers: A Three City Study. Working Paper 00-01. Johns Hopkins University, Baltimore, MD.

Pear, Robert. 2001. Nominee's Focus on Married Fatherhood Draws Both Praise and Fire. *New York Times*, 7 June.

Piven, Frances Fox and Richard Cloward. 1993. *Regulating the Poor*. Updated ed. New York: Vintage.

State Policy Documentation Project. 1999a. Pending Application Requirements. Available at http://www.spdp.org/tanf/applications. Accessed May 1999.

———. 1999b. Personal Responsibility Contracts: Obligations. Available at http://www.spdp.org/tanf/applications/appsumm.htm. Accessed June 1999.

———. 1999c. Sanctions for Noncompliance with Work Activities. Available at http://www.spdp.org/tanf/sanctions/sanctions_finding.htm. Accessed June 1999.

Study Group on Work, Poverty and Welfare. 1999. *Assessing Work First: What Happens After Welfare?* New Jersey: Study Group on Work, Poverty and Welfare. Cited in Women of Color Resource Center 2000.

Toussaint, Pierre. N.d. Empowering the Vision: Abstinence Education Grant Proposal to the Florida State Human Services Division. Duplicated.

U.S. Bureau of Labor Statistics. 2000. *Highlights of Women's Earnings in 1999*. Report 943. Washington, DC: U.S. Department of Labor.

U.S. Census Bureau. 2000. *Poverty in the United States, 1999*. Washington, DC: U.S. Department of Commerce.

U.S. Department of Health and Human Services. 1999. Administration for Children and Families. *Characteristics and Financial Circumstances of TANF Recipients, Fiscal Year 1998*. Washington, DC: U.S. Department of Health and Human Services.

———. 2000a. HHS Awards Adoption Bonuses and Grants. *HHS News*, 20 (Sept).

———. 2000b. *HHS Fatherhood Initiative: Improving Opportunities for Low-income Fathers*. Washington, DC: U.S. Department of Health and Human Services.

———. 2000c. *HHS's Fatherhood Initiative: Fact Sheet*. Washington, DC: U.S. Department of Health and Human Services.

———. 2000d. Administration for Children and Families. Office of Family Assistance. *Helping Families Achieve Self-Sufficiency: Guide for Funding Services for Children and Families Through the TANF Program*. Available at http://www.acf.dhhs.gov/programs/ofa/funds2.htm.

U.S. Department of Labor. 1999. The 1999 Welfare to Work Amendments. Available at http://wtw.doleta.gov/laws-regs/99amedsum.htm.

U.S. House. 1997. *Adoption Promotion Act of 1997*. 105th Cong., 1st sess., H.R. 867.

———. 2000a. *Child Support Distribution Act of 2000*. 106th Cong., 2nd sess., H.R. 4678.

———. 2000b. Committee on Ways and Means. *Child Support Distribution Act of 2000: Report to Accompany H.R. 4678*. 106th Cong., 2nd sess.

———. 2000c. Committee on Ways and Means. *2000 Green Book: Overview of Entitlement Programs*. 106th Cong.,

———. 2000d. *The Responsible Fatherhood Act of 2000*. 106th Cong., 2nd sess., H.R. 4671, Jesse Jackson Jr., sponsor. 2nd sess.

U.S. Public Law 104-193. 104th Cong., 22 Aug. 1996. *Personal Responsibility and Work Opportunity Reconciliation Act*.

U.S. Public Law 105-89. 105th Cong., 19 Nov. 1997. *Adoption and Safe Families Act*.

Wider Opportunities for Women. 2000. *Job Retention and Advancement Issues*. Washington, DC: Wider Opportunities for Women.

Women of Color Resource Center. 2000. *Working Hard, Staying Poor: Women and Children in the Wake of Welfare "Reform."* Berkeley, CA: Women of Color Resource Center.

Women's Committee of One Hundred/Project 2002. 2000. *An Immodest Proposal: Rewarding Women's Work to End Poverty*. Available at http://www.welfare2002.org. Accessed 23 Mar. 2000.

Welfare Reform and Neighborhoods: Race and Civic Participation

By JAMES JENNINGS

ABSTRACT: Welfare reform is weakening the social and institutional fabric of neighborhoods with relatively high levels of poverty and is, therefore, antiurban and antineighborhood policy. This article is based on an in-depth study of three Massachusetts communities that finds that welfare reform is increasing regulatory and service demand pressures in inner-city neighborhoods, thereby altering the mission, organizational capacities, and planning activities of community-based organizations. These findings support recent research that examines the problematic connections between welfare reform and race, neighborhood development, and civic participation. The emerging lesson is that the building of civic consciousness and the strengthening of institutional capacities to pursue community and economic development are ignored in the push of welfare reforms to change individual behavior. Neighborhood revitalization initiatives, as well as the call for increasing citizen participation and self-help strategies, are similarly being weakened or ignored.

James Jennings is professor of urban and environmental policy and planning at Tufts University. He has written and lectured extensively on urban politics and community development. His books include Understanding the Nature of Poverty *and* Race, Politics, and Economic Development: Community Perspectives.

THE latest stage of welfare reform is a major impediment both to building social capital and to encouraging civic participation in black and Latino urban neighborhoods with relatively high proportions of families on public assistance. At its heart, the current policy is a top-down reform driven by faulty, but historically rooted, presumptions about the behavior of poor people and fueled by a political rhetoric reflecting misinformation about the nature and causes of persistent poverty in the United States. In fact, welfare reform has little to do with attempts to alleviate urban poverty but instead seeks to control the economic mobility and behavior of poor people and families.

An examination of how the institutional fabric and social and economic capital of poor neighborhoods are affected by welfare reform shows that this policy can be characterized as antineighborhood or antiurban public policy. It is producing negative effects on neighborhood organizations, and it forces community-based agencies to chase low-paying jobs for their clients rather than strengthening the economic infrastructure of the area as a way of producing jobs or preparing and educating people for higher-wage employment. Welfare reform also undermines the development of economic capital in inner cities and generally ignores important lessons about neighborhood revitalization that have emerged over many years of local victories and examples of improving living conditions (Richman, Chaskin, and Ogletree 1992).

This article is based on a forthcoming study assessing the institutional impact of welfare reform in three poor and working-class neighborhoods in Massachusetts.[1] For the most part, as I will explain below, we found that welfare reform is increasing regulatory and service demand pressures in inner-city neighborhoods and thereby altering the mission, organizational capacities, and planning activities of community-based organizations. The major conclusion of the study is that welfare reform, as embodied in Massachusetts Temporary Aid to Needy Families (TANF) policy (specifically, time limits to benefits, regulations forcing individuals to find any available job, regulations against schooling as a way to earn benefits, and work-first rules), coupled with erroneous misperceptions and civic biases against our poorer black and Latino neighborhoods, is weakening the social and institutional fabric of neighborhoods with relatively high levels of poverty.

WELFARE REFORM
AND RACE

The legislative and policy debates preceding welfare reforms at federal and state levels indicate that the target issue was reducing the use of public assistance, not resolving structural causes of poverty. The underlying rationale of this law is that by combating dependency the problem of persistent poverty associated with families and children will be alleviated because indigent people will be forced into employment and poor single mothers will be forced to marry and/or be employed (*Personal Responsibility and Work Reconciliation Act of 1996*).

According to the goals of welfare reform, dependency and lack of a work ethic represent key factors explaining persistent poverty, and therefore public policy should be aimed at combating such dependency through work-first initiatives. This assertion is challenged by the fact that the composition of the poverty population in this country includes many demographic groups, including children and the elderly, working and nonworking people, single and married-couple families, and people with disabilities. Millions of people who do work full- and part-time are still poor (Jennings 1994). Further, the history of antipoverty efforts shows that this welfare reform does not represent new thinking about the causes or responses to widespread poverty in our society (Brown 1999; Hamilton and Hamilton 1997).

Civic and political discourse surrounding the adoption of welfare reform reflected two implicit messages about poor people. First, poor people were viewed as being impoverished due to their own dependency on government dole, but the second message is that the undeserving poor are mostly black and Latino people. Poverty was thereby racialized in a way that facilitated the adoption and support of welfare reform. This racialization was conducted in several ways, beginning with polemical works by both liberal and conservative scholars and writers who created a genre of literature proposing that

poverty is not only a social and cultural aberration but primarily ensconced in the urban culture and even native intelligence of black people (Banfield 1973; Auletta 1983; Herrnstein and Murray 1994).

Our study and others find that welfare reform has differential racial and ethnic impact in those predominantly black and Latino neighborhoods with high numbers of recipients compared to other neighborhoods. Since many neighborhoods reflect high levels of residential segregation and even hypersegregation, even neutral or universal public policies can carry racial and ethnic implications in terms of their impact on neighborhood services or resources (Massey and Denton 1993). In Massachusetts, the concentration of poor people and families on public assistance that are affected by the institutional effects of welfare reform occurs precisely in the same places where we find the highest number and concentration of black, Latino, and Asian residents. For example, our study found that the zip codes with at least 400 or more families on public assistance in 1999 were the same zip codes with the highest concentration of blacks, Latinos, and Asian-descent people across the whole state.[2]

Building social capital and increasing citizen participation as a tool for improving the quality of public policy and responding to local economic problems is an utmost concern of poorer communities. Growing demands exist for improving living conditions and enhancing opportunities for residents of low-income communities by the building of social capital through strengthening and tapping neighborhood resources. Yet the federal context of devolution and welfare reform means fewer resources for urban programs and provides a significant obstacle to interorganizational cooperation and collaboration between neighborhood organizations.

Increasing evidence, including our study, points to racial and ethnic differences in how welfare reform is being implemented at the local level. In some places, for example, black and Latino recipients of public assistance may not be receiving the same kinds of benefits that are doled out to white recipients. In a study of clients in Illinois who were denied benefits due to sanctions, for instance, it was reported, "Latinos were more likely to experience case closings due to non-compliance than non-Latinos. Fifteen percent of Latinos reported such a closing compared to 8 percent of non-Latinos. Communication problems may have contributed to Latinos with low English proficiency either missing meetings, or failing to comply with regulations" (Chicago Urban League 2000, 35). This study concluded that the likelihood was greater for white recipients than black or Latino recipients to be referred to education programs before being required to accept a job (64).

Another study compared the employment experiences of black and white welfare recipients and concluded that "among black and white welfare recipients with similar barriers to employment, blacks have more negative employment outcomes than whites. In general, blacks

earn less than whites, are less likely to be employed full-time and are over-represented in lower paying occupations" (Gooden 1998, 24). Gooden shows that these racial differences are due to discrimination and a workforce that is culturally unbalanced, as well as the role that caseworkers perform in the implementation of welfare reform. Case workers have wide discretion in assisting welfare recipients at various levels of interaction and activity, including the point of assessing needs and setting goals, adopting actions for meeting these goals, referring clients to services, and monitoring the behavior of clients.

Our study, among a few others on the topic, suggests that welfare reform is adversely influencing the mission, work, and capacity of community-based organizations in black and Latino neighborhoods to meet the social and economic needs of residents. Community-based organizations are involved in activities that seek to provide resources to individuals, families, and neighborhood organizations in the areas of human services, education, youth activities, health, public safety, housing, and economic development. Ironically, it is these kinds of community organizations that could help poor people and families to acquire the resources and necessary services for social and economic mobility. If these kinds of institutions are bypassed, then it tends to weaken efforts to enhance the social mobility of poor people and families or to improve living conditions in some places.

WELFARE REFORM
AND NEIGHBORHOOD
REVITALIZATION

Overall neighborhood characteristics, including the state of community-based organizations, can play a major role in ensuring the success of welfare reform in terms of moving people into meaningful employment. Economist John Fitzgerald (1995) notes, for example, "A weakness in previous studies is that they do not adequately account for local labor market conditions or other local area effects. This omission may bias the estimated effects of policy and labor market variables" (43). He adds that

neighborhood can have other effects as well. Information about jobs may be lacking in poor areas. The degree of stigma associated with welfare will influence choices and reflects neighborhood (peer) tastes, as well as state welfare policy and personal tastes. Neighborhood may affect human capital, and hence the values of job options, directly through school quality and indirectly through peer pressure to continue education. (45)

A serious oversight in welfare reform is inattention to the role of community organizations in those neighborhoods most affected by the changes. Coulton (1996), for example, highlights the role of neighborhood institutions and local processes for understanding how the social and economic mobility of individuals can be enhanced: "To respond to the challenges of the new era . . . more intricate knowledge of the workings of low-income communities and low-skill labor markets is required, particularly knowledge about how these factors support or undermine individuals' chances of finding a job that provides a living wage" (510). She argues that "understanding what needs to be done to create and support opportunity within communities, however, requires a focused and multidisciplinary program of community research. To date little of the research on welfare dynamics and welfare-to-work programs has been embedded in a social context" (511). Another urbanist reiterates this observation:

The ability for a welfare recipient to move from welfare to work depends to some extent on the quality and competence of the set of local institutions that are in place to serve and assist her—in particular, local welfare, employment and training and other labor market intermediary institutions (e.g. employment agencies, vocational schools, community colleges, local economic development agencies). We can assume that the quality of these institutions varies across areas as does the degree to which this set of institutions perform in a cooperative, integrated, and coordinative manner. Where local welfare and employment and training agencies co-operate closely, and where these, in turn, are well-integrated with other community institutions, welfare recipients should, ceteris paribus, have an easier path moving from welfare to work. (Wolman 1996, 6)

Professors Avery M. Guest and Susan K. Wierzbicki (1999) add, "The degree of social interaction among neighbors is a key indicator of the strength of localized communities in urban society" (92). And in a study about factors that explain the state of children's social and health conditions, Jason M. Fields and Kristin E. Smith (1998) report that certain kinds of neighborhood characteristics are associated positively with the well-being of children. Such arguments imply that the chances of poor people, including individuals on public assistance, to become self-sufficient is related to the capacity of community-based organizations to work effectively in certain kinds of neighborhoods. As a matter of fact, one researcher discovered that the quality of life in a neighborhood, including its institutional richness and support networks, was a major factor in explaining the likelihood of recipients of the previous public assistance program, Aid to Families with Dependent Children, to leave its rolls (Vartanian 1997; see also Bratt and Keyes 1997; Schwartz and Vidal 1999).

Many representatives of community organizations in our study reported that they had to change the direction and activities aimed at neighborhood improvements as a result of welfare reform. These organizations had to shift from community and economic development planning and related activities and instead respond to public assistance recipients seeking information about the availability of services needed to comply with new welfare regulations. Areas such as employment and training, community development, and planning for economic development strategies had to take a secondary role in those organizations that were assisting TANF recipients. Staffing could not be devoted to creative or strategic planning either because resources were not available or because TANF recipients generated added fiscal and personnel pressures. The origins of such pressures are the regulations and procedures that agencies had to follow, accompanied by new needs forced upon TANF recipients seeking referrals for child care, housing, and transportation assistance.

Under welfare reform it is difficult for community organizations in these neighborhoods to plan strategies and activities aimed at growth since there is little information about the impact of time limits or how new welfare regulations might affect their own operations. Interviewees noted that the new welfare reform regulations functioned in a way that inhibited or discouraged collaborative planning and networking between their organizations. This development is problematic in that welfare reform is causing a shift in the mission and capacities of community-based organizations at a point when the call and need for cooperation has started to emerge as necessary for the survival of some of these organizations (Keyes 1990).

Competition between agencies for showing that clients are successful within a work-first strategy weakens the call for organizational collaboration. As lamented by one interviewee in our study,

Before, many of us used to get together once in a while to talk about problems we were all having in helping the Latino community. Now . . . they see everyone as competition. . . . Now, everyone is doing outreach trying to get the welfare clients from the agencies your friends work for, and they are doing the same to you.

Competition is also encouraged because there is a need to count successful clients regardless of whether people are being really helped or not. Another interviewee, for example, stated that

some people around here are taking our clients who are still on welfare to give them other services that they don't really need. . . . Some clients have complained about this. They come to me to help them find an apartment, and the next thing I know someone from one of our job training programs is trying to push them into their program.

This kind of environment is not conducive to community revitalization strategies where organizations have to plan and implement activities collaboratively for the benefit of people and the neighborhood.

Welfare reform further weakens neighborhood institutions because it is implemented within a specter of big government and a highly regulatory bureaucracy used for monitoring poor people. President Ronald Reagan helped to trigger the devolution revolution by calling for "getting government of our backs" in his 1980 inaugural speech. Today's welfare reform shows that this was not meant for poor people or their neighborhoods. The presence of state government and centralization mandated by welfare reform in inner-city communities is enormous.

An example of this problem is the requirement that all welfare recipients have to report to newly created employment and training centers for assessment. They can no longer first approach a local community agency for employment assistance. Welfare recipients must now be processed by a central bureaucracy that emphasizes a quick stamp of "job readiness" in order to comply with policies and regulations pushed by state agencies administering welfare reform. Only clients with the most extreme debilitating conditions tend to be referred to training programs, which, in turn, are mostly short term and aimed at entry-level employment. Some job-ready clients are referred to community-based organizations that are forced to accept contracts seeking any job placements rather than providing supportive services and skills training to the clients.

The punitive monitoring of poor people on public assistance mandated by welfare reform in states like Massachusetts adds burdens and pressures to community-based organizations because highly centralized procedures dictated by the state must be followed in order to assist people. This new red tape requires management information and personnel systems that smaller neighborhood organizations may not be able to afford, and thus they become less competitive with larger agencies that may be disconnected socially from the community. Community-based organizations in black and Latino neighborhoods tend to rely to a greater extent on public funds since they serve a poorer clientele. Private sector initiatives and larger service agencies can compete better for reduced funding than can neighborhood-based organizations due to the possibility of operating economies of scale.

In many places, welfare recipients are treated as pariahs who are not to be trusted and must be forced to the first available jobs. Indirectly, this contributes to social divisions in poor neighborhoods. It encourages divisive blame-the-victim attitudes on the part of citizens living in the same neighborhood rather than building networks of citizens who could be working together on behalf of their neighborhood interests. Racial and ethnic divisions were identified as a potential problem created by the implementation of welfare reform in Massachusetts in a study conducted by the Radcliffe Institute for Public Policy in 1998 (Dodson, Joshi, and McDonald 1998).

As resources for local programs are reduced either directly through lesser budgetary allocations or as a result of increased demands for assistance, competition between community-based organizations for scarce public funding is exacerbated, as suggested by Bailey and Koney (1996): "With the focus on expanding state control of welfare and reducing social spending, competition for finite resources is increasing as well. Community-based organizations are particularly vulnerable to these changes" (604).

Another study similarly documented greater competitive pressures for community-based agencies as a consequence of welfare reform in many urban neighborhoods across the nation (Withorn and Jons 1999). It was reported that welfare reform generated new internal and external tensions for many neighborhood

agencies surveyed during 1998. They also noted that agencies serving immigrants believed that they have become more politically vulnerable in neighborhoods where other agencies are serving nonimmigrant but impoverished sectors.

Similar observations were echoed in our interviews and meetings with many representatives of community-based service agencies in the three neighborhoods. In the predominantly Latino neighborhood of Lawrence, the director of a community-based organization noted that "not only is the agency competing for welfare clients with other agencies, but programs within the agency are fighting one another for eligible people." This kind of competition produces an informal practice that one observer describes as "churning," which occurs when

CBO [community-based organization] consumers of one program are directed to other agency programs, not because they need the services but because they are eligible in social characteristics, for the agency to bill or justify their existence to another funding source. . . . We see this with Medicaid where a welfare client comes into the CBO for housing, but because they have Medicaid are forced to get a mental health assessment just for the agency to bill Medicaid.

Thus, rather than government partnering with successful and effective community-based organizations, welfare reform encourages yet greater institutional efficiencies and waste rather than productive collaboration.

WELFARE REFORM AND
CIVIC PARTICIPATION

There is also a disconnection between major themes in the literature on civic participation in local places and welfare reform in black and Latino urban neighborhoods. The foundation sector in this nation has taken the lead in identifying civic consciousness and the building of social fabric and social capital as fundamental elements for comprehensive urban revitalization. The role of neighborhood organizations involved in community and economic development has been highlighted in numerous reports and national discussions. But while praising the work and role of community-based organizations in places with relatively high poverty, the foundation sector has been passive and reactive to the adoption and operationalization of welfare reform. This is occurring at the very time that welfare reforms across many states discourage civic participation in poor communities and at the same time that it seeks to fight dependency.

The contradictions and inconsistencies between the rhetorical call for self-sufficiency and reduction in dependency and the effects of welfare reform are evident in the findings of a recent online seminar sponsored by Handsnet (Gross 2000). The online proceedings state that "if self-sufficiency for poor families is the goal of welfare reform, welfare clients must be perceived in more than just economic terms; their social and political roles as parents, family members, and community members cannot be ignored." The proceedings included several ways in which current welfare reform inhibits the development of self-sufficiency that parallel the concerns of community representatives in the three neighborhood areas we studied: "Self-sufficiency may demand long-term supports not provided by TANF. Indeed, TANF time limits can short-circuit welfare clients' attempts to achieve self-sufficiency." Further, "Human service providers need additional tools and resources to help their clients overcome major barriers to self-sufficiency including lack of adequate education, job training, health care, housing, transportation and child-care."

This online report indicated that welfare reform is undermining the development of the self-sufficiency of clients and their families. Through the testimony of a wide range of people, including representatives of agencies providing direct services to clients, it suggests that self-sufficiency requires comprehensive approaches and tools optimally within a framework of developing and supporting stronger communities.

The inconsistency between "ending welfare as we know it" through current welfare reform and building self-sufficiency is suggested by other observers. Delgado (1999) writes that self-sufficiency involves much more than the values or actions of individuals (see also Bratt and Keyes 1997). Community-based support systems also have to be intact and effective in order to encourage and sustain self-sufficiency in low-income urban neighborhoods. Delgado's review of the history of self-help movements in this country indicates that these supporting factors include building a sense of community on the part of institutions; the geographical and psychological accessibility of institutions; institutional practices that accentuate affirmation rather than stigmatization on the part of clients; support and respect for cultural heritages; encouraging the development of community leadership; and building trust between clients, citizens, and institutions.

The staff members of one organization we interviewed, however, expressed concern that their work in encouraging entrepreneurship and self-help is being undermined by welfare reform: "Dollars to be earned by welfare clients are not sufficient for entrepreneurship. Day care and other life issues make it difficult for welfare recipients to advance beyond low-level paying jobs." Welfare reform is not aimed at satisfying this kind of criteria for building or maintaining effective local self-help strategies and programs.

CONCLUSION

While the language of welfare reform is directed at changing presumed antiwork individual behavior, the fact that some urban locations have relatively large and concentrated numbers of families receiving public assistance raises questions about the effect of this policy on these places in terms of institutional, social, and economic effects. Welfare reform policy avoids the issues of the quality of life in neighborhoods, investment in the economic development of these places, and the investment of resources necessary for strengthening community-based organizations and for revitalization strategies. It focuses not on strengthening neighborhood institutions but rather on eliciting a prescribed social behavior of individuals and families that presumably, in turn, leads to their own economic mobility. But the negative consequences of welfare reform on neighborhood organizations involved with enhancing or maintaining the social and economic health of predominantly black and Latino neighborhoods cannot be ignored.

Although generally not treated as such, welfare reform is manifestly a community development and urban policy matter. It must be considered within the ongoing debates about effective policy and institutional strategies for improving living conditions in inner cities—where both the processes and effects of welfare reform bolster the views of scholars and observers who believe that social and economic investments in black and Latino neighborhoods should be discouraged because they will be ineffective or wasteful.

Some scholars have advocated place-based strategies as a way to revitalize inner cities, while other scholars would use opportunities for residents to move to other neighborhoods. Commentators such as Robert Halpern argue that investment of time and money in urban neighborhoods is not a panacea to systemic problems: "The idea that poor neighborhoods contain the resources and capacities for their own regeneration can be, and often has been, used to promote self-help without the requisite external supports and linkages" (Halpern 1995, 222). Halpern adds, "Creating local governance bodies and mechanisms can seem somewhat empty when the local community has few public resources of its own to govern" (223).

However, this often valid criticism does not, a priori, invalidate the call for neighborhood empowerment but perhaps forces us, along with urban scholar Clarence N. Stone, to see it as a "mixed picture." Stone (1999) argues against,

Dismissing bottom-up efforts to strengthen civic capacity in poorer neighborhoods, paying little attention to the engagement of lower socioeconomic status citizens in developing an agenda of their fashioning, and writing off activities that might enhance their skills in pursuing that agenda relegate economically marginal people to the nonpolitical condition of forever being acted upon without a prospect of being able to have a voice in their own fates. (854)

Welfare reform, by discouraging the social and economic revitalization of poor neighborhoods and by ignoring the role that neighborhood organizations can play in improving living conditions, can be seen as serving this dismissal. We found that welfare reform is not only hurting families and children but also the neighborhoods in which relatively high numbers and proportions of poor people live and work and where many residents are actively striving for change. It is, therefore, an antineighborhood public policy because the building of civic consciousness and the strengthening institutional capacities to pursue community and economic development are ignored. Neighborhood revitalization initiatives, as well as the call for increasing citizen participation and self-help strategies, are similarly being weakened or ignored.

Community-based organizations and a healthy institutional infrastructure are key pieces for urban revitalization strategies. Strong neighborhoods allow citizens from different backgrounds and with different racial and ethnic characteristics to work together on common problems facing their cities. Today, welfare reform is undermining the building of this kind of foundation. Unfortunately for poor people and, ultimately, others in the neighborhood as well, "ending welfare as we know it" has little to do with the lessons learned over the years about revitalizing poor and working-class neighborhoods and thereby equipping the citizenry to come and work together across racial and ethnic boundaries.

Notes

1. The study includes interviews conducted between 1997 and 2000 with many community representatives working in three neighborhood areas in the cities of Boston, Lawrence, and Brockton. These places have relatively high number of families on TANF and predominantly black and Latino populations with a high rate of poverty and near-poverty status. The following individuals assisted in this research project with interviewing and related tasks: Dr. Jorge Santiago, Maria Estella Carrion, Barbara Gomes Beach, and Danielle Wilson.

The questions posed to civic and neighborhood representatives were aimed at highlighting changes or new pressures that community-based organizations have experienced as a result of welfare reform, both in terms of level and kinds of services in demand and the resources available for meeting new demands or regulations. The three neighborhood areas were studied in terms of how institutions involved with community and economic development revitalization strategies are influenced by welfare reform.

2. From monthly reports provided by the Massachusetts Department of Transitional Assistance; population projections and estimates provided by Applied Graphics Solution (for 1999).

References

Auletta, Ken. 1983. *The Underclass*. New York: Random House.

Bailey, Darlyne and Kelly McNally Koney. 1996. Inter-organizational Community-Based Collaboratives: A Strategic Response to Shape the Social Work Agenda. *Social Work* 41(6): 602-11.

Banfield, Edward C. 1973. *The Unheavenly City Revisited*. Boston: Little, Brown.

Brown, Michael K. 1999. *Race, Money, and the American Welfare State*. Ithaca, NY: Cornell University Press.

Bratt, Rachel G. and Langley C. Keyes, with Rhae Parkese, Kim Phinney, and Diana Markel. 1997. *New Perspectives on Self-Sufficiency: Strategies for Nonprofit Housing Organizations*. Medford, MA: Tufts University and the Department of Urban and Environmental Policy.

Chicago Urban League and the Center for Urban Economic Development. 2000. *Living with Welfare Reform: A Survey of Low Income Families in Illinois*. Chicago: Chicago Urban League and the Center for Urban Economic Development.

Coulton, Claudia J. 1996. Poverty, Work, and Community: A Research Agenda for an Era of Diminishing Federal Responsibility. *Social Work* 41(5):509-19.

Delgado, Melvin. 1999. *Social Work Practice in Nontraditional Urban Settings*. New York: Oxford University Press.

Dodson, Lisa, Pamela Joshi, and Davida McDonald. 1998. *Welfare in Transition: Consequences for Women, Families, and Communities*. Cambridge, MA: Radcliffe Public Policy Institute.

Fields, Jason M. and Kristin E. Smith. 1998. *Poverty and Family Structure, and Child Well-Being: Indicators from the SIPP*. Population Division Working Paper, no. 23, Apr. Washington, DC: U.S. Bureau of the Census, Population Division.

Fitzgerald, John M. 1995. Local Labor Markets and Local Area Effects on Welfare Duration. *Journal of Policy Analysis and Management* 14(1):43-67.

Gooden, Susan. 1998. All Things Not Being Equal: Differences in Caseworker Support Toward Black and White Clients. *Harvard Journal of African American Public Policy* 4.

Gross, June. 2000. *Pressure from All Sides: Living Through the Conflicting Realities of Poverty*. Working Families Online Roundtable (30 Mar. 2000). Available at www.igc.org/handsnet/whitepaper2.html.

Guest, Avery M. and Susan K. Wierzbicki. 1999. Social Ties at the Neighborhood Level: Two Decades of GSS Evidence. *Urban Affairs Review* 35(1):92-111.

Halpern, Robert. 1995. *Rebuilding the Inner City: A History of Neighborhood Initiatives to Address Poverty in the United States*. New York: Columbia University Press.

Hamilton, Charles V. and Dona C. Hamilton. 1997. *The Dual Agenda: Race and Social Welfare Policies of Civil Rights Organizations*. New York: Columbia University Press.

Herrnstein, Richard J. and Charles Murray. 1994. *The Bell Curve: Intelli-*

gence and Class Structure in American Life. New York: Free Press.

Jennings, James. 1994. *Understanding the Nature of Poverty in Urban America.* Westport, CT: Praeger.

Keyes, Langley C. 1990. The Shifting Focus of Neighborhood Groups: The Massachusetts Experience. In *The Future of National Urban Policy,* ed. Marshall Kaplan and Franklin James. Durham, NC: Duke University Press.

Massey, Douglas S. and Nancy A. Denton. 1993. *American Apartheid: Segregation and the Making of the Underclass.* Cambridge, MA: Harvard University Press.

Personal Responsibility and Work Reconciliation Act of 1996. U.S. Public Law 104-193. 104th Cong., 22 Aug. 1996.

Richman, Harold A., Robert J. Chaskin, and Renae Ogletree. 1992. *The Ford Foundation's Neighborhood and Family Initiative: Toward a Model of Comprehensive Neighborhood-Based Development.* Chicago: University of Chicago, Chapin Hall Center for Children.

Schwartz, Alex F. and Avis C. Vidal. 1999. Between a Rock and a Hard Place: The Impact of Federal and State Policy Changes in Housing in New York City. In *Housing and Community Development in New York City,* ed. Michael H. Schill. Albany, NY: State University of New York Press.

Stone, Clarence N. 1999. Poverty and the Continuing Campaign for Urban Social Reform. *Urban Affairs Review* 34(6):843-56.

Vartanian, Thomas P. 1997. Neighborhood Effects on AFDC Exits: Examining Social Isolation, Relative Deprivation, and Epidemic Theories. *Social Science Review* 71(4):548-74.

Withorn, Ann and Pamela Jons. 1999. Worrying About Welfare Reform: Community-Based Agencies Respond. Unpublished paper, Academic Working Group on Poverty, University of Massachusetts Boston.

Wolman, Hal. 1996. *Welfare to Work: The Need to Take Place Differences into Account.* Technical Analysis Paper, no. 45. Washington, DC: U.S. Department of Health and Human Services, Office of the Assistant Secretary for Planning and Evaluation.

ANNALS, *AAPSS*, **577**, September 2001

Friends or Foes?
Nonprofits and the
Puzzle of Welfare Reform

By ANN WITHORN

ABSTRACT: Nonprofit human service agencies are in the middle of the welfare reform mess. They may have the opportunity to obtain more public dollars for delivering more services to low-income families, and from their position, they have the potential to be effective witnesses to what is happening. On the other hand, the effects of welfare reform on the constituencies they serve call for advocacy and challenging action that they do not know how to do. The author uses comments from interviews with workers in the system to argue that, if agencies are not very careful, it will be extremely hard for them to play a dependable role in whatever future welfare state evolves.

Ann Withorn is professor of social policy at the University of Massachusetts Boston. She has written extensively about welfare and women's poverty and is most proud of her long history of welfare activism, including her arrest, along with 30 others, for sitting in at the governor's office in protest against the imposition of Massachusetts' two-year welfare time limit.

108 THE ANNALS OF THE AMERICAN ACADEMY

Things have changed. . . . If people can't get cash from the system, and contact with agencies may get them in trouble with children's services, INS, or the law, then why should they want anything to do with us?

—Human service administrator (2001)[1]

Welfare reform as we know it has exposed long-standing tensions within the world of nonprofit human service agencies. The rules and possibilities for agencies have changed, and yet few actors within the system have explored the implications (Jennings 1999). Most significant, the dramatic changes the Personal Responsibility and Work Opportunity Reconciliation Act (PRWORA) has wrought in the structure of the system and the options available to poor people have simultaneously and radically altered the capacity of community-based agencies to be active players in efforts for economic and social justice.

Nonprofit human service agencies have, since the beginning of the twentieth century, embodied a classic, well-documented contradiction (McKnight 1995; Sachs and Newdom 1999; Wagner 1999). Service programs allowed professional and nonprofessional workers a chance to help people deal with a wide range of personal, economic, and social problems and even, sometimes, to support them in collectively addressing those problems. Yet nonprofit agencies have also been, to a greater or lesser degree, themselves a part of the system whereby public and religious organizations attempted to impose order—either the larger order of the political economy or the particular

moral order of a specific religious faith—in exchange for service.

This brief speculative essay is based on years of research into the changing roles of human service workers and agencies (Withorn 1982, 1984, 1996, 1998) and most recently into how community-based agencies are responding to welfare reform (Withorn and Jons 1999). It attempts to open a discussion of how human service agencies are responding and might operate differently in the puzzle of postwelfare reform. After a cursory analysis of the history of nonprofit human service agencies within antipoverty efforts of the U.S. social state, I summarize the changed environment created by welfare reform and the worries generated by it for service agency staff. Next, the dangers posed by the current climate are explored, and finally, some suggestions for positive action hinted at.

Before proceeding, my initial bias must be noted. As a young radical, grassroots organizing and social service work in a Head Start program allowed me to hone my anger at the U.S. political economy via day-to-day involvement with the real people who were both hurt by that system and using it as part of their effort to be "heroes of their own lives"—in Linda Gordon's (1988) apt phrase. Since then, in teaching welfare recipients and service workers—as well as in my writing and activism—I have argued that, however difficult, an integration of service work with the long- and short-run struggles for justice is both healthy and, ultimately, essential (Withorn 1999). Today, however, I am more fearful than ever that the contradiction inevitably contained in service work is well nigh impossible to maintain. This article is an effort both to explain and to overcome that fear.

INSIDERS OR OUTSIDERS?
NONPROFITS WITHIN
AN EVOLVING SYSTEM

We have been around for more than 10 years, and over that time have become, essentially, a new type of service agency, one where the focus is entirely on employment. People come to us seeking employment and we find it for them. The old "social worker" types tended to leave as it became clear what we do and don't do.

—Employment agency
administrator (2001)

This is not the space to contextualize how the history of nonprofit human services for low-income people has helped create the U.S. welfare state. But a basic review of key elements of the story helps explain the current reconfiguration of longstanding tensions (Jansson 2000).[2]

Since before the days of the settlement houses and charity organization societies, nonpublic organizations have existed alongside (emerging) public social welfare institutions. Indeed, from the earliest days of the nation, many of the oldest nonpublic services were providing charity in what we are now calling the faith-based sector. Sometimes, as in the Progressive Era or the 1960s and 1970s, a subset of professional and/or community leaders of nonprofit organizations saw their role as explicitly that of social reform. Occasionally, certain ethnically based organizations or social movement organiza-tions decided to provide services to their members or to people they saw as suffering from injustice and therefore as potential members (Withorn 1984). But, most often, what was called the voluntary sector existed to respond to a wide range of human needs—services to blind or deaf people, alcoholics, people with various disabilities, and so forth—that were seen as unmet by public programs.

A central tension throughout this history has been the nature of the relationship between the public sector and the private sector. Liberal social welfare theorists argued that the relationship was a progressive process whereby private agencies would identify needs, begin to meet them, and realize that they were too big to be handled without public resources, and then gradually public social policies would provide funding, set standards, and at least oversee direct provision of services. Social welfare textbooks documented this trend, often summarized as a journey from charity to justice.

An underlying assumption of such a historical understanding, at least after the 1940s, was that public services would always be around to provide the basic safety net of income and institutional services and that nonprofit organizations would provide vital but less institutionally provided and universally needed social and community services. Political liberals would push for more public services, or at least public funding, while conservatives would want fewer services and less funding. Radicals would criticize the social control aspects, and reactionaries would expose how the growing welfare state undermined individual initiative.

In the 1960s, the world of social welfare services experienced another change, in what can now be seen as the beginning of today's devolution. For a range of political reasons, community action programs began to funnel federal funding directly into cities in a mixed effort to circumvent presumably racist and patronage-ridden city halls. Community control, in many areas, meant that community-based nonprofit organizations began to be seen as inherently more responsive than public programs. Community-based services began to spring up as a self-conscious part of community empowerment strategies. By the 1970s, community mental health and normalization initiatives (coupled with the availability of drug therapies and increasing costs of maintaining big institutions) lead to a process of the deinstitutionalization of large mental health, mental retardation, and youth services facilities and to the growth of community-based nonprofits as a substitute for public care, not just as a supplement or as a base for strengthening neighborhoods.

In the mid-1960s, state social services agencies (providing a variety of family services) were split off from public welfare departments in a response to arguments that service provision should be separated from income support. The argument initially was that social services would not be stigmatized as poor services and that income assistance should be a simple matter of eligibility. The reality was that most new state social service agency became purely child welfare agencies responding to child abuse, neglect, and abandonment, and Aid to Families with Dependent Children, or "welfare," became an increasingly inadequate and punitive income program staffed by people without mandate or training for responding to the complex social needs associated with poverty. As one community service worker described it in 1998, "All the county used to do was pass out or withhold checks. They never did help families in a real way, and now what they do is tell them to find a job, no matter what."

A related tension over all the years of agency growth and change centered on the quality and professionalization of service workers. Unionized workers might sometimes be portrayed as representing bureaucratized nonperformers and at another time be blamed for setting pay levels too high. Training and professional education were sometimes, in some areas, equated with good service, while at other times, in other areas, they were seen as precursors to increasing distance from the community and a reduction in the quality of care that comes from connectedness to the issues. One long-time activist put it this way in 2000: "We want 'our people' who live in the community to provide services. But all the contracts make money management hard . . . they pull your contracts if you lack professional staff. And then if something bad happens because people weren't trained properly, or paid enough, everybody suffers."

Nevertheless, amid these and other tensions, public social services grew for 20 years, primarily through increases in services purchased from private agencies. New management models emerged as contracted services with fee-for-service, performance-based arrangements replaced more open-ended grant programs, creating an environment where the nonprofit sector began to see itself as an industry. By the end of the Reagan era, many traditional nonprofits began to be attacked by the Right as interest groups that could not be trusted on policy issues because of their enmeshment in the system (Payne 1998).

At the same time, grassroots advocates began to develop more full critiques of how the expanding network of nonprofits had become part of the system that directly oppressed them. Former recipient Theresa Funicello (1993) articulated the criticism most baldly as a *Tyranny of Kindness*: "As the misery of poor people increased, so did the cacophony of private interests competing for government contracts, foundation grants, donations by individuals and corporations, and tax advantages for the donations to 'correct' their vision of the problem" (xviii).

The precursor to PRWORA, the Family Support Act of 1988, further institutionalized the involvement of nonprofits in welfare reform by encouraging states to develop job placement, training, and education programs through existing or newly created nonprofits. In short, the welfare state across the nation came to mean a set of state-by-state systems that had evolved into a continuum of services—from public direct provision of income, criminal justice, and a few other direct services (which vary depending on state history), to a set of large nonprofit agencies funded largely by state contracts (which may themselves subcontract to smaller, more specialized nonprofits), to a set of neighborhood or issue-based nonprofits that combine public funding with other sources of income, and finally, to a few advocacy or faith-based groups that provide services entirely with private funds.

AGENCY WORRIES IN THE POST-WELFARE-REFORM ERA

We're the ones left holding the bag after welfare ends. People come to us and all we know to do now is the same thing we have always done before. Something has to change but we don't know what.

—Family service worker (1998)

Structurally, the implementation of national welfare reform has intensified changes for nonprofits, and its repercussions in the lives of low-income people have created additional new challenges (Friedman 2001). Briefly, staff members at today's nonprofit agencies share at least seven worries as they struggle to be of real use to poor people and to stay alive in the current climate.

First worry. The lack of federal controls and monitoring standards, coupled with the possibility of privatization to profit-making companies (like Lockheed Martin) or large nonprofit providers (like the Salvation Army), has changed the rules and the players at the core of welfare-related services. Most states changed the names of their prime welfare agency—Massachusetts, a typical example, went from the Department of Public Welfare to the Department of Transitional Assistance. In 1998, all staff members who were interviewed for our study of 42 agencies described "confusing rules" and "new organizational structures" as creating problems in their ability to participate in the welfare reform process.

Second worry. The growth of new players and service providers at the state and county levels has created competition for years; however, now there are many new actors at the table. As one long-time community worker described it,

They hold these meetings to describe the proposal process for new money and we see people in the room who have never worked with poor people before . . . then we hear that they got big money to make people "job-ready" . . . pretty soon they call us up asking for help because their clients have too many problems to hold jobs.

Third worry. The national shift to a work-first strategy, combined with time limits and full family sanctions, means that many multipurpose family service or community service agencies find that their broader antipoverty and proactive missions are no longer appreciated. As one director put it in 1998, "As a prevention program we worry if we are going to have a place in parents' lives and in the world of social services anymore. If only self-sufficiency programs are what is valued, then how does a long-

term prevention program like ours—even if it works—get attention?"

Fourth worry. Changes in conditions for poor families now make it more likely that those low-income families who do seek services are in more dire need. A settlement house worker commented, "I always worried about my families. But now I don't know where they are until they call us desperate when they lose a job and aren't eligible for welfare or unemployment, and, unlike before, there is nothing we can do except call the food pantry."

Many staff members worry about worker overload or distraction. Hours have to shift to accommodate employed clients, and then staff members cannot work the extra hours. Staff members who were good at counseling often do not do well with mandated time constraints. As one young program coordinator said, "It's too depressing to hear about how this is all so bad. Most of the time I just keep my head down and try to help my workers cope." Good workers leave as the agency mission is reframed. One child care advocate commented, "Anyone who wanted to work with families about anything other than employment just left, and we all suffered."

The level of concern that many people expressed in 2001 was sometimes intense: "I often wonder why some of our staff don't go 'postal' because it feels so hard." But, in a similar study of New York agency staff, preliminary findings suggest that those staff members who stay feel that their work matters and that they can make a difference if they stick with it (Abramovitz 2001).

Fifth worry. Some administrators fear for their survival and seek an alternative path. One mental health program director planned to relocate to the suburbs. Others seek to find their way around restrictive rules: "We should find sources of funding for what we do [serve immigrants], but then we will be caught in the foundation merry-go-round and I'm not sure we can handle that."

Sixth worry. More politicized staff members worry that the only hopes are for organizing between agencies and with clients. However, few agencies interviewed were doing much collaboration for anything beyond joint grant writing, because they do not have staff, or time, or connections and because the people they serve are so hard to organize. One long-time activist complained in 2001, "Nobody wants to admit they receive assistance now, and old stalwarts are too busy trying to make ends meet . . . and the situation is so different now that stories from the old days don't resonate. It's hard."

Seventh worry. Faith-based organizations are often already in the mix of service agencies, but they are not sure what to think about charitable choice. Some, who do not receive public funding, see it as an opportunity to "get support for what we already do," but others are worried about being blamed when they cannot do it all, eventually being controlled by bureaucratic rules or by church or state

litigation. One minister with years of experience warned some eager peers, "Watch out. We can't do it all, and they will want us to. Or they will tell us we can do what we want 'but just not call it prayer.' But that's what we do, is pray. Maybe we should slow down."

The cumulative effect of such worries should deeply worry advocates of a contradictory welfare state, much less those of us who seek to keep the struggle for economic justice alive. While many agency staff members can still find some hope in the possibility to help, many others (and their academic and activist allies) who are not so overwhelmed by the daily disasters have to raise more critical questions, quickly.

DEEPER DANGERS

After listening to over 40 people around the country at the beginning of 2001, I found that at least five dangers exist that are not easily fixed under the current system or in immediately likely changes to PRWORA. A full review of each is not possible here, but I present them hoping that they do not come to pass.

First danger. Money going directly to faith-based organizations, not to existing nonprofits linked to religious organizations, is a recipe for disaster for a dependable welfare state—not just as a threat to church-state division. The dangers here are immense and involve everything from the inevitable lessening of options for the many people who cannot abide overly faith-based environments, to the denial that the scope of economic and social needs of those at the losing end of this society's reward structure simply cannot be addressed privately, to the fear that funneling money to churches is a right-wing effort to buy off the most conservative elements of the black community. As one religious leader said in an individual interview, "We know who will be first at the trough. It will be those churches who haven't done anything about poor people until now, who don't know how, and want to live in a dream world about our community."

Second danger. A devolved welfare state, with no respectful accountability, will be further discredited and undefended—and along with it the community-based agencies that still have the potential to be one of the last places where people can make democratic demands. The welfare windfall created by block granting based on an old formula of the recipient population will live on, to be spent unwisely by state legislators on anything but income for poor people. The increasing misery will be invisible except to those activists brave enough to speak up, and many service providers will find themselves unable to defend the system. As one community leader said,

We can speak up here, with each other, but it is hard before the legislators—and not because we are afraid for our funding. A strange dynamic happens, they don't want to hear us whine; they want us "to think outside the box." So we try to speak so that we won't threaten anybody with how bad it is and our limits in dealing with it.

Third danger. Social service organizations have never received public money to free people from the oppression of capitalism, racism, and sexism. It has always been possible to do more harm than good (Withorn 1984, 1998). But now, with welfare's end and the possibility of full family sanctions (plus changes in child welfare and criminal justice policies), for those few who remain eligible, the pressures on agencies and workers have intensified. Those who work with immigrants saw this first—agency staff members repeatedly say that eligible families stopped wanting to use any service for fear of being a public charge or for fear that some nondocumented relative would somehow be "caught in a net."

Efforts to follow-up with welfare leavers have been hampered because

people have heard through the grapevine that we will take their kids away. And it is hard for us to promise not to, because if we see a child left alone or staying with a bad family member while the mother works, we might have to report them. And then it is out of our hands.

I met some workers who had even started to feel that this was inevitable. "If they don't work, and there is no money, then maybe it is best for the kids to go."

Fourth danger. Workers in 2001 spoke often about disabilities that don't get labeled, such as the reasons why their customers or job seekers are not earning enough to survive. They talked about how much harder it seems for people to be labeled disabled. Their analysis may be both true and a two-edged sword: must all mothers who find the best way to manage their lives and their kids is not to be fully employed be labeled disabled? What happens to workers and programs whose only help is to find disability status as a respite from punitive programs?

Finally, I see the fifth biggest danger as a systemwide game of let's pretend that discredits us all. Public agencies pretend that they are not in control of the money they dole out to the most loyal agencies first and that "any job is a good job" for anyone. Either nonprofit administrators and workers pretend to go along with punitive but lucrative policies in order to stay in the system, or they pretend to oppose these policies in order to connect with their long-standing community allies while making compromises they are unable to mention. Low-income people pretend they are all right and do not need those enrichment or substance abuse or training or parenting programs because they are "working now" and do not have the time or the money.

Workers pretend they are helping; it is those other agencies that are "failing to hold up their end."

In the midst of the game, everyone—workers, administrators, and poor people—in the system or proud to have avoided or escaped it keeps denying that the human problems associated with poverty, and sometimes responsible for maintaining it, are real. The problems do not go away because we end welfare, and they will only be alleviated if human service workers find a way to demand cash backup to low wages or no wages so that they can be of true service and not a poor alternative. As one homeless services provider put it,

We know folks need a place to be, and we are the only place. If we make them lie and tell us they are job seeking or sober every day and it is the only way for them to have a bed, then they will lie and we will know they are lying. And that discredits everybody. It's the same old dysfunctional stuff that got us all here.

CAN THIS CONTRADICTION BE RESOLVED?

Maybe the fallout of all this will be better. Lockheed Martin has already been forced out of, or left, several places because it could not earn a profit.

Maybe, as one agency director observed, "Those social workers who left us to earn more money and get people jobs are coming back; they want to do 'real work' again. And the ones who haven't learned their lesson are better off gone."

Maybe agencies will learn to work together, as one activist hopes, on more than just finding money. Those workers with activist roots seem to find more hope for this, as one argued in 1998:

Maybe our agencies aren't getting depressed like some others are because we are meeting with each other. . . . We want to keep going and we know that we have to keep talking to each other. . . . If you are isolated, and all you have are lines of people asking for what you can't give, you get depressed.

And maybe poor peoples' groups and citizens' groups will stay alive somehow and find ways to broaden the analysis and work with more allies, as Willie Baptist and Mary Bricker-Jenkins suggest in this volume. After a long talk about all the problems, one veteran of 35 years of civil rights and community struggles gave me hope:

Whenever I get discouraged I go talk to someone who's fighting against bigger odds than I am, and I remember those who were lost along the way. It's the same fight now, for dignity and justice; we just have to keep going, keeping talking and remember who we are and why we have to do this.

Notes

1. Unless otherwise indicated, all quotations come from interviews associated with my ongoing study of the responses of community-based agencies to welfare reform, "Worrying About Welfare Reform" (Withorn and Jons 1999), originally published in 1999 and currently being updated in 2001. Because of the nature of this work in progress—I am still interviewing agency staff—this article is presented as a speculative essay, not in any sense as a presentation of findings.

2. The historical summary presented here is an amalgam of most standard, progressive histories and of my own work over the years. Unless otherwise cited, Bruce Jansson's The Reluctant Welfare State (2000) provides the fullest overview of the approach I take and the fullest treatment of the development of nonprofits.

References

Abramovitz, Mimi. 2001. The Impact of Welfare Reform on Non-Profit Social Service Agencies in New York City. New York City Association of Social Workers.

Friedman, Donna Haig. 2001. Parenting in Public: Family Shelter and Public Assistance. New York: Columbia University Press.

Funicello, Theresa. 1993. Tyranny of Kindness: Dismantling the Welfare System to End Poverty in America. New York: Atlantic Monthly Press.

Gordon, Linda. 1988. Heroes of Their Own Lives: The Politics and History of Family Violence. New York: Viking.

Jansson, Bruce. 2000. The Reluctant Welfare State. 4th ed. Belmont, CA: Brooks/Cole.

Jennings, James. 1999. The End of Welfare as We Know It? Or Ending Neighborhoods as We Have Come to Know Them? Newsletter of the Neighborhood Funders Groups 6(4):1-5.

McKnight, John. 1995. The Careless Society. New York: Basic Books.

Payne, James L. 1998. Overcoming Welfare: Expecting More from the Poor and from Ourselves. New York: Basic Books.

Sachs, Jerome and Fred Newdom. 1999. Clinical Work and Social Action: An Integrative Approach. New York: Haworth Press.

Wagner, David. 1999. What's Love Got to Do with It? A Critical Look at American Charity. New York: New Press.

Withorn, Ann. 1982. The Circle Game: Human Services in Massachusetts 1965-1978. Amherst: University of Massachusetts Press.

———. 1984. Serving the People: Social Services and Social Change. New York: Columbia University Press.

———. 1996. For Better and for Worse: Women Against Women in the Welfare State. In For Crying Out Loud: Women's Poverty in the United States, ed. Ann Withorn and Diane Dujon. Boston: South End Press.

———. 1998. No Win: Facing the Ethical Dilemmas of Welfare Reform. Journal of Families and Society 79(3).

———. 1999. Not for Lack of Trying: The Fight Against Welfare Reform in Massachusetts. Special Publication, Center for Women in Politics, University of Massachusetts Boston, Winter.

Withorn, Ann and Pamela Jons. 1999. Worrying About Welfare Reform: Community Based Agencies Respond to Welfare Reform. Boston Area Academics' Working Group on Poverty.

ANNALS, *AAPSS*, **577**, September 2001

Learning from the History of Poor and Working-Class Women's Activism

By MIMI ABRAMOVITZ

ABSTRACT: The long but largely untold history of activism among poor and working-class women in the United States since before the twentieth century reveals that low-income women activists developed a class- and race-based gender consciousness that fueled their activism at three key sites: the point of production, the point of consumption, and the point of state intervention. While their issues and strategies have varied over time, at each site low-income women consistently became active to fulfill their community-defined gendered obligations—which included helping to improve the standard of living of their families and communities. For African American women, this meant fighting for racial as well as economic justice. The long record corrects historical distortions, offers inspiration, and provides lessons for the next round of welfare rights struggles in the twenty-first century.

Mimi Abramovitz, professor of social policy at Hunter School of Social Work, is author of Regulating the Lives of Women: Social Welfare Policy from Colonial Times to the Present *(1996) and* Under Attack, Fighting Back: Women and Welfare in the United States *(2000). A cofounder of the Welfare Rights Initiative, a student-led organization of women on welfare at Hunter College, and a member of the board of Community Voices Heard, a community-based welfare rights organization in New York City, she is a long-time welfare rights activist.*

NOTE: This is a shorter and significantly revised version of chapter 4 of *Under Attack, Fighting Back: Women and Welfare in the United States* (Monthly Review Press, 2000). Research for this article was supported by a grant from the Lois and Samuel Silberman Fund and an award from the Professional Staff Congress—City University of New York Research.

WELFARE reform has spawned a new round of social welfare activism among poor and working-class women in the United States. As the adverse impacts of the 1996 Personal Responsibility and Work Opportunity Act (PRWORA) have intensified and spread, groups of women across the country have joined forces to press for change. Contrary to popular wisdom, today's activism is part of a long tradition that includes poor and working-class women. Unlike white middle-class feminists who became active to secure equal rights with men, black and white low-income women mobilized to fulfill their community-defined gendered obligations, which included helping to sustain or improve the standard of living of their families and communities. Consistently locked into "women's jobs" (which were often further segregated by race) as well as caretaking roles in the home, low-income women developed the grievances, organizational networks, and consciousness that allowed political struggle. A glance back at the last century of low-income women's activism reveals that they asserted their power in several key spheres, the "point of production," the "point of consumption" (Frank 1991), and the "point of state intervention" (Levi 1974). Their efforts played a critical role in making private enterprise and the welfare state more responsive to low-income women's needs.

WORKPLACE ACTIVISM AT THE POINT OF PRODUCTION

Low-income women have always worked for wages at the point of production. The gender and race division of labor shaped their collective action and contributed to a distinct working-class women's consciousness that feminist scholars have termed "trade union" (Milkman 1985), "industrial" (Orleck 1995), and "working-class" (Frank 1998; Greenwald 1989) feminism. African American women's activism was shaped by racism, the legacy of prior black struggles, and the capacity to survive simultaneously in two contradictory worlds. Shaped by what Patricia Collins (1990) termed the "black women's standpoint," their calls for economic security depended as well on securing racial justice.

More than 5 million women of all races worked outside the home by the 1900s, and many gravitated to the burgeoning labor movement. Young Jewish and Italian women emerged as key leaders in the massive 1909-10 strikes of the New York shirtwaist makers, also known as the Uprising of 20,000. Still, in most industries, women had to fight union resistance to women as members and shop leaders, not to mention top officials (Kessler-Harris 1985; Greenwald 1996). After World War I, anger at being returned to the home, combined with the rising cost of living, long hours of work, and stagnant wages, spurred massive strike waves by women telephone operators and garment workers, among many others. Having won the vote, but unable to win the support of employers or unions, low-income women formed an uneasy alliance with the Women's Trade Union League, the National Consumers League, and other white middle-class reformers (Orleck 1995;

Kessler-Harris 1985). These cross-class coalitions frequently turned to the government in their fights for a minimum wage, a shorter work day, and other labor market changes needed by women workers.

During World War I, southern black household workers organized clandestinely to control wages, hours, and volume of work agreed to with white employers. In 1916, black women in Houston formed the Domestic Workers Union and affiliated with the American Federation of Labor. With some limited success, in 1917, in Norfolk, Virginia, black domestics, waitresses, oyster shuckers, and tobacco stemmers established a branch of the Women Wage-Earners' Association and organized strikes for higher wages (Frederickson 1985; Scott 1990; Hunter 1997). Activist black women also turned for support to the National Association for the Advancement of Colored People, the Urban League, and the National Association of Colored Women.

In the 1930s, falling wages, high unemployment, and strong efforts to keep women (and most blacks) out of jobs and unions remobilized working women. In 1933, some 60,000 members of the International Ladies Garment Workers Union, mostly white, but some black, struck in the Northeast. That same year, the St. Louis strike of mostly black women nutpickers also aroused nationwide attention (Foner 1979, 1980). Even women participating in a Florida Works Project Administration's sewing project protested their unequal pay (Tidd 1989). The women's auxiliaries formed by wives to support

male trade unionists also played important roles, especially in coal-mining struggles in Illinois, New Mexico, and elsewhere (Foner 1979, 1980; Strom 1985). In the late 1930s, the new Congress of Industrial Organization began to recruit white and black female (and male) workers who were ignored by the elitist, craft-based American Federation of Labor. Quickly, thousands of unskilled women in the mass production industries signed up.

After World War II, a small but growing number of female unionists reactivated their networks and placed more women's issues on the labor agenda. They called for equal pay for equal work, nondiscriminatory seniority lists, protection of women's jobs during the conversion to peacetime production, and female representation in union leadership roles (Kates 1989; Kannenberg 1993). As in the past, occupational and industrial segregation by race often interfered with joint activism among black and white women, but the hostility of both employers and unions to women's postwar demands exposed workplace sexism to rank-and-file women. Pressed by increasingly militant women, who began to win leadership posts, the unions gradually included their demands in collective bargaining (Gabin 1985).

The explosive growth of the female labor force and the reemergence of a mass women's movement emboldened women activists during the 1960s and led to important legislative gains. Still pressing their claims on employers and unions, women began to insist on government remedies for sex and race discrimination.

The 1962 Presidential Commission on the Status of Women, the 1963 Equal Pay Act, and the 1964 Civil Rights Act gave new credibility to the idea of equality for women workers and fueled both low-income women's activism and women's gains.

Contrary to popular wisdom, women unionists also played a fundamental, if uneven, role in building the feminist movement of the 1960s (Kates 1989; Deslippe 1997). Women unionists supported the Equal Rights Amendment, helped to found the National Organization of Women in 1963, pressed for equal opportunity laws in employment, and then flooded the Equal Employment Opportunities Commission with sex discrimination complaints. These actions by working-class women helped to legitimize the middle-class women's feminist agenda, especially its strong call for the fair treatment of women on the job (Deslippe 1997).

In the early 1970s, more unions created women's departments and included women's needs in collective bargaining. Meanwhile, activist women developed their own labor networks, including Union Women's Alliance to Gain Equality (1971), United Union Women (1972), and Nine-to-Five (1973) (Milkman 1985). In 1974, the Coalition for Labor Union Women convened 3200 delegates from 58 unions to hear Myra Wolfgang of the then–Hotel Employees' and Restaurant Employees' and Bartenders International Union tell them, "We didn't come here to swap recipes" (Kennedy 1981).

However, by the mid-1970s, downsizing, deindustrialization, global-ization, and the massive assault on organized labor by business and the state undercut women's workplace gains. Even so, working women won Social Security retirement program changes, the Pregnancy Discrimination Act, recognition of sexual harassment as sex discrimination, the Family and Medical Leave Act, and other protections from the courts and Congress. And since the early 1990s, a reinvigorated labor movement, grounded in public employee unions, seems to have learned a lesson from its own past. Based on principle or survival needs, organized labor has hired more women, recognized working-class feminist issues, and begun to pay considerably more attention to serving its female base.

THE COMMUNITY:
ACTIVISM AT THE
POINT OF CONSUMPTION

Contrary to stereotypes of homemakers as passive and apolitical, poor and working-class housewives have a long history of activism at the point of consumption. Clustered together by the gendered division of labor in the community, poor and working-class homemakers shared their concerns about family and community life in parks, local clubs, neighborhood groups, laundries, child care facilities, and women's associations. When they could not feed, clothe, shelter, or otherwise maintain their families and communities, they reflected what Kaplan (1982) has called "female consciousness": they asserted their right to protect their families and fulfill their community-defined gendered roles by pressing their claims on local merchants and then the state.

Women's activism on behalf of a just price for food and housing has a long history in the United States (Orleck 1995). In the early twentieth century, many immigrant homemakers conducted militant boycotts to protest the high price of milk, bread, and meat in various East Coast cities (Hyman 1980; Hine 1994). This early activism reflected both women's responsibility for consumption and the lingering influence of the European notion of a moral economy. This community tradition held that local grocers and landlords should not take advantage of their customers who shared membership in the same ethnic group. When charged too much for food or rent, low-income women periodically protested collectively. Their demands brought down prices for a while, exposed what the economy could not provide, and prefigured what the welfare state would later have to furnish.

After World War I, the moral economy gave way to the consumer economy. The discrepancy between the promises of consumerism and the realities of rising prices provoked new cost-of-living protests among low-income homemakers. During the 1920s, the United Council of Working-Class Women assailed the high cost of food, fuel, housing, and education in various cities. High rents also provoked numerous rent strikes by the large Brooklyn Tenants Union. The Housewives Industrial League insisted that the state government investigate the health and housing conditions of unwaged women working at home. Trade union women's auxiliaries also called on legislators to establish children's bureaus, maternal and health care programs, local health departments, and other social welfare programs (Orleck 1995).

In the 1930s, the consumer economy transformed into a depression economy, stimulating a new round of homemaker activism. In 1935, women's groups closed 4500 butcher shops in New York City alone. Hundreds of African American women in Harlem marched through the streets and successfully demanded that butchers lower their prices by 25 percent. Representatives of groups from major cities traveled to Washington, D.C., met with the secretary of agriculture, and demanded government regulation of the meat trusts. Washington's equivocal response fueled more meat boycotts, which brought meat prices down in hundreds of low-income urban neighborhoods across the country (Orleck 1995). Black homemakers in Detroit, Chicago, Baltimore, and Washington, D.C., organized "Don't Buy Where You Can't Work" boycotts using their role as consumers to demand jobs for unemployed black men and women (Hine 1994). The housewives' protests subsided during World War II (1941-45). But huge price increases in 1946-47 and 1951 sparked two of the largest consumer strikes in U.S. history (Stein 1975).

Low-income African American homemaker activists had always furthered a civil rights agenda. With the end of World War II, however, the increasingly militant movement captured their energy. Acting as "bridge women" or "micromobilizers," these unheralded foot soldiers forged critical links between national organizers and local residents (Robnett 1997). In the mid-1950s, local black women launched the 381-day Montgomery bus boycott (Robinson 1987). During the late 1950s and 1960s, local black women across the South insisted on a governmental response. They assisted the Freedom Riders, fought to desegregate public schools, struggled to end racial discrimination in employment and public accommodations, and registered thousands of new voters (Jones 1985). In this context, many black women on public assistance began to organize for more adequate welfare benefits so that they could care for their families. And when the welfare state came under attack in the late 1970s and early 1980s, women on welfare and other low-income women remobilized to protect their hard-won gains.

WELFARE STATE ACTIVISM
AT THE POINT OF
STATE INTERVENTION

The historic povertization of women, the predominance of women among welfare state recipients and workers, and the state's role in supporting families led low-income women to create their own complex relationship with the state. Prior to the Great Depression, when low-income women sought economic security or racial justice from the public sector they turned to local and state governments. However, the federal government loomed larger as a target during the Great Depression. Pressed by organized labor, house-wife cost-of-living protests, and left political parties, the federal government assumed greater responsibility for the economy, family maintenance, and the general welfare.

Using tactics pioneered in the meat boycotts, the homemakers' movement staged large and successful protests of various kinds. In 1937, some 3000 poor and working-class women sat in at New York City's relief centers to demand a 40 percent increase in benefits (Stein 1975). Their squads also blocked evictions, returned furniture to apartments, and warned housing court judges to be prepared for resistance (Kelly 1990; Foner 1979, 1980). Low-income women also played a large but unsung role in the neighborhood-based Unemployed Councils organized by the Communist Party—but filled with hundreds of nonparty members—in numerous northern cities.

Black women in various northern African American communities became very active in these Depression-era protests for better public relief and unemployment insurance. In the South, black women joined the Arkansas-based Southern Tenant-Farmer's Union, which resisted evictions caused by the Agricultural Department's decision to raise farm income by paying farmers to destroy their crops (Stein 1975). Women also participated in the 1932 Hunger March on Washington (Foner 1979, 1980). Once the temporary social welfare programs became permanent, poor and working-class women pressured the government to build affordable housing, improve public schools, create jobs, and otherwise underwrite the services that they as women needed to fulfill their household commitments. In the 1940s, when President Roosevelt cut social welfare spending to placate conservative critics, white and black housewife activism exploded again (Orleck 1995).

The welfare state expanded from 1935 to 1975, fueled by postwar liberalism and pressure from social movements. Emboldened by greater economic security resulting from the more prosperous postwar social welfare economy, white and black welfare recipients from Watts, California, to Mud Creek, East Kentucky, to Boston, Massachusetts, began to organize. They formed the National Welfare Rights Organization (NWRO) to coordinate their activities, worked to shore up public assistance, and demanded a federally guaranteed annual income. NWRO claimed 20,000 members nationwide at its height in 1968, with thousands more participating in local affiliates. In a 1972 *MS* magazine interview, Johnnie Tillmon (1976), the first woman president of NWRO, defined welfare as a women's issue. Influenced if not supported by the women's movement, shortly thereafter, NWRO's cadre of politicized, battle-tested women wrested control from the organization's male-dominated leadership. Increasingly, the names of local welfare rights groups explicitly referred to gender. Although NWRO closed its doors in 1975 due to lack of funds, it politicized many women and changed the debate over welfare in the United States.

By the mid-1960s, the welfare state became the target of activism for employed and community women as well as women on welfare. Indeed, these categories themselves began to merge as welfare policy began to push women on welfare into the workforce and as more women with young children became employed within the social welfare system. At the same time, the expansion of the welfare state and the wider use of public benefits by more low-income households brought many more women into contact with child care, housing subsidies employment, and other government services.

By the mid-1970s, the sagging economy, the more conservative political climate, and budget cuts converted more low-income homemakers into activists. In Brooklyn, New York, working-class women organized against cutbacks in day care, nutrition, fire protection, and other public services (Susser 1982). When the government reduced public housing funding after years of neglect, women tenants in Chicago (Feldman and Stall 1992); South Central, Los Angeles (Leavitt 1992); and other "projects" fought to restore services. In 1974, the National Congress of Neighborhood Women (NCNW) pressed the government for improved education, health care, housing, employment, child care, street safety, financial aid, battered women's services, and transportation facilities (Haywoode 1979). In 1975, the Coalition of Labor Union Women, the NCNW, and Housewives for the ERA opposed President Carter's 1976 welfare reform bill because it neither valued women's work at home nor provided adequate child care provision. Meanwhile millions of low-income women volunteered or worked in new antipoverty programs—which attempted to formally involve poor people in decisions that affected their lives. Seeking to improve their communities' standard of living, these female antipoverty warriors became activists in towns and cities around the country (Naples 1998).

By the early 1980s, President Reagan launched an economic growth strategy, which promoted economic recovery by lowering labor costs, shrinking the welfare state, discrediting the federal government, promoting conservative family values, and reducing the influence of popular movements best positioned to resist the conversion of the social welfare economy into an austerity economy.

Welfare reform became the testing ground for this program based on limited government and family values. From the state-level welfare experiments in the 1980s to the 1996 PRWORA, the welfare reformers won public support for punitive policies by racializing the welfare debate, stigmatizing single motherhood, and discrediting the welfare state. In the late 1990s, while the nation's politicians celebrated a 50 percent drop in the national welfare caseload, most of the women who left welfare reported that they could not make ends meet due to below-poverty wages, irregular employment, and lack of access to Medicaid, food stamps, and child care. However, welfare reform did benefit low-wage employers whose profits depend on cheap labor and politicians who won votes by bashing the poor.

Like their foremothers, low-income women did not take the pain and punishment lying down. Instead, the intense assault on poor people and social programs reactivated welfare rights and advocacy groups with prior roots in the NWRO and sparked the emergence of new ones in numerous cities around the country. The National Welfare Rights Union began to mobilize and coordinate low-income women's antipoverty and welfare rights efforts. For several years, its Up and Out of Poverty Now campaigns and Survival Summits drew hundreds of women from around the country. Over time, more of the welfare rights groups began to define welfare as a matter of gender as well as economics. The names of their groups—Aid to Needy Children (ANC) Mothers Anonymous in Compton, California; Justice, Economic, Dignity, and Independence (JEDI) for Women in Salt Lake City, Utah; Mothers for Justice in New Haven, Connecticut, and the Women's Economic Agenda Project (WEAP) in Oakland California—reflected this increased women's consciousness. In 1992, WEAP convened over 400 poor women for the first ever Poor Women's Convention. On Valentine's Day 1995, JEDI for Women mobilized groups in 77 cities and 38 states for a national day of action to defeat welfare reform. In the 1990s, the Kensington Welfare Rights Union worked to form a poor people's movement arguing that welfare reform represented a violation of human rights.

By the mid-1990s, the *Directory of Welfare Organizations* published by the New York City–based Welfare Law Center listed some 200 organizations. Many of these groups, aided by the Internet, joined forces at the state, regional, and national levels. Faced with the upcoming debate on the reauthorization of Temporary Aid to Needy Families (TANF) funds, their coalitions plan to let Congress know that its version of welfare reform simply cannot stand. Their goals range from fixing TANF, to improving the labor market, to building a wider movement of poor people.

BROADENING
THE AGENDA

Compared to their forerunners, the current welfare rights/advocacy struggle possesses unprecedented political and organizational skills and in some cases greater financial resources. At the same time, it continues to face the historic race, class, and gender dilemmas that have consistently plagued working-class women's organizing for more than a century. The upcoming TANF reauthorization may be just the right time to take up these interrelated unresolved issues.

Class struggle

Low-income women's activism contains internal class conflicts. Composed of young mothers, college students, employed women, and women who cannot work, its future strength depends on unifying these groups along with women not on welfare. However, welfare policy's emphasis on work and the advocacy communities' tendency to focus just on working families risk dividing the welfare community into a new set of deserving and undeserving poor. If tolerated, this would both leave the most vulnerable women behind and undercut the movements' burgeoning strength.

Racial discrimination

The emphasis on work has intensified the racial divide within welfare. Recent studies suggest that fewer women of color than white women have left welfare work due largely to racial discrimination. Gooden (1998, 1999) found that, despite similar skills and backgrounds, black women received far less job-search support from welfare caseworkers than did white women and far fewer job offers from employers.

A connection has also been made between the racial composition of a state's welfare caseload and its adoption of sanctions and other harsh policies. Citing a 1999 unpublished study by Soss and colleagues, Neubeck and Cazenave (forthcoming) reported that states with higher proportions of African American and Latino recipients have adopted the child exclusion, which denies aid to children born on welfare and a shorter time limit than the five-year maximum permitted by the PRWORA and other harsh policies. Many immigrants of color no longer are eligible for welfare benefits, and those who are suffer sanctions, a lack of translators, and overall disrespect (Neubeck and Cazenave forthcoming).

By "push[ing] the minority share of the caseload to the highest level on record" (DeParle 1998, 1) and forcing those who leave into the lowest paid jobs, these practices hand the race card to welfare's opponents. In the past, advocates could refute racial stereotypes by pointing to a numerical predominance of white women on welfare. This is no longer possible. By making racial discrimination a talking point, welfare activists will help low-income women and may help to forge stronger ties to the civil rights movement.

Gendered obligations

Women still have near exclusive responsibility for caregiving even when they work outside the home, which raises special issues for them at several different "points."

The point of production. With the demise of welfare income, low-income women once on welfare now have to balance work and family responsibilities. Not surprisingly, the bottom line for today's welfare activists includes quality, affordable child care; expanded educational and training options; effective health insurance coverage; adequate transportation; and other work supports needed by all working women. Welfare advocates seeking to end poverty also support a higher minimum wage and local living wage campaigns and call for more education, training, and job creation.

However, waged-based labor market demands do not account for labor market risks faced primarily by women: pregnancy, child rearing, and caretaking. A gender-sensitive labor market policy would include women- and mother-friendly policies such as pay equity, a shorter work week, affordable quality child care, paid family medical leave, gender-sensitive unemployment insurance benefits, and an end to sex discrimination, sexual harassment, and sex-segregated occupations and jobs.

The point of consumption. Since the well-being of families and the economy rely heavily on women's unpaid labor in the home, many low-income women activists have a dual agenda. To ensure that they no longer have to put welfare mandates or their jobs before the needs of their children, today's low-income women need both a solid income support system and nonsexist labor market policies. To create the conditions for effective parenting and homemaking, many low-income women activists have joined a long line of women seeking to redefine work to include caregiving. To this end, groups have variously called for counting caregiving as a way to fulfill welfare's work requirements, raising the public assistance grant, enforcing child support orders, expanding the earned income tax credit and/or child tax credit, and replacing TANF with a guaranteed income for caregivers. These proposals, along with protections against male violence, recognize the value of women's work in the home, allow women to decide how they will balance work and family activities, and ensure that neither caregiving nor the loss of male support will expose women to greater poverty and economic inequality. A strategy that combines income support and labor market policies acknowledges the realities of low-income women's lives. It can also help to bridge the divide between the so-called welfare poor and working poor and forge ties to feminist groups.

The point of reproduction. TANF's work requirements have captured most of the public interest, but welfare reform also directs our attention to what might be termed the point of reproduction—long a site for activism for the feminist movement and many middle-class women. In its effort to promote marriage as the foundation of a successful society, welfare reform stigmatizes single mothers and unduly controls the marital, childbearing, and child-rearing choices of poor and working-class women. To this end, TANF includes the family cap noted earlier but also an illegitimacy bonus, which provides extra funds to the five states that reduce their nonmarital birth rates the most without increasing abortions, and abstinence-only funds for school programs that try to limit teen pregnancy by replacing comprehensive sex education with abstinence-only programs. The reformers built support for these harsh policies by evoking racialized stereotypes of hypersexed black women who have additional children to increase their welfare grants. The new Fatherhood and Marriage initiative, currently under discussion in Congress, suggests that family values will become a major issue during the upcoming reauthorization debate.

CONCLUSION

The historical record reviewed here suggests that the next round of organizing will need to recognize that the points of production, consumption, state intervention, and reproduction are less discrete than before. Despite differences of race and income, both the welfare poor and the working poor must deal with issues that arise for them as workers, caretakers, and welfare state beneficiaries. With the lines blurred by changing social and economic and political conditions, the opportunity exists to design a more inclusive platform attractive to large groups of women. Such a platform would call for more jobs, living wages, and government benefits and services and link reproductive rights and economic justice issues more closely. Since many middle-class women already support many of these issues, a platform that focuses on them has the potential to produce new allies, build new alliances, and if we are lucky, generate a strong movement for social justice.

References

Collins, Patricia. 1990. *Black Feminist Thought: Knowledge, Consciousness and the Politics of Empowerment.* London: HarperCollins.

DeParle, Jason. 1998. Shrinking Welfare Rolls Leave Record High Share of Minorities. *New York Times,* 28 July.

Deslippe, D. 1997. Organized Labor, National Politics and Second-Wave Feminism in the United States, 1965-1975. *International Labor and Working Class History* 49(Spring):143-65.

Feldman, Roberta and Susan Stall. 1992. The Politics of Space Appropriation: A

Case Study of Women's Struggles For Homeplace in Chicago Public Housing. Unpublished manuscript.

Foner, Philip. 1979. *Women and the American Labor Movement*, vol. 1. New York: Free Press.

———. 1980. *Women and the American Labor Movement*, vol. 2. New York: Free Press.

Frank, Dana. 1991. Gender, Consumer Organizing and the Seattle Labor Movement, 1919-1929. In *Work Engendered: Toward a New Labor History*, ed. A. Baron. Ithaca, NY: Cornell University Press.

———. 1998. Working Class Feminism. In *The Reader's Companion to U.S. Women's History*, ed. W. Mankilller, G. Mink, M. Navarro, B. Smith, and G. Steinem. New York: Houghton Mifflin.

Frederickson, Mary. 1985. "I Know Which Side I'm on": Southern Women in the Labor Movement in the Twentieth Century. In *Women, Work and Protest: A Century of U.S. Women's Labor History*, ed. Ruth Milkman. Boston: Routledge Kegan Paul.

Gabin, Nancy. 1985. Women and the United Automobile Workers' Union in the 1950s. In *Women, Work and Protest: A Century of U.S. Women's Labor History*, ed. Ruth Milkman. Boston: Routledge Kegan Paul.

Gooden, Susan T. 1998. All Things Not Being Equal: Differences in Caseworker Support Toward Black and White Welfare Clients. *Harvard Journal of African American Public Policy* 4:23-33.

———. 1999. The Hidden Third Party: Welfare Recipients' Experience with Employers. *Journal of Public Management and Social Policy* (5)1:69-83.

Greenwald, Maurine. 1989. Working Class Feminism and the Family Wage Ideal: The Seattle Debate on Married Women's Right to Work, 1914-1920.

Journal of American History 76(1):118-49.

———. 1996. Women and Pennsylvania Working-Class History. *Pennsylvania History* 63(1):5-16.

Haywoode, Terry. 1979. Putting It Together. Conference report for the National Congress of Neighborhood Women, 24-26 Oct., Washington, DC.

Hine, Darlene. C. 1994. The Housewives League of Detroit: Black Women and Economic Nationalism. In *Hine Sight: Black Women and the Reconstruction of American History*, ed. Darlene C. Hine. Brooklyn, NY: Carlson Publishing.

Hunter, Tera. 1997. *To "Joy My Freedom": Southern Black Women's Lives and Labors After the Civil War.* Cambridge, MA: Harvard University Press.

Hyman, Paula E. 1980. Immigrant Women and Consumer Protest: The New York City Kosher Meat Boycott of 1902. *American Jewish History* 70:91-105.

Jones, Jacqueline. 1985. *Labor of Love, Labor of Sorrow: Black Women Work and Family, from Slavery to the Present.* New York: Basic Books.

Kannenberg, Lisa. 1993. The Impact of the Cold War on Women's Trade Union Activism: The UE Experience. *Labor History* 34(2-3):309-23.

Kaplan, Temma. 1982. Female Action and Collective Action: Barcelona. *Signs: A Journal of Women, Culture and Society* 7:4-56.

Kates, Carol. 1989. Working Class Feminism and Feminist Unions: Title VII, the UAW and NOW. *Labor History Journal* 14(2):28-45.

Kelly, Robin. 1990. *Hammer and Hoe: Alabama Communists During the Great Depression*. Chapel Hill: University of North Carolina Press.

Kennedy, Susan. 1981. *If All We Did Was to Weep at Home: A History of White Working Class Women in America.*

Bloomington: Indiana University Press.

Kessler-Harris, Alice. 1985. Problems of Coalition Building: Women and Trade Unions in the 1920s. In *Women, Work and Protest: A Century of U.S. Women's Labor History*, ed. Ruth Milkman. Boston: Routledge Kegan Paul.

Leavitt, Jacqueline. 1992. Women Under Fire: Public Housing Activism, Los Angeles. *Women's Studies* 13(2):109-31.

Levi, Margaret. 1974. Poor People Against the State. *Review of Radical Political Economics* 6(1):76-98.

Milkman, Ruth. 1985. Women Workers, Feminism and the Labor Movement. In *Women, Work and Protest: A Century of U.S. Women's Labor History*, ed. Ruth Milkman. Boston: Routledge Kegan Paul.

Naples, Nancy. 1998. *Grassroots Warriors: Activist Mothering, Community Work and the War on Poverty*. New York: Routledge.

Neubeck, Kenneth J. and Noel A. Cazenave. Forthcoming. Welfare Racism and Its Consequences: The Demise of AFDC and the Return of the States' Rights Era. In *Work, Welfare and Politics*, ed. Frances Fox Piven, Joan Acker, Margaret Hallock and Sandra Morgen. Eugene: University of Oregon Press.

Orleck, Annelise. 1995. *Common Sense and a Little Fire: Women and Working-Class Politics in the United States, 1900-1965*. Chapel Hill: University of North Carolina.

Robinson, Joan. 1987. *The Montgomery Bus Boycott and the Women Who Started It*. Knoxville: University of Tennessee Press.

Robnett, Belinda. 1997. *How Long? How Long? African American Women in the Struggle for Civil Rights*. New York: Oxford University Press.

Scott, Anne Firor. 1990. Most Invisible of All: Black Women's Voluntary Associations. *Journal of Southern History* 56(1):3-22.

Stein, Ann. 1975. Post War Consumer Boycotts. *Radical America* 9(July-Aug.):156-61.

Strom, Sharon H. 1985. "We're No Kitty Foyles": Organizing Office Workers for the Congress of Industrial Organizations, 1937-1950. In *Women, Work and Protest: A Century of US Women's Labor History*, ed. Ruth Milkman. Boston: Routledge Kegan Paul.

Susser, Ida. 1982. *Norman Street: Poverty and Politics in an Urban Neighborhood*. New York: Oxford University Press.

Tidd, James. 1989. Stitching and Striking: WPA Sewing Room and the 1937 Relief Strike in Hillsborough County. *Tampa Bay History* 11(1):5-21.

Tillmon, Johnnie. 1976. Welfare Is a Women's Issue. In *American Working Women: A Documentary History 1600 to the Present*, ed. Rosalyn Baxandall, Linda Gordon and Susan Reverby. New York. Vintage.

ANNALS, *AAPSS*, **577**, September 2001

Closing the Care Gap That Welfare Reform Left Behind

By LUCIE E. WHITE

ABSTRACT: This article begins by drawing from an interview with Johnnie Tillmon, a grassroots leader of the National Welfare Rights Organization, to locate welfare reform in the context of cultural anxieties about an eroding racial order and shifting gender roles. It then considers the sorts of state policies and legal entitlements that could resource the care-work that has heretofore been subsidized by low-income women's labor and argues that such innovations are not beyond the reach of a pragmatic postmodernist democracy.

Lucie E. White is the Louis A. Horvitz Professor of Law at Harvard Law School. She is a founder of the Kitchen Table Conversations Project, a group of low-income women who support one another while advising the City of Cambridge on social policy issues. She is the coeditor, with Joel Handler, of Hard Labor: Women and Work in the Post-Welfare Era.

JOHNNIE Tillmon was one of the grassroots leaders of the National Welfare Rights Movement in the late 1960s. She stood for the idea that the welfare rights movement should be anchored in strong community-based groups, like the one that she founded in Los Angeles (Quadagno 1994; Davis 1993; West 1981). In a 1993 interview with the author, Tillmon wanted to make one thing clear: she had always worked for wages, from when she was a child, cleaning white folks' houses and taking care of their children. After she settled in Los Angeles, she took a job in a laundry, doing the best that she could to find care for her children while she was at work. It was only after she got hurt on the job in the mid-1960s that it occurred to Tillmon to apply for welfare for a time. She found the whole experience profoundly humiliating.

As she told her story, Tillmon underscored several points. First, she felt morally entitled to welfare because of her solid work record, even as a single mother. Second, although her work at the laundry was hard, she was proud that she had done it. Third, it was the injustices she confronted when she went on welfare that turned her into a welfare rights activist.

The biggest problem with the old welfare system, according to Tillmon, was its race prejudice. For Johnnie Tillmon, welfare seemed like a system that was set up to tear down the self-esteem of the women who used it, especially black women, like herself, who had come upon hard times. If the government was going to have welfare at all, it should not injure the very people it was supposed to be helping.

The second problem with the welfare system, according to Tillmon, was that to get welfare you had to swear that you were not working under the table. Yet welfare did not pay you enough to live on. Furthermore, getting welfare made you say that you wanted to stay at home all the time, rather than working. Johnnie Tillmon and the other women that she knew had always been both mothers and workers, from the days of slavery (Jones 1995).

Johnnie Tillmon and the other grassroots women who took to the streets in the 1960s sought a welfare system that would respect their dignity. They dreamed of a welfare system with rules that would admit to, rather than make them deny, the bread-and-butter realities of their lives. They dreamed of a system in which getting welfare would not make them deny that they were workers and mothers at the same time. They just wanted decent working conditions and decent pay. They wanted some extra help when they got sick or could not find a good job or needed some time off of work to take care of their children. They wanted a welfare system that they were not cut out of, a system that their lives and their ideas had played some part in shaping.

WHY A WORK-BASED
WELFARE SYSTEM?

In August of 1996, the federal government enacted the Personal Responsibility and Work Opportunity Reconciliation Act, which requires states to put most Temporary Aid to Needy Families (TANF)-funded welfare recipients into workfare jobs for between 20 and 30 hours a week and limits their lifetime maximum access to TANF to five years. Congress rationalized these requirements by declaring that low-income single-parent families, just like all other American families, should be expected to support themselves through work.

Should progressive scholars endorse a work-based alternative to a stay-at-home welfare entitlement? There are several reasons to give serious consideration to the idea. First, to many low-income women, like Johnnie Tillmon, a work-based safety net seems far superior to a stay-at-home cash entitlement, even one that, unlike Aid to Families with Dependent Children (AFDC), pays a decent level of benefits. A web of social policies for assuring all families a decent life through waged work would fit more closely with the historically embedded values, the real-life practices, and the aspirations of many low-income women, including but not exclusively African Americans (Schultz 2000).

Second, a work-based safety net would align social policy with the social science data suggesting that working outside of the home can be a very good thing for women's well-being and their children's development. Working outside of the home can help to combat the intense isolation that many low-income single mothers feel and the emotional suffering that often goes with it (Bassuk et al. 1998; Dodson 1998; Weissbourd

1997). Work, even low-wage work, has the potential to enhance a single mother's feelings of self-esteem, competency, and social connection. It can give her a bulwark of social and institutional support against the risk of intimate violence. It can provide positive role models for her children.

Finally, a work-based safety net would bring low-income single mothers into the mainstream of social and civic life in our work-centered society. As many of the liberal proponents of welfare reform have insisted, a work-based safety net would enable low-income single mothers to pursue the goals of personal autonomy, gender equality, and social inclusion on the same basis as elite women.

So while there are many good reasons to endorse the idea of a work-based safety net, it is the concrete social policies that might realize this idea, especially here in the United States, that are so hard to imagine. The web of policies it would take to create a real work-based safety net in this country would mean nothing less than ending low-wage work, at least as we know it today. Furthermore, that web of policies would soften the rigid boundaries that separate the nuclear family from the wider community and that wall off the formal sector low-wage workplace from both of these spheres.

A work-based safety net that starts from what Lisa Dodson (2000) calls "the groundtruth" of low-income single mothers' lives would bring workplace and state-based social policies into closer alignment with the interweaving of workplace, family, and community that has marked the lifeworlds of African American women throughout our country's history. It would also undermine the rigid dichotomy between worker and mother that the old, Mothers' Pension/AFDC welfare regime imposed.

In this article, I use the example of child care to outline some of the features that a realistic work-based safety net would need to include. Crafting a realistic work-based safety net is not a technical problem that can be solved through the expertise of lawyers and policy experts. Rather, it will require a major reshaping of the values and practices in the domains of waged work, the family, and the community (Fraser 1997; Harrington 1999; Williams 2000). Let's start by looking at some of the trends that have shaped public policies here in the United States regarding race, gender, work, and care.

THE HISTORICAL ROOTS
OF THE CHALLENGE

*The demise of the family wage
and rise of the care gap*

In the first half of this century, the family wage was the dominant social policy in the United States for socially resourcing the care of children, elders, and other non-wage-earning persons. According to the family wage idea, employers would pay each male worker enough to support his entire nuclear family. The Mothers' Pension/AFDC welfare regime reinforced the family wage care deal by giving a state-funded cash pension directly to single mothers, especially widows, who fit the domestic ideal of the family wage era. The family wage was a normative arrangement rather than a widespread social practice. It was common among elite white working- and middle-class households, in which the male worked in a unionized job or professional/managerial position.

The family wage norm failed to penetrate the work-family arrangements of single-parent households that were not deemed to be worthy of the Mothers' Pension either because they brought on their own single motherhood or because they failed to comply with Euro-American cultural norms of domesticity. Nor did it penetrate the work-family arrangements of African Americans or other non-white racial groups at all, as access to family-wage-level jobs was rigidly segregated. Thus, in all but the most affluent two-parent families of color, both husband and wife routinely worked outside of the home.

Caretaking in these households was typically handled through extended family networks and community-based caretaking institutions, such as churches, fraternal organizations, and what were often very elaborate locally organized social welfare networks. The care work was resourced, for the most part, through a noncash economy in which goods and services were donated and exchanged informally, in accord with a value system that was rooted in faith, family cohesion, and race solidarity (Collins 2000; hooks 1984; White 2000). Sometimes older children did substantial portions of the household's waged work and care work, while younger children were often left without care or taken by charities or the state.

In the 1960s and 1970s, the family wage formula, and the cult of domesticity that went with it, came under challenge from the liberal, second-wave women's movement, which promoted a vision of women's liberation that was premised on women assimilating themselves to a male-identified ideal-worker norm. The well-to-do wives of family-wage-earning males were no longer satisfied to stay at home minding the children (Williams 2000).

But how would this modern woman respond to the care gap that her exit left behind? Some simply put off having children altogether. Others found partners willing to take over the caretaking work. Many tried to buy the services of care workers, nannies, house cleaners, preschool and after-school programs, and elder care. This last solution is prohibitively expensive, even for families with two high-wage workers, especially if the care work that is purchased with one's income is paid at salary levels that will permit the care workers themselves to purchase care for their dependents while they work.

Furthermore, there are some care needs that money just cannot buy. These "interstitial" care needs, as Nancy Fraser (1997) has labeled them, are hard to farm out to paid caregivers, no matter how much money one has to spend, and all but impossible if one's budget for care has its limits. They range from giving birth, to shuttling kids between different caretakers, to dealing with kids or caretakers who are too sick to follow the routine, to responding to a loved one's need for the kind of attention that just cannot be delegated.

The commodification solution to the post-family-wage care gap has been a recipe for frustration among the middle- and upper-income households that have tried to make it work. Modern women, as well as their families, have found themselves increasingly caught between a rock and a hard place as they try to be equal with men in the workplace while coping with the care gap that they have left behind in the home.

Conservative forces have responded to this crisis by invoking religious and moral themes to urge households to turn back the clock. They have urged families and the society at large to reaffirm nuclear marriage and, within it, the traditional division of the breadwinning and caretaking household roles.

Yet these backward-looking solutions have not been feasible. Since the late 1970s, U.S. firms have been downsizing and restructuring in order to remain competitive in a shifting economy. Many secure family-wage-paying jobs have been eliminated. Wage levels have stagnated for many low- and middle-income men. This trend has forced many two-parent families to send mommy as well as daddy out to work, simply to help pay the mortgage.

This was the setting in which, in the early 1980s, a conservative social movement zeroed in on the AFDC program as one of its key symbolic targets. The conservative attack on welfare played into both the resentment of families in which wives were unwillingly drawn into the labor market and the frustration of liberal women who sought to pursue careers. To the resentful, unwillingly working wives, the rhetoric went something like this: It is patently unfair for the government to pay poor single mothers a dole to have children when so many taxpaying families have to send their women out to work to make ends meet. If poor women choose to have children, they should work, just like the rest of us, to support them. The government should not be taking money from hard-working families to pay poor women to sit at home, watch TV, and have more babies.

To the women who were struggling, often unsuccessfully, to have both career and family, the rhetoric went something like this: We all know that work outside of the home is a good thing for everybody. It connects women to the wider society. It raises their self-esteem. It turns them into responsible citizens. It provides a dynamite role model for their children. No matter how hard it may seem to get out there and work at the same time you are trying to raise children, every woman can, and should, be expected to do it. The transition may be difficult, but the payoff will be enormous, both for the women who are nudged out of dependency and for the fabric of the nation.

The symbolic appeal of welfare reform was so compelling that there were almost no serious efforts, among any of welfare reform's proponents, to think through the post-family-wage care-gap question for low-income single mothers, or indeed for the wider society, in any realistic way.

As we saw above, when elite women in two-parent households decided to go to work for long hours to break the glass ceiling, they would find it almost impossible to solve their care problem, both because of the astronomical costs of living-wage-level care services and because of those interstitial care needs that cannot be easily bought and sold. The "arithmetic," to use Mona Harrington's term (1999), just would not work out. How, then, could the lowest-income single-parent families be expected to solve their care problem?

The only response to this dilemma from welfare reform's proponents was to pay lip service to child care and earned income tax credits and then to be silent. Clearly, a good deal of magical thinking was going on, especially among welfare reform's liberal proponents, when the federal welfare reform law, complete with stringent work requirements and a five-year drop-dead time limit for most recipients, was enacted.

Welfare as a threat to the nation's racial order

But widespread societal frustration about the demise of the family wage care deal was not the only anxiety that was driving welfare reform. A second, and even more potent, wellspring of social anxiety converged with this gender trouble to give the welfare reform movement an obsessional sense of urgency.

Between the New Deal and the 1970s, the civil rights movement gradually opened up the AFDC system to racial and ethnic minorities, most notably African Americans. This racial integration posed a major shock to the AFDC system because it extended an open-ended, cash entitlement into African American social networks, thereby destabilizing segregated local labor markets.

The biggest shock waves came in the deep South, where access to welfare gave African Americans an alternative to working for very low wages in harsh conditions, both on the plantations and in white people's homes. In urban centers, access to AFDC enabled African American women like Johnnie Tillmon to become more politically active, both in their workplaces, where AFDC worked like a union strike fund for women who risked getting fired for organizing on the job, and against the welfare system itself, as the realities of AFDC taught them a bitter lesson about a basic flaw in the American version of democracy.

At the same time, wide access by African American women to the AFDC entitlement made the distinctive family practices among low-income African Americans, shaped as an adaptive response to slavery and its aftermath, uncomfortably visible to white elites. These family practices entailed young women giving birth in households that included older women. This arrangement assured that children were born before their mothers' health had been eroded by the stresses of poverty and before their grandmothers were too old to help with their care. These practices also included geographically dispersed intimate partnerships, shaped by a racially segregated national labor market, which compelled African American men to move about for work while women took domestic care jobs that allowed them to maintain a homeplace for the family.

The central roles for women in these extended, geographically dispersed families clashed sharply with the notion of wife as husband's helpmate that the family wage norm presumed. AFDC had been designed to buttress domesticity. Yet once its color bar was broken, AFDC became, Pandora-like, a threat to the entire race-gender order. Beginning in the 1960s, the "black family" became a code word among whites for the anxieties they felt about both the rebellion against Jim Crow and the demise of the family wage. Politicians began to look for ways to limit the AFDC entitlement by imposing new work requirements and snarling the program in new red-tape rules.

By the early 1980s, a cultural narrative that blamed welfare, point-blank, for provoking black women's sexual promiscuity and promoting their dependency was crafted in conservative think tanks (Murray 1995). This story was then masterfully interwoven with the magical belief that compelling poor single mothers to work full-time for wages would somehow close the care gap that had come with the erosion of the family wage.

A CARE GAP EMERGES

Even before the federal welfare reform bill became law, data confirming the inescapable realities of poor single mothers' work/care economies began to emerge. Kathryn Edin and Laura Lein's (1997) work showed that low-income single mothers in several U.S. cities were simply unable to earn enough income in the nation's low-wage labor markets to make ends meet. If they tried to increase their hours, they were caught in a catch-22 situation. The longest of days has just 24 hours, and the more of those hours you work, the more you have to pay for child care.

Recently conducted cost-of-living studies document the income levels that would be required to meet basic living expenses, including housing, child care, food, transportation, health care, and the like. In Boston, for instance, a three-person household composed of an adult, a preschooler, and a school-age child would require a budget of $3,263 a month to meet basic expenses. That translates into a full-time wage level of $17.47 per hour. The highest single budget item, of $985 per month, would be for child care (Bacon, Russell, and Pearce 2000). To make ends meet with very low wages, one has to work very long hours. But long hours on the job only increase the gap between income and expenses because of the increased need for care. A care gap that is merely intractable for middle-class and elite working women becomes an insane vicious circle for the poor.

A REALISTIC POLICY RESPONSE

As a start, a realistic, work-based safety net for low-income working families, particularly those headed by single mothers, would have to assure that high-quality, affordable, developmentally sound care is readily available for children, elders, and other household members in need of care, for all of the hours that the parents are at work. This in itself creates several big challenges for social policy.

The first challenge involves the timing of care. Routine and interstitial care would have to be available. Thus, care would have to be available for irregular needs, like doctor appointments and school assemblies, as well as the parents' regular work hours. And wraparound, or odd-hours, care would have to be available to accommodate to the wraparound work schedules that are common in low-wage jobs (Dodson, Joshi, and McDonald 1998). Family and medical leave-type policies, in which the state requires employers to allow workers time off to deal with family and medical emergencies, are the most feasible for dealing with unpredictable care needs (Heymann 2000).

The challenge here is to link those mandates to policies for promoting the kinds of postbureaucratic innovation in the organization of work itself, at the shop-floor level, that will make such flexibility in work scheduling seem less of a threat to employers' economic interests (Schultz 2000). A post-Fordist, high-road approach to the organization of work at the firm level will also be a lynchpin of policies for accommodating the varying needs of low-wage workers themselves, not just for personal leave time but for a work environment that affirms their capacities rather than aggravating their health risks.

With respect to care services for workers who work long or odd hours, the challenge is different. Close study of best practices for firm-based day care for second- and third-shift workers demonstrates how hard it is to make such programs work well for children. It simply is not developmentally optimal for a 3-year-old to be roused from sleep every night to be taken to a day care center so his mother can report for her third-shift job. So, once again, the policy challenge here is more on the side of work organization and community care networks. Is this an industry that could move away from a 24-hour model of production? If not, are there innovations at the community level that could ensure odd-hours child care for the parents who need it— innovations such as cooperative, service-enhanced congregate housing for single parents—that governmental housing and community policies could more consciously promote? Could subsidies for kith-and-kin care be targeted to parents with these odd-hours care needs and enhanced by features that ensure that kin caregivers will be well paid, well trained, and well connected to community supports and that ensure funding for the removal of obvious health hazards like lead paint from the homes in which this care takes place?

The second challenge involves making care affordable to low-income families. Here, the consensus of economists who have looked at the issue closely is that, at the very least, the state must step in to correct what are patent failures in care markets, at least for low-income families (Vandell and Wolfe 2000). Because the market failures are multiple and complex, it is unlikely that they can be corrected by a single form of state intervention. A whole range of state policies will have to be coordinated to achieve a good care system. Public education will have to be extended to include services for children from ages 0 to 6 and to expand services into after-school hours and school vacations. The money that is available to families to spend for fee-based care will have to be increased substantially, through vouchers, tax credits, or mandates on employers, from unions or the state itself, to pay wages that are high enough to cover the costs of care.

Even with substantial demand-side subsidies, the most expensive components of care, that is, the costs of paying professional-level care workers the kinds of salaries that will both attract and hold them in these jobs and the costs of constructing and maintaining good care sites, will have to be supported by additional supply-side subsidies, such as state-subsidized loan pools for capital expenses and caregivers' educational expenses.

The third challenge is that the quality of care will have to be assured through creative forms of state action. This action must move beyond rigid command-control regulation to regulatory innovations that generate both the funding and the know-how to provide good-enough care for all children. Beyond that, however, state action in the area of quality assurance will be most successful if it creates the networks and structures for parent and peer monitoring and for encouraging providers to innovate outside-the-box improvements in their own practices and to design techniques for benchmarking, documenting, and disseminating their success (Morgan 1995).

As should be apparent from this brief outline, the kinds of state action that are called for to entitle low-income working parents to adequate day care look very different than the old notion of entitlement as a legally enforceable claim, by an eligible citizen, to a lump-sum of cash. To take the challenge of a work-based safety net seriously, then, we need to begin thinking of entitlements as legally enforceable commitments to the creation of public goods. Rather than a single law that guarantees day care for all, such commitments would be set forth through webs of inter-related constitutional standards, federal and state statutes and regulations, local ordinances, judicial precedents, and the like, dispersed across all levels of government. These laws would use the full range of policy instruments to intervene simultaneously in all of the societal domains that are relevant to the issue. It is only through this conception of entitlement that the law can begin to guarantee that the real programs and services that are called for to enable low-income women to work have a good chance to emerge.

Shaping this kind of entitlement framework takes a new, much more pragmatic, institutionally grounded kind of policy design work than the old, rigidly rights-based notion calls for. In many circumstances, this will mean preserving and enhancing the cultural norms, social institutions, and legal frameworks that are already out there, rather than bulldozing them away like a 1950s-era urban planner. For instance, in the case of child care, this might mean mapping out the ways that low-income families in a particular neighborhood are already weaving together care for their children through a combination of kin, neighbors, paid babysitters, and church- or community-based care sites. On the basis of this picture, changes could be written into existing federal and state day care block grant laws to permit quality improvement funds to be used to enhance social support, training, and resource sharing among such networks of providers.

One of the big challenges in this approach to entitlement is to ensure that the law affords family- and neighborhood-based groups clear, legally enforceable rights to participate in the shaping, monitoring, and evaluation of all relevant policies through processes that identify benchmarks for evaluating progress toward clear goals. Another challenge is to ensure that individual citizens have an enforceable right to defend themselves against legal obligations, like workfare or welfare time limits, that are premised on the assumption that the public goods in question, like good child care, are already available.

We are obviously quite far from that goal in the case of child care (White 1999). We are also quite far from that goal in the other two bedrock features of a real work-based safety net—the assurance of adequate wage levels in low-income jobs and the assurance of workplace environments that will accommodate the realistic needs of low-income women. As the case of child care illustrates, getting from here to there is not just a question of mustering up the political will to fund the deep subsidies that a good care system will require.

It is not that simple. To ensure both productive work and good care for all who need it, citizens will have to be engaged to seek structural innovations in the family, community institutions, and the workplace and to evaluate and improve on those changes. How much can or should workplaces change their production processes to enable workers to spend more time away from the workplace in order to give direct care to family or community members? When does it make sense for firms to provide onsite care? How can the jobs of paid caregivers be brought into the mainstream of real, formal sector work without imposing the rigidities of a Fordist work culture? How should families change to distribute the care they provide more equitably between men and women? How should communities change to provide social support for isolated at-home caretakers and to handle care needs when families and regular care providers are not available?

Processes for answering these questions must tap into the personal commitments of citizens while engaging their creativity and public-oriented interests. These processes must bridge different social domains, encouraging dialogue between peoples with different histories, economic priorities, and cultural values. The law should both structure and resource these processes of democratic engagement. At the same time, these processes should shape and reshape the law in ways that can gradually move us beyond the care

gap that was left in the wake of the family wage.

CONCLUSION: A GROUND
OF INCOME SECURITY

When we are at so early a stage in this transition, it does not make good policy sense to require low-income women to work for long hours in the hope that they can somehow close the care gap on their own. A more sensible approach to moving toward a work-based safety net would encourage work outside the home by creating the care resources that will make it more feasible. At the same time policies would be devised to enable low-income parents to participate more actively in the care of their own children and to link home-based caretakers, whether they are family members or paid workers, to social connection and fiscal support.

An income support policy consistent with this approach would ensure every family a modest, means-tested basic income that is large enough to permit them to care for their own dependents. Other laws and policies should encourage them to try public sector work and socially networked parenting to the degree that those options are feasible in their own lives (Ackerman and Alstott 1999). Such a policy would place the responsibility for closing the care gap on the institutions with the power to make it happen—legislatures, employers, community groups, faith-based organizations—rather than on impoverished single mothers.

This is the sort of approach to welfare policy that Johnnie Tillmon was calling for when she spoke so passionately against American welfare policies that show no respect for the real commitments and real constraints of low-income women's lives.

References

Ackerman, Bruce and Alstott. 1999. *The Stakeholder Society*. New Haven, CT: Yale University Press.

Bacon, Jean, Laura Russell, and Diana Pearce. 2000. The Self-Sufficiency Standard: Where Massachusetts Families Stand. Report prepared by the Women's Educational and Industrial Union in collaboration with Wider Opportunities for Women, Boston, MA.

Bassuk, Ellen, J. C. Buckner, J. N. Perloff, and S. S. Bassuk. 1998. Prevalence of Mental Health and Substance Abuse Disorders Among Homeless and Low-Income Housed Mothers. *American Journal of Psychiatry* 155(11):1561-64.

Collins, Patricia Hill. 2000. *Black Feminist Thought: Knowledge, Consciousness, and the Politics of Empowerment*. New York: Routledge.

Davis, Martha. 1993. *Brutal Need*. New Haven, CT: Yale University Press.

Dodson, Lisa. 1998. *Don't Call Us Out of Name: The Untold Lives of Women and Girls in Poor America*. Boston: Beacon Press.

———. 2000. The Hidden Work of Children. *Radcliffe Quarterly* (Fall):20-21.

Dodson, Lisa, Pamela Joshi, and Davida McDonald. 1998. Welfare in Transition: Consequences for Women, Families, and Communities. Report prepared by the Radcliffe Public Policy Institute, Cambridge, MA.

Edin, Kathryn and Laura Lein. 1997. *Making Ends Meet: How Single Mothers Survive Welfare and Low-Wage Work*. New York: Russell Sage Foundation.

Fraser, Nancy. 1997. *Justice Interruptus: Critical Reflections on the "Postsocialist" Condition*. New York: Routledge.

Harrington, Mona. 1999. *Care and Equality: Inventing a New Family Politics*. New York: Knopf.

Heymann, Jody. 2000. *The Widening Gap: Why America's Working Families Are in Jeopardy and What Can Be Done About It*. New York: Basic Books.

hooks, bell. 1984. *Feminist Theory: From Margin to Center*. Boston: South End Press.

Jones, Jacquelyn. 1995. *Labor of Love, Labor of Sorrow: Black Women, Work and the Family from Slavery to Freedom*. New York: Vintage.

Morgan, Gwen. 1995. *New Approaches to Regulation*. Boston: Wheelock College, Center for Career Development in Early Care and Education.

Murray, Charles. 1995. *Losing Ground: American Social Policy 1950-1980*. New York: Basic Books.

Quadagno, Jill. 1994. *The Color of Welfare*. New York: Oxford University Press.

Schultz, Vicki. 2000. Life's Work. *Columbia Law Review* 100(7):1881-964.

Vandell, Deborah Lowe and Barbara Wolfe. 2000. Child Care Quality: Does It Matter and Does It Need to Be Improved? Special report no. 78 of the Institute for Research on Poverty, Madison, WI.

Weissbourd, Richard. 1997. *The Vulnerable Child: The Hidden Epidemic of Neglected and Troubled Children Even Within the Middle Class*. New York: Perseus Press.

West, Guida. 1981. *The National Welfare Rights Movement: The Social Protest of Poor Women*. New York: Praeger.

White, Lucie. 1999. Despair, Impasse, Improvisation. In *Hard Labor: Women and Work in the Post-Welfare Era*, ed. Joel Handler and Lucie White. Armonk, NY: M. E. Sharpe.

———. 2000. "That's What I Growed Up Hearing": Race, Social Provision, and the Redemption of American Democracy. In *Who Provides*, ed. Brent Coffin, Mary Jo Bane, and Ronald Thiemann. Boulder, CO: Westview Press.

Williams, Joan. 2000. *Unbending Gender: Why Family and Work Conflict and What to Do About It*. New York: Oxford University Press.

ANNALS, *AAPSS*, **577**, September 2001

A View from the Bottom:
Poor People and Their Allies
Respond to Welfare Reform

By WILLIE BAPTIST and MARY BRICKER-JENKINS

ABSTRACT: The Personal Responsibility and Work Opportunity Reconciliation Act (PRWORA) is construed as simply affecting or attacking "welfare moms." The authors see welfare recipients as only the first and most visible targets of this and related welfare reform measures. The ultimate objective, the authors argue, is a downsized standard of living for the majority of Americans, justified by a restricted vision of human rights. Like the 1857 Dred Scott decision and the abolition of slavery, the PRWORA is a clarion call about the necessity of building a powerful movement to abolish poverty once and for all. Such a movement must be grounded in the unity, leadership, and widespread organization of the poor and guided by an unrestricted vision of economic human rights for all. This article describes the authors' approach to building this new movement.

Willie Baptist is the education director of the Kensington Welfare Rights Union (KWRU), a member of the War Council, and co–lead organizer of the University of the Poor, the educational arm of the Poor People's Economic Human Rights Campaign. He was formerly homeless. With his family, he was on welfare for 10 years, participating in workfare as a condition for survival.

Mary Bricker-Jenkins does odd jobs in the movement as a member of the Temple Depot of the Underground Railroad, a network of allies of KWRU. She is a member of KWRU's Education Committee and an honorary member of the War Council. She teaches social work practice at Temple University School of Social Administration and is convener of the School for Social Workers of the University of the Poor.

NOTE: Authors are listed alphabetically; neither is the senior author. We thank the members of the KWRU Education Committee for their participation in this project.

I had three kids. I was paying $275 every two weeks. . . . I was only getting $247 by that time. One day I came home, there was a padlock on the door. So I took my kids to a friend's, but it was too crowded, then I moved to another friend's, then another. . . . I tried to get into the shelters, but the shelter system turned me away. . . . [I realized] it's got to be something not just wrong with me. It's got to be something wrong in the world, in the system.
—Kensington Welfare Rights Union member

This work is not about pitying the poor. It is about making common cause with people living in poverty because we share a common plight, a common position in relation to forces that are working to define the conditions of our existence—indeed, to claim the right to define the very history of this planet. We are reclaiming that right.
—Underground Railroad member

The Personal Responsibility and Work Opportunity Reconciliation Act (PRWORA) of 1996 was said to signal "the end of welfare as we know it"; for us, it signaled the end of welfare rights organizing as we knew it. For decades, most antipoverty efforts in the United States had pursued a civil rights strategy designed to wrest concessions from the welfare state. But we saw the PRWORA as another indication that we had moved into a new period of human history, one in which ending poverty is both necessary and eminently possible. Thus, shifting our organizing focus from civil rights to economic human rights, we are pursuing the goal of ending poverty to secure for all the rights to life, liberty, and happiness. Nothing less.

While the political environment appeared to offer little hope, we excavated it from history and our experience working in organizations of poor people and their allies. The message of both history and experience was clear: build a broad movement based on the development and growth of the unity and leadership of the poor as a class—one that reflects the real demographics of poverty in terms of race/ethnicity, gender, geographic environment, and connection to the workforce. Such a movement must embrace the majority of Americans but necessarily be rooted in the immediate needs and demands of the 35-60 million people living in poverty in the United States today. Their program, not a program ultimately benefiting the wealthy, must constitute the vision of the movement.

The lessons of history gave us hope: as was the case during the growth of the abolition movement, this period in history offers a vision that can be embraced by people who unite with the poor out of common analysis and shared interest. If the political environment appears to offer only a shrinking (or compromising) resource base for organizing, we can rely primarily on our resourcefulness for resources and on commitment over compensation. If the contemporary global context of welfare reform appears to place the sites of controlling power beyond our reach, we can extend our grasp by organizing both locally and globally, building new foundations of power.

In short, we see the period of welfare reform as a period of mounting contradiction and crisis—one that portends heightened suffering to be sure, but one that provides a new opportunity to build a successful movement to end poverty. For this task, we need to clarify and consolidate our responses intellectually, strategically, and organizationally. In this article, we present the scaffolding we are using to construct these dimensions of our program.

THE INTELLECTUAL SCAFFOLDING: OUR ESTIMATE OF THE SITUATION

We are readers of history. Especially for leaders and organizers from the ranks of the poor, reading and interpreting history is a matter of survival. When discussions, explanations, and theories about us and our situation have been controlled by others—people who currently control the institutions of society—we must make our own, rooting them in our experience and interpretation of history. In this section, we present our current reading of history in relation to welfare reform, focusing on the ways that two key mechanisms, economic and ideological, have been operating in the interest of others and to our detriment. We are not posing a conspiracy theory but a consensus theory; that is, we see an alignment of interests among a tightly networked group of individuals representing major corporations, foundations, government entities, and intellectual circles, all pursuing a logic of global capitalism around which a tacit consensus has emerged (Draffan 2000; Grugan 2000; Kincheloe forthcoming; Polychroniou 1995).[1]

The economic mechanisms: Lessons from history

Particularly relevant to our situation is the history of the American antislavery movement. This included the first broad-based movement of the poor in American history, involving the industrial poor and agricultural poor of the North as well as the slave poor—all challenging the economic and two-party political systems of the slaveholding power nexus. Studying this period in history helps us to grasp that the PRWORA had as much to do with welfare recipients as the Dred Scott decision had to do with slaves.

When in 1857 the U.S. Supreme Court ruled in *Dred Scott v. Sandford*,[2] the manifest issue was Scott's right to claim freedom. The proslavery majority, in extending the purview of the case to include matters of "Negro citizenship" and the constitutionality of the Missouri Compromise, revealed the latent function of the decision: to reinforce the legal and judicial infrastructure needed by slaveholders for the continued expansion of their economic institution. Against the backdrop of the spent soil of the South and the emergence of industrialism in the North, industrial classes of the North collided with the slavocracy and its claim on the resources it needed—land and labor. In this time of economic transformation, inexorable but as yet uncertain in outcome, the Supreme Court used its power to support the economic interests of its class.

Significantly, in his inaugural address, President-elect Buchanan backed the decision and the Supreme

Court's right to decide the matter, thereby taking the issue out of the realm of the people's political discourse and enshrining it in the allegedly nonpartisan sphere of the judiciary. To the Court's authority and wisdom, "in common with all good citizens, I shall cheerfully submit," Buchanan said (cited in Kutler 1967, 5). This endorsement of the "good judgment" of presumably benign experts is as much a part of the ideological apparatus of the ruling class today as it was then and serves the same function: it conceals the nullification of the right of the people whose economic destiny is at stake to participate in the decisions that affect their lives. Similarly, the contours of the decision's two primary pillars bear chilling resemblance to our contemporary situation: (1) the property rights of slaveholders were, in effect, expanded, and (2) not only did slaves and free blacks lose the rights of citizenship, but opponents of the slavocracy understood that this extension of judicial purview placed in jeopardy the rights of the majority of the American people.

For those of us who look at welfare reform from the bottom up, there are compelling lessons in the Dred Scott decision. First, we believe that both Dred Scott and the PRWORA used the mechanisms of government to legitimate and support the interests of a key element of the country's economic structure at a time of profound and permanent economic transformation. Second, while both were purportedly about a particular targeted element of the population, both had the effect (and, quite likely, the intent) of controlling the economic latitude and liberty of the majority of the population.

Neither Dred Scott nor the PRWORA appeared suddenly on the scene; both reflected changing attitudes and positions that developed over decades. In the case of welfare reform, the poor—both employed and unemployed, able to work and not, men and women, white and people of color alike—had been experiencing for decades an ever-increasing erosion of viable work opportunities, social services, and income supports. Indeed, prior to the enactment of PRWORA, the so-called middle class had lost ground in living standards, the ability of women to choose work outside the home was constrained by the falling value of welfare grants and partner income, and poverty among whites was increasing at a faster rate than among people of color.[3] Nevertheless, the U.S. economy was doing well by conventional indicators. Why, then, would Congress and the president—a Democrat at that—enact punitive and controlling legislation that eliminated at most 2 percent of a robust budget and that reflected wholly disprovable myths and legends about the poor? Of course, the answers to this question are many and complex, but two are key to our daily lives and to our organizing: the nature of the economic shifts under way and the erosion of the rights of all Americans.

As was the case in the era of Dred Scott, technology has made possible whole new ways of organizing production and distribution of goods and services around the globe. While academics, including many on the Left, have argued heatedly about the existence and nature of globalization, we are merging our analysis and lived experience to generate a position from which we do our work: that a technology-enabled globalization process is under way that fundamentally and permanently alters the value of labor, the nature of work (now including both jobs and "work activity"), and the composition of a new class that stands in a contingent and precarious relationship not only with the boss but with the boss's electronic labor force as well. Davis (1998-99) puts it well:

Employment under these circumstances can increase while new technologies are, at the same time, destroying the value of labour power. The capitalist does not care if production is done by the "gratuitous labour of machines" or by the "free" labour of slaves. With electronics driving down the value of labour power and, therefore, wages, more members of the household are compelled to enter the job market, or to work past the traditional retirement age, or to take on multiple jobs in attempts to maintain a slipping standard of living. Workers pushed out of the top of the labour market scramble to hold on by re-entering waged work at lower wages. Others are driven into the job market at the bottom by the end of welfare programmes, *temporarily* providing a cheaper alternative to technology. And others are driven by circumstance into the sex trade or the illegal drug industry or other illicit activity, and from there into forced labor prisons. (42)

The role of government in creating the conditions amenable to this transition is apparent: ensure the survival of internal production and distribution capacities and enhance the competitive position of U.S.-based su-

pranational corporations by any means necessary (Grugan 2000; Polychroniou 1995). Seen in this way, the congressional/presidential embrace of the principles embodied in PRWORA makes perfect sense: like the Taney court of 1857, they represented the interests of the people who put them in power, people whose class interests pursue the logic of global capital. The premises of that logic include a flexible, contingent—and terrified—workforce and the substitution for real jobs of mandatory work activity. That arrangement is terribly like what was once called slavery in America, an arrangement also protected and promoted by the state.

This assessment has important strategic implications for those who organize to end poverty, for if we are correct that the economy has entered a new stage and the role of the nation-state has therefore changed, there are no large concessions to be won from the state. The liberal welfare state will be a thing of the past, buried (significantly) by a Democrat. If we are wrong, not everything will have been lost, because our organizing will have produced a populace that questions, that demands, that moves. In those circumstances, concessions might be possible. But we believe that this is a new period of history in which ending poverty is eminently possible. If we educate and organize around the realities and possibilities of this moment, the PRWORA could have the same galvanizing effect that the Dred Scott decision had in 1857. It is worth remembering that the abolition movement did eventually prevail. Poverty is no more inevitable or permanent than slavery.

The ideological mechanisms

Like the economic infrastructure for globalization, the ideological apparatus was constructed over time through the normal operations of a range of social institutions. Three of these are particularly relevant to welfare reform: the interlocking directorates that produce the concepts and rules around which programs are organized; the media; and the two-party system.

We see the interlocking directorate as both an informal club of the major controlling figures in America's political economy and the organizational structures and mechanisms used by this group to pursue their class interests (Draffan 2000). At every level of government, we find examples of the latter dominated by the former—councils of business representatives, public officials, foundation leaders, and intellectuals from the academy and think tanks brought together to develop and, increasingly, to implement and manage public policy. These alignments are nothing new, of course; what is new is the degree to which visible formal structures and methods are being created through which these networks conduct the public's business. From privatization to business roundtables to policy commissions, we see the dissolution of the boundaries between public and private spheres, an insistence that private individuals (mostly women) perform the social welfare functions of society, and the appropriation of the public's decision-making purview by private entities. Indeed, at the transnational level, the instruments and institutions governing global trade and development operate altogether beyond the gaze of democratic processes.

These interlocking directorates generate and legitimate components of the ideological apparatus that get translated into public policy. One of these, the changing notions of rights and entitlements, is particularly significant to us: corporate class interests require a broad acceptance of a new social compact, one that involves a significant change in the function of government and the relationship between government and the people. This notion was marketed to the public as early as 1980: in a special issue of *Business Week* (June 1980), a team of scholars and businesspeople appraised the preconditions for the recovery of the American economy in a multinational environment. One such condition was stated unequivocally: the notion of entitlements must go (84). To us, it is most significant that the focus was not on the poor but on all Americans, and particularly the worker. Here we see another historical analogy: in 1857, the court used Dred Scott's status as a slave to restrict the rights of "all Negroes," thereby establishing the foundation for government abrogation of the rights of all and consolidating the class interests of slave owners; in 1996, the government's ending of welfare entitlements was the visible front in an assault on the rights of all Americans, one designed to consolidate the class interests of today's rich. Pursuing this course, Americans' rights will never include government protection of, much less provision for, economic human rights. This is a primary reason that we have invoked the United Nation's Universal Declaration of Human Rights—specifically the economic human rights provisions—in our organizing.

The interest of the interlocking directorate is also seen in the media. The power of the media to produce a collective and uncritical consciousness is readily apparent. In *Why Americans Hate Welfare*, Gilens (1999) examines the role of the media in the production of an ideology of shame and blame regarding poverty. His study also illuminated the ways that racism is folded into the mix as he directly connected economic conditions and racial images of poverty: when increases in poverty and unemployment occurred during economic slumps, media images of the poor were primarily of luckless and presumably blameless whites; during periods of economic boom, "lazy blacks" predominated the images and explanations of poverty.

Corporate iconography also plays a role: Kincheloe's *Sign of the Burger* (forthcoming) explores "the corporate colonization of consciousness" in his exploration of the ways in which the company teaches, in a global classroom, the new marketplace rules. This study points to one of the taproots of media power: it insinuates itself into our everyday lives, purveying the symbols that define normal and correct and just and valued as we eat and dress and go about our business, spending our money and relating to each other. The power of the media to affect the self-images of poor and homeless people has not

been lost on the apologists of welfare reform—nor on us. Using media, arts, and culture to create countervailing images and messages is an integral part of our program of organizing and education.

Finally, we note the way in which the ideology of a two-party system has contributed to an illusion of inclusion while consolidating the power of a ruling elite. To us, the alignment of the two major parties around a common corporate agenda was clearly revealed in their consensus on welfare reform. We believe the two-party system places an ideological headlock on the American people: it ensures that the boundaries within which legitimate dissent can take place are clearly defined and (ideologically) enforced. Nothing but the loyal opposition lies within the arc of legitimacy determined by this two-party system. This assessment also has implications for our organizing approach, including the alliances we have made with the Labor Party.

A summation

So what is the meaning of welfare reform to us? For many, it means nearly absolute control of the most intimate spaces of our lives, the constant specter of psychological and physical danger, and even death itself. But it also means that we are clearer and stronger. We are aware of our unity with the ever-growing numbers for whom a gilded cage for the workers of the globalized economy is being constructed. The PRWORA is but one tiny wire in the cage but, interwoven with dozens more, has this purpose: that the majority of Americans adjust to a lowered standard of living, one sustained by a constricted vision of our rights. Whether we are locked together in the cage depends in large measure on our ability to act from a consciousness of our common circumstances and our ability to organize strategically to counter the forces that would contain us. In the next sections, we describe the ways we are working toward those objectives and, beyond them, the goal of ending poverty.

ORGANIZATIONAL
SCAFFOLDING

In 1991, five "welfare mothers" began meeting in the basement of a church in the Kensington section of Philadelphia to share their experiences, define their needs, and use their study of history and social movements to figure out ways to meet their needs through unified, organized efforts. Kensington was and is the poorest section of Philadelphia. Until the 1970s, Kensington had been a thriving area built around light industry and the residences and commercial services that clustered around the factories. By 1990, it was emblematic of the deindustrialized Northeast—a multiethnic, multiracial area of deteriorating and abandoned housing where the dearth of legal jobs left welfare and illegal drugs as the primary options for most families' incomes. In this environment so starkly at odds with the prevailing rhetoric of the 1980s, the founding members of the Kensington Welfare Rights Union (KWRU) grasped the necessity and opportunity of organizing around immediate,

felt needs and educating about the economic and political contexts of those needs.

Today, KWRU is a membership organization of poor and homeless people with a program that encompasses neighborhood-based organizing to meet basic needs and national, even global, organizing to address the political and economic structures that produce those needs. Through direct-action campaigns, including the takeover of empty HUD (Department of Housing and Urban Development) housing by homeless families, we have housed over 500 families, fed and obtained utility services for thousands, and educated on the streets for basic skills and the literacy of political survival. We have organized or hosted several national and international marches and meetings, including the fall 2000 Poor People's World Summit to End Poverty, attended by over 400 poor people and their allies representing 135 organizations from the United States and 80 organizations from abroad.

We recognize that the movement to end poverty, like the abolition movement of the 1800s, must include other sectors of the population who are affected by the forces that produce poverty. The new Underground Railroad (URR) is one implementation of that analysis, one way for people who are not currently living in poverty to become involved in this new abolition movement. The URR is both an informal network of individuals and organizations that have allied themselves with KWRU (or other poor people's groups in the movement) and a somewhat more formal association of "depots"—groups of allies that have come together specifically to work in the movement. The URR Temple Depot is an example of the depot model.

THE STRATEGIC SCAFFOLDING: BUILDING A MOVEMENT TO END POVERTY

Structural inequalities and conflicts are necessary but not sufficient preconditions for the emergence of a social movement. Our organizing experiences have taught us that new conditions require new thinking and tactics, including the formation of a new collective identity and the application of "five main ingredients" (Baptist 1998): teams of indigenous organizers, bases of operation, networks of mutual support, lines of communication, and consolidated cores of leaders. In this section, we describe the way that we build on and foster these elements.

Since KWRU's inception, we have been part of a larger collectivity, the National Welfare Rights Union (NWRU). Through NWRU, we have benefited from the experiences of chapters, particularly Minnesota Women, Work, and Welfare and the Michigan Welfare Rights Organization. We also inherited the lessons of the Homeless Union, a national organizing effort that fell victim to the drug war, dollar co-optation, and lack of strategic consciousness. Given this history and experience, the need for a broad-based movement was clear and compelling by the mid-1990s, and an organizational base was needed. KWRU's leadership, in response to our study of history and the looming enactment of welfare

reform, constructed a strategic approach to building this movement that would (1) shift the focus from civil rights to economic human rights, (2) incorporate all who are affected (the majority of the people) by the attacks on the poor (the visible target), and (3) be based on the unity, leadership, and organization of the poor (those most directly affected). Given the lack of available resources and the opportunities posed by technology, we decided to use the Internet as a primary organizing tool.

Economic human rights

On 10 December 1948, the General Assembly of the United Nations adopted the Universal Declaration of Human Rights, which contained several articles commonly referenced as economic human rights. By 10 December 1997, we had begun a national campaign to document violations of these rights in the United States, focusing specifically on Article 23 (employment and income support), Article 25 (basic human needs), and Article 26 (education). In announcing the documentation campaign, our executive director signaled the unifying strategy: "If you are part of that 95% that doesn't own anything, you need to link up to this growing movement for human rights" (Honkala 1997). Speaking to the KWRU leadership, representatives of several other poor people's groups, and some allies, Honkala also established the role of the poor:

To bring this movement to everybody out there, we in this room have to see ourselves as leaders. . . . We have got to get people out of their intoxication in every sense of the word, to get people to put down the drugs, the alcohol, the television, and the despair.... If we can inspire them to get involved, then we can win the fight because we are the majority of the people and we can truly take our country back.

The following summer, we organized and led the month-long New Freedom bus tour of the United States, visiting poor people's groups in over 40 cities and towns, collecting documentation, and building a network of dissimilar groups with similar concerns about the effects on their communities of concurrent economic dislocations and the erosion of rights portended by the PRWORA as well as social and economic take backs in housing, labor rights, environmental protection, health care, and other areas.[4] The tour, which had begun at the Liberty Bell in Philadelphia, culminated at a rally at the United Nations; in a nearby church, a people's tribunal heard the evidence and declared the United States to be in violation of the economic provisions of the Universal Declaration of Human Rights.

Momentum continued to build that fall as KWRU and the URR Temple Depot cohosted the Poor People's Summit in October 1998. Attended by representatives of poor people's groups from 40 states, Puerto Rico, and Canada, the summit provided an opportunity for dialog between groups about their varied perspectives and programs but culminated in a call for a March of the Americas to occur in the fall of 1999. The call signified the growing consensus around the use of economic human rights as a consolidating

focus for organizing as well as the need to place the matter of U.S. poverty in the context of global poverty.

Thus, in the fall of 1999, poor people's groups and their allies from all over the United States united with representatives of poor people's groups from nearly all South and Central American nations in a month-long march from Washington, D.C., to the United Nations. For the U.S. groups, the departure from Washington amplified the message that their government could not be counted on to protect and promote the economic human rights of its residents. We therefore turned toward the court of world opinion symbolized by the U.N. Social and Economic Council. Uniting poor from the hemisphere, the march also aimed to link inextricably the fallout of economic dislocations in the United States with the dynamics of globalization, including the superexploitation of labor, heightened disregard for rights, and the widening gulf between rich and poor around the world.

By this time, the network of groups that had come together through the initiative of KWRU had adopted a name, the Poor People's Economic Human Rights Campaign (PPEHRC). The notion of a campaign signified the commitment to a long-term struggle to translate the concepts of economic human rights into real programs for real people. The campaign did not—and has not—prescribed specific programs, opting instead to emphasize the imperative of organizing a mass base for change, to "win people's hearts and minds" to the notion that economic justice is both necessary and possible. Each organizational member of the PPEHRC retained its own goals and programs but came together in a network to pursue two shared initiatives: organizing events that span the boundaries of their communities, and education facilitated through its community-based, Web-centered University of the Poor. Representatives of constituent groups formally adopted this program in February 2000. Strategically, it was designed to build a movement while synergistically strengthening the constituent groups: each would benefit from having a boundary-spanning organizing focus and an accessible place to share among themselves knowledge, skills, and strategy as well as questions and dilemmas posed for peer consultation.

The next major event of the PPEHRC was the March for Economic Human Rights held in Philadelphia on the opening day of the Republican National Convention 2000. From its base of operation— Bushville, a tent city in the midst of closed factories and abandoned houses with a magnificent view of Philadelphia's downtown skyline— the PPEHRC led 10,000 people down the city's main artery to the shadow of the convention hall in defiance of a city ban on the march. National news media reported a "clear victory" for the marchers, who carried the message that the poor and their allies would refuse to be "disappeared" in America despite the repudiation by both major political parties of the legitimacy of their claims to economic human rights in the world's richest country. Through individual, coordinated, or collective programs,

the members of the PPEHRC network will continue to bring this message to every corner of the country.

"For All Who Are Affected"

A fundamental supposition from which we act is that the poor are only the first and most visible targets of an assault on the economic human rights of the majority by those whose class interests are thus served. We are reaching out to all elements of society that do not belong to that latter group. As corporate consolidations and mergers result in the downsizing of managers as well as line workers, more and more people are becoming aware of the nature and extent of economic dislocations under way in the United States and abroad. The KWRU and the PPEHRC are creating both an analysis and a program around which people can unite for a long-haul change effort.

The relationship between the undermining of labor rights and other economic human rights is clear to many workers, as is the vitiating consequence of pitting employed and unemployed against each other. Increasingly, labor is clarifying its class interests, resisting a long history of corporate co-optation of labor leadership, propaganda about the poor, and government action to undercut unionization. Two formal relationships signify the unity of interests between labor and the poor: KWRU is an affiliate of the National Union of Hospital and Health Care Employees, AFSCME, AFL-CIO, and of the Labor Party.

Another means of recruiting individuals and organizations to the movement is the URR project composed of people who are not (currently) living in poverty but have come to believe that poverty must end for the sake of all. These are the allies (not advocates) in the movement: pro bono lawyers who defend the KWRU in civil disobedience actions and who file complaints of violations of economic human rights on its behalf; social workers who organize the social work community to work shoulder-to-shoulder with movement groups; individual men and women who donate time and money to help with day-to-day operations; students who handle event logistics, raise money and awareness, and align other student movements with the movement to end poverty; legislators who strategize with KWRU; religious leaders who preach and teach about this new abolition movement; artists who create symbols and a cultural base for the movement; educators who conduct research in collaboration with KWRU; and videographers who document and support the development of the movement.

In sum, community organizers often distinguish between horizontal and vertical organizing. KWRU has adopted a central role in horizontal organizing among poor people's groups to constitute a foundation for the movement. Vertical organizing is, however, supplanted by a diagonal approach—an engagement with those elements of society who have not yet been as directly assaulted as the poor but who have come to understand in this period that their class interests lie more with the poor than with the rich. The history we envision and

seek to make together is one that is now possible—one in which everyone's economic human rights are nonnegotiable. As readers and makers of history, despite and because of welfare reform, we look to this future as we begin each day.

Notes

1. Draffan (2000) provides a specific who's who in the power nexus, listing the major players in and interconnections between corporations, foundations, think tanks, universities, and government and quasi-government bodies.

2. The court had heard the case in 1856 but ordered a reargument in the 1857 session, most likely to avoid deciding the volatile case during the 1856 election campaign.

3. Supporting data has been compiled by many scholars. Particularly accessible is Axinn and Levin (2001, chap. 9).

4. See Skylight Picture's 1997 documentary film *Outriders*.

References

Axinn, June and Mark J. Stern. 2001. *Social Welfare: A History of the American Response to Need*. 5th ed. Boston: Allyn & Bacon.

Baptist, Willie. 1998. On the Poor Organizing the Poor: The Experience of Kensington. Available at http://universityofthepoor.org/library/kwrumodl.html.

Davis, Jim. 1998-99. Rethinking Globalization. *Race & Class* 40(2-3):37-48.

Draffan, George. 2000. *The Corporate Consensus: A Guide to the Institutions of Global Power*. Seattle, WA: Public Information Network. Available at http://www.endgame.org/.

Gilens, Martin. 1999. *Why Americans Hate Welfare*. Chicago: University of Chicago Press.

Grugan, Pat. 2000. Personal communication, 11 Dec.

Honkala, Cheri. 1997. Speech to the Next Step School, convened by Kensington Welfare Rights Union, 5-7 Sept., Philadelphia, PA. Quoted in *People's Tribune*, Oct.

Kincheloe, Joe L. Forthcoming. *The Sign of the Burger: McDonald's and the Culture of Power*. Philadelphia: Temple University Press.

Kutler, Stanley I. 1967. *The Dred Scott Decision: Law or Politics?* Boston: Houghton Mifflin.

Polychroniou, Chronis. 1995. Rise and Fall of US Imperialism. *Economic and Political Weekly* 30(29 July):PE54-PE64.

Book Department

INTERNATIONAL RELATIONS AND POLITICS

BRONNER, STEPHEN E. 2000. *A Rumor About the Jews: Reflections on Antisemitism and the* Protocols of the Learned Elders of Zion. Pp. ix, 154. New York: St. Martin's Press. $24.95.

Before the publication of Hitler's *Mein Kampf*, the *Protocols of the Learned Elders of Zion* was the most famous and influential anti-Semitic work in the world. Bronner's fascinating volume presents a number of selections from the *Protocols* themselves and offers a thoughtful analysis of their background and political significance. Produced by the czarist secret police at the turn of the twentieth century, the *Protocols* purports to be the minutes of meetings held by the "innermost circles of the rulers of Zion" outlining the Jews' plans to infiltrate all modern institutions, including the government, the media, the schools, and the banks. The *Protocols* purports to reveal that through these institutions, the Jews plan to corrupt the Gentile world, confusing the minds of the Gentiles with subversive notions of liberty and equality and, ultimately, seek to seize behind-the-scenes control of every important Gentile state. Though clearly a work of fiction, the *Protocols* was widely read as fact and frequently cited by anti-Semitic movements during the first half of the twentieth century as evidence of the insidious machinations of the Jews.

The immediate political purpose of the *Protocols* was to unmask liberalism and the liberal regimes of the West as nothing more than the puppets of the Jews. Through this unmasking, the authors of the *Protocols* sought to discredit their liberal political opponents. Liberalism, according to the *Protocols*, was the Jews' way of undermining the "aristocracy of the *goyim*" and confusing the "intellectuals of the *goyim*" with ideas designed to enhance the power of the Jews. This use of anti-Semitic references to attack liberalism is, perhaps, the most interesting and significant feature of the *Protocols*.

In a sense, the *Protocols* could be read as a tribute to the importance of Jews in the development of liberalism during the nineteenth century. Where liberal forces were strongest—in France, Britain, and, of course, the United States—Jewish support was not critical to liberalism's success. However, Jewish support for liberal movements was very important in southern and central Europe, where liberalism faced its greatest challenges. Jews in substantial numbers supported Mazzini's Young Italy movement and took part in the uprisings of the 1830s. In addition, Mazzini received considerable financial aid from the Jewish banking firm of Todros in Turin. Subsequently, the Jewish banking houses of Rothschild, Bendi, and Tedesco financed Cavour's efforts to unify Italy. Jews were also important in Cavour's inner circle, serving as publicists for his cause and members of his cabinets. Significant numbers of Jews participated in the liberal revolutions of 1848 in central Europe. In Germany, Jews fought at the barricades in

Berlin and helped to lead the Prussian National Assembly and Frankfurt Parliament. Such intellectuals as Heinrich Heine and Ludwig Borne were major publicists and propagandists for the liberal cause. In Austria, Jews participated in the Vienna uprising and helped to formulate a new liberal constitution. In Hungary, 20,000 Jews enlisted in the national army formed by Louis Kossuth. The distinctive role of the Jews in the development of liberal regimes was in the domain of political mobilization and opinion formation. Liberal regimes removed religious disabilities and opened up opportunities for Jews in business and the professions. This cleared the way for a great expansion of the Jewish business class and fostered the emergence of an important urban Jewish stratum consisting of lawyers, journalists, writers, physicians, and other professionals. These businessmen and professionals became important figures in the popular politics of the liberal era as publishers, editors, writers, politicians, political organizers, and party financiers. In these capacities, Jews were staunch supporters of the liberal state and important allies for those leaders who sought to strengthen it.

The authors of the *Protocols* were fully aware of the relationship between Jews and liberalism and sought to exploit this identification as a political weapon. In so doing, they were following a well-worn path. In a number of different political and historical contexts, forces opposed to regimes in which Jews have played important roles have sought to discredit the regimes by unmasking the government and its institutions as puppets of a cunning alien race. Even in recent American history, political commentator and presidential candidate Pat Buchanan referred to a then–Democratically controlled Congress as "Israeli-occupied territory." Like the authors of the *Protocols*, Buchanan sought to discredit his political foes by revealing them to be agents of the Jews. Thus the *Protocols* is significant for both historical and current political reasons. Bronner is to be commended for preparing an excellent volume that makes these important documents accessible to contemporary readers.

BENJAMIN GINSBERG

Johns Hopkins University
Baltimore
Maryland

ROSALES, RODOLFO. 2000. *The Illusion of Inclusion: The Untold Political Story of San Antonio*. Pp. viii, 236. Austin: University of Texas Press. Paperbound, $14.95.

Beyond its catchy title, *The Illusion of Inclusion* should command attention for its insightful analysis of power and politics in San Antonio, Texas, and its theoretical contributions to the literature in urban studies and race and ethnic politics. Focusing on the development of San Antonio from the 1950s to the 1990s, Rodolfo Rosales presents a history of the Mexican American demands for inclusion in local governing institutions and a share in the economic prosperity associated with San Antonio's rise as one of America's major cities. Rosales's account of this "untold story" of Mexican American mobilization, in itself a contribution to both Chicano and Texan history, also addresses a number of significant issues in contemporary urban politics.

Drawing upon archival research and interviews with key participants, Rosales provides a detailed account of how the Chicano middle class mobilized, largely through electoral politics, to challenge the political and economic marginalization of the city's Mexican American population. New political arrangements resulted that ultimately led to greater Chicano political representation in city government, notably exemplified by the 1981 election of Henry Cisneros as San Antonio's first Chicano mayor. While acknowledging the significance of San Antonio's more pluralistic political environment, Rosales questions the broader effects of political change as he points to "continuing social and economic exclusion . . . of major sectors of San Antonio's Chicana and Chicano working class and poor." In the end, Rosales finds that the imperatives of a market economy guide urban governance and the city's development, privileging the priorities and interests of the Anglo business community over those of other groups.

Rosales's narrative draws relationships between structure and agency—that is, how political institutions and their rules affect political activity and how political behavior, in turn, affects political structures and outcomes. Underlying his theoretical approach are considerations of race and class. To illustrate, Rosales demonstrates how in the 1950s, under the banner of municipal reform, middle-class Anglos dislodged San Antonio's political machine and instituted new rules of the game, such as nonpartisan, at-large city elections. Using the new electoral arrangements to their advantage, Anglo business interests consolidated their dominance in city affairs through their establishment of a "nonpartisan" political organization, the Good Government League (GGL), which controlled the nomination process for city council elections for two decades. The GGL's exclusive hold over city politics was eventually broken as Chicanos and other groups successfully mobilized for political representation using new rules of engagement, such as those mandated

by the Voting Rights Act and fostered through community-based organization.

Importantly, Rosales inserts Mexican Americans into San Antonio's documented history while revealing a complexity and multidimensionality to their politics as well. Generational and ideological differences become manifest in how Mexican American activists defined and pursued political inclusion. A World War II generation placed its faith in coalition building within the Democratic Party to advance Mexican American interests. But a Chicano generation heavily influenced by the identity politics and social protest of the Chicano Movement of the 1960s and 1970s eschewed traditional politics in favor of electoral strategies that established independent bases of power for the Chicano community.

The implications of gender differences are also addressed, albeit largely in one chapter that features two prominent Chicana activists, one of whom is Rosales's wife, Rosa, a visible figure in the League of United Latin American Citizens. While one may question whether family connections unduly influence Rosales's interpretations of Chicana women's activism, his study affirms arguments made by Carol Hardy-Fanta and others on the mobilizing and democratizing role Latina women play in the politics of their communities.

Rosales's pessimistic assessment of the economic and political consequences of San Antonio's changing political face may be somewhat overdrawn or, at least, premature. The shape and meaning of political inclusion for Mexican Americans is still evolving, in both electoral politics and community-based organizations. But his study is compelling in its suggestive, if troubling, conclusions.

CHRISTINE MARIE SIERRA

University of New Mexico
Albuquerque

SMITH, ANTHONY D. 1999. *Myths and Memories of the Nation*. Pp. 288. New York: Oxford University Press. $65.00. Paperbound, $24.95.

Those who have followed Anthony Smith's substantial contributions to the professional literature on nationalism and ethnicity over the years will be pleased to see so many of his essays brought together in the present volume. Those unacquainted with his work will now have an opportunity to explore the evolution of historical ethnosymbolism, an approach to the study of ethnicity and nationalism that he has helped to develop.

While the 10 chapters of this book have appeared previously as journal articles, the introduction provides a theoretical retrospective that lays out the conceptual underpinnings of his distinctive perspective. His emphasis on myths and memories, perceptions and beliefs, draws our attention to the subjective and ideological dimensions of nations and nationalism.

This approach insists on the importance of the historical origins of nations, especially premodern roots, in the forms of symbols, rituals, and shared memories. These vernacular cultural resources prove critical in the later processes of nation building, and they point to the popular basis of nations. Smith argues that, although the ethnosymbolic approach focuses on subjective cultural and symbolic elements, "their long term patterning produces a structure of relations and processes . . . which can provide a framework for the socialization of successive generations of ethnic and national members." New members learn the myths of the community's origin and descent as recollected and transmitted through memory and as interpreted by earlier generations. This subjective version of a nation's origins is understood through ethnohistory rather than any official historian's lens.

The collection includes chapters on the historical roots of national identity; the myths of ethnic descent; ethnic nationalism and its impact on minority groups; the territorial issues associated with ethnic and national groups; the role of nationalists as "political archeologists" as they go about the work of reconstructing nations; chosen peoples; Zionism and diaspora nationalism; and the prospects for European unity in light of European nationalisms.

The first and last chapters are the most interesting because they deal most specifically with the theoretical questions of how we account for the persistence and depth of ethnic and nationalist attachments. While historical ethnosymbolism is a useful lens through which we can learn much about nationalism and ethnicity, it leaves out too much to stand on its own as an explanatory framework. For heuristic purposes, it is probably helpful to compare Smith's approach with other theoretical perspectives as he does in the introductory chapter. Our understanding of nationalism and ethnicity is enriched by Smith's insights, and historical ethnosymbolism is a useful addition to our understanding of the subject matter, but it does not pose a sufficient or satisfactory alternative, as is suggested in the introduction to the book. Furthermore, Smith's critique of other approaches—specifically, social constructionism—is weak. He says, for example, that "the idea that thousands, even millions, of men and women have let themselves be slaughtered for a construct of their own or others' imaginations, is implausible, to say the least." That argument is characteristic of intellectuals whose knowledge of the world is quite literally derived from books. If Smith were to talk with people who have fought in the wars of secession in the former Yugoslavia, for example, he would quickly discover that these wars, and probably most others, have been fought by reluctant warriors, people who were conscripted into armies against their will, who had no inclination to fight, and who certainly would rather flee a war than fight in one.

Nonetheless, this is a first-rate and welcome contribution to the literature on ethnicity and nationalism. It is bound to advance our understanding of one of the most complex and powerful phenomena of our time.

REED COUGHLAN

S.U.N.Y Empire State College
Utica
New York

STEVENS, JACQUELINE. 1999. *Reproducing the State*. Pp. xv, 307. Princeton, NJ: Princeton University Press. $49.95. Paperbound, $18.95.

The purpose of *Reproducing the State* is to demonstrate that "as long as there are political societies based on kinship forms, there will be far-reaching practices of violence that follow from the corollary forms of nationality, ethnicity, race, and family roles." Stevens is convinced that political theorists are much more interested in trying to resolve group conflicts than in determining how the conflicting groups initially came into existence, despite the fact that all of the characteristics generally thought to be acquired naturally at birth—sex, kinship, race, and ethnicity—are constructed politically. She argues that

political societies institutionalize the relation between birth, history, and kinship rules in ways that make concrete the attachments of parents and children. Immigration laws, laws regulating personal names, the taxonomy of the earth through the aggregation of state-nations, the taxonomy of populations by reference to these places of origins as racial, and the political constitution of maternity (and matri-

mony) as natural all borrow from the birth connotations wrought through political societies to constitute and regulate certain forms of being. (268)

Through sheer fabrication, the state constitutes membership practices of "naturally occurring characteristics." Stevens supports her argument by examining birth-based theories of membership and group affiliation in a wide range of historical and contemporary societies. By examining the origins of intergenerational constructs such as marriage, nationality, race, gender, ethnicity, and family, Stevens explores the ways in which political societies constitute these categories and depend on their constitutive forms to delineate membership and group affiliations.

Stevens's analysis of the interconnection between ostensibly natural characteristics, on the one hand, and the determination of who belongs to a political society, on the other, is one of the book's major strengths. Others are her use of history to demonstrate the intrinsically political nature of race, gender, kinship, sexuality, and nationality, as well as her detailed account of the importance of intergenerational affinities in the reproduction of political societies and the state-sanctioned divisions between individuals that result in oppression and inequality. Throughout the book, Stevens consistently relies upon "an approach . . . [that] has an affinity with some strains of both deconstruction and Foucauldian methods, which, broadly defined, refer to examinations of discourse in scientific fields, legal institutions, and philosophy, as well as in more popular texts." Simultaneously, her approach navigates the difficulties inherent in this method.

While Stevens acknowledges that there exists no definitive answer to the question of what is to be done, she maintains that there are two ways of reproducing political societies so that kinship principles might play a diminished role: all state involvement in marriage must be eliminated, and all citizenship requirements based on birth or ancestry must be curtailed. By abolishing political societies based on kinship forms, the possibility exists that the state would no longer be a crucial source of oppression and hardship for human beings. It is naïve, however to assume that states will voluntarily withdraw their imprimatur on race, gender, ethnicity, sexuality, marriage, nationality, and kinship. Fortunately, naïveté is not one of Stevens's flaws. She recognizes that her solutions "challenge the prevailing laws of familial taxonomies [and] dislodge the centrality of birth to membership in political societies and their related forms of affiliation." She is equally clear that "the purpose of positing the conditions of history and kinship rules for considering the salience of birth . . . reveals the specific contexts that render birth such a crucial practice for political societies to control." Political societies do not readily relinquish control over their citizenry, despite the larger interest such as an action serves.

MARTHA T. ZINGO

Oakland University
Rochester
Michigan

EUROPE

GASCOIGNE, JOHN. 1998. *Science, Politics and Universities in Europe, 1600-1800*. Pp. viii, 581. Brookfield, VT: Ashgate. $89.95.

The volume under review reproduces, with original pagination, essays by John Gascoigne that appeared between 1984 and 1995. During these years, Gascoigne

also published *Cambridge in the Age of the Enlightenment: Science, Religion and Politics from the Restoration to the French Revolution* (1989), and it is indeed the University of Cambridge that occupies center stage for the majority of the nine studies in *Science, Politics and Universities*. This is not a parochial viewpoint, however, Gascoigne's exploration of developments at Cambridge encompass the political dynamics of church and state, and his accounts of intellectual developments during the Scientific Revolution range across the universities of Europe.

England's two universities, like virtually all their Continental counterparts, were creatures of both political rulers and established churches during these two centuries. Indeed, the volume begins with an account of Cambridge's vicissitudes during the turbulent era of the English Revolution. The university remained bonded to the Anglican Church through more tranquil times to such an extent that reform did not become possible until the Anglican monopoly was broken in the 1820s. Due to this nexus, the university's role in English society was monumentally conservative. Yet this role of largely serving the aristocracy coexisted with a remarkable degree of intellectual vitality. Not only did the university harbor Sir Isaac Newton and the Scientific Revolution, but it also evolved the Mathematical Tripos in the eighteenth century, one of the most rigorous and meritocratic forms of academic competition.

The studies that treat the Scientific Revolution more widely portray a similar kind of duality. Gascoigne shows that the large majority of the scientists of that era were university trained. However, intellectual change in the universities was a glacial process. For most of this period, the new doctrines of what we now call science coexisted with logically incompatible philosophical systems. The universities largely fulfilled the role of merely imparting knowledge, not discovering it. For that reason, scientific academies became the eighteenth-century venues for serious scientific inquiry. But this distinction, too, is qualified in Gascoigne's nuanced account. Within universities, schools of medicine managed better than other faculties to nurture a spirit of scientific inquiry.

The six principal studies of this volume treat the following subjects: the academic milieu of Isaac Barrow, Newton's predecessor and senior colleague at Cambridge; Newton at Cambridge as an exemplar of the Scientific Revolution; the influences of politics and patronage of the institutionalization of Newtonian natural philosophy; the emergence of the Mathematical Tripos; the failure of Parliament to reform the English universities in the eighteenth century; and the role of the universities in the Scientific Revolution throughout Europe.

Gascoigne's style is consistently helpful to the reader. Each section begins by setting out fundamental issues that are in some sense in dispute. The ensuing text then brings to bear evidence to clarify these points. The explanations provided are chiefly contextual. Indeed, the great merit of this scholarship is to reveal how academic doctrines, and individuals who espoused them, carried implications for factions in the church or state that consequently affected events. These studies deserve re-publication as a collection. Despite an occasional redundancy, they provide a penetrating view of the interplay of intellectual and political currents in the universities of the seventeenth and eighteenth centuries.

ROGER L. GIEGER

Pennsylvania State University
University Park

UNITED STATES

GARCIA, IGNACIO M. 2000. *Viva Kennedy: Mexican Americans in Search of Camelot.* College Station: Texas A&M University Press. $29.95.

The focus of this book is on the Viva Kennedy Clubs established during the 1960 election by Mexican Americans to support a candidate few knew but from whose presidency many expected great things. The latter never materialized, but the Viva Kennedy Clubs gave birth to a new series of related political groups up through Adelante Clinton! and ultimately helped incorporate Mexican Americans, whose culture was largely invisible and ignored during the 1950s, into the processes and norms of American politics. The trade-off, Ignacio Garcia suggests, may have been a broader commitment to a more radical, community-based social reform agenda in turn for the episodic and piecemeal approach more characteristic of policy making in the United States. Divisions within the Mexican American ranks would emerge. These focused on the more socially reform-minded Chicago movements; those espousing a politics built more on incremental American-style approaches and seeking government-sponsored welfare state remedies; and, of less concern to Garcia's conception of the study, a broader passivity and noninvolvement in the Mexican American community generally. Among the outgrowths of the Viva Kennedy experience were the adoption of the Mexican American political agenda as a national one and the emergence in politics of the most successful generation of Mexican American public officeholders to date. The more prominent of these political leaders receive extended attention.

Garcia traces the evolution of the Viva Kennedy Clubs into the Political Association of Spanish-Speaking Organizations and the latter's eventual demise (the primary concern is the time period 1960-64), the victim of changing times as well as conflicts over goals, ideology, community and political commitments, factionalism, personalities, and individual ambitions. The national scope of the movement and its broader ambitions are examined, but attention is paid mostly to developments in Texas.

The evolution of a distinctive Mexican American political identity and a recognition of its cultural achievements and distinguishing characteristics is a multifaceted, nuanced, and complicated undertaking. Garcia chooses this broader approach and manages to include a considerable number of contextual and social perspectives in what could have been a fairly dry, basically chronological rendering of a stage in the evolution of one (very broad) group's political awakening. The principal concern and unifying focus is with the Viva Kennedy Clubs and the forces they managed to set in motion in terms of a more politically conscious, better-organized, and, although this was not their intention, long-term series of political movements.

The developments are significant and the period in question an important one for crystallizing Mexican American objectives and giving them political voice. Garcia does a skillful job in weaving a variety of themes into a cohesive exploration of a marking point in an evolving political drama. In this context, he has made a perceptive and insightful contribution to our understanding. As he observes, the Mexican American presence in, and contribution to, American politics and social development are underexplored, often not well understood or appreciated, and seldom included in most school curricula.

Latinos will soon constitute the largest ethnic group in the United States. This book, in Garcia's concluding words, helps to tell the Mexican American story,

in itself a "testament to the *mexicano*'s quest to find his or her niche in American society and to [his or her] tenacity in achieving it with dignity and pride." More such studies would be welcome.

WILLIAM CROTTY

Northeastern University
Boston
Massachusetts

PESTRITTO, RONALD J. 2000. *Founding the Criminal Law: Punishment and Political Thought in the Origins of America*. Pp. x, 197. DeKalb: Northern Illinois University Press. $36.00.

Ronald Pestritto's *Founding the Criminal Law* has four main parts. The first discusses efforts to reform the criminal law—primarily by reducing the number of crimes punishable by death and replacing corporal punishment with incarceration—in Pennsylvania, Virginia, and New York around the time of the founding of the American Republic. This first part emphasizes the appeal to reformers such as Benjamin Rush of the Enlightenment principles of punishment identified chiefly with Beccaria's utilitarian approach. The second part surveys theories of punishment: utilitarian/deterrent (Beccaria and Bentham, Hobbes and Locke), moral idealist/retributive (Kant and Hegel), and "ancient and medieval" (Plato and Aquinas), among others. The third part returns to Founding-era views of criminal law, now emphasizing the appeal of nonutilitarian sources: religion, higher law, and just deserts. Pestritto aims to show that the reform efforts were based not simply on the appeal of Enlightenment utilitarianism but on a mixture of that and the nonutilitarian sources just mentioned. This is done convincingly enough. The fourth part of the book is a conclusion arguing that contemporary criminal justice policy can learn from the comprehensive approach of the Founding era, particularly from its inclusion of just desserts as a basis for punishment.

The historical sections of the book, parts 1 and 3, are interesting and well documented. They would make good reading in courses on legal and American history. The survey of theories of punishment is adequate. However, there is an odd lack of fit between this section and the others, in that it takes up theorists who are not mentioned in the historical chapters (Kant and Hegel) and theories not known in the Founding era (Foucault's). Moreover, there are several misinterpretations. For example, discussing Locke, Pestritto claims that *"by definition,* there is no crime in the state of nature,"* crime existing only in the state of war. Locke, however, clearly allows that the state of war can occur in the state of nature without it stopping being the state of nature, so there surely can be crime in the state of nature. Purporting to explain Kant's retributive theory of punishment, Pestritto writes, "Everyone wills that criminals ought to be punished. That criminals suffer the pain of punishment is a universalizable maxim." But these and other related statements by Pestritto do not explain Kant's theory of punishment. They do not explain the strict application of lex talionis that Kant demands. Nor do they explain how, for Kant, retributive punishment is a duty. Acting on a universalizable maxim is permitted, but it is not a duty. ("I should go to the movies for relaxation" is a universalizable maxim.) What is a duty, for Kant, is that one *not* act on a maxim that *cannot* be universalized.

Pestritto's conclusion is sadly out of date. What he calls "contemporary rehabilitation" is the work of Ramsey Clark and Karl Menninger, published more than 30 years ago and long out of vogue among criminal justice policy makers. He bemoans the mildness of American prison sentences at a time when—due to mandatory minimum sentences, tough sentencing guidelines, and truth-in-sentencing laws—sentences are at their harshest, the prison population has quadrupled in the space of 30 years, and a higher percentage of our population is behind bars than in any other modern nation. And he calls for adoption of just desserts as a foundation for criminal penalties when that has been the reigning policy for decades. Witness the adoption of capital punishment by 38 states since 1976, in the face of consistent research showing its inability to deter murder more effectively than imprisonment.

JEFFREY REIMAN

American University
Washington, D.C.

PONDER, DANIEL E. 2000. *Good Advice: Information and Policy Making in the White House.* Pp. xii, 244. College Station: Texas A&M University Press. $39.95.

Daniel E. Ponder has continued his excellent research in the field of presidential leadership and presidential decision making in his latest book, *Good Advice.* Ponder examines how presidents and their staffs "use, misuse, and even decide not to use the advice they get in the process of formulating policy."

Using the Carter presidency as a model, Ponder has carefully negotiated the volumes of presidential papers at the Carter presidential library in Atlanta and the current Carter scholarship to evaluate the degree to which the president relied on his White House staff for policy advice. Ponder argues that the Carter White House can be adequately used to evaluate the policy processes in the modern presidency and serves as a clear model for later administrations.

Like all modern White House policy structure, the Carter White House relies on the Domestic Policy Staff to centralize domestic policy development and evaluation. Established in the Nixon administration as the Domestic Council, the Carter policy staff simply had the name changed to "Domestic Policy Staff." Every successive administration has also utilized a strong White House–based policy staff, although the name generally changes from administration to administration.

Ponder sees how this now institutionalized domestic policy staff is a central focus of presidential decision making, for it provides not only continuity in presidential policy but also both political and policy input into the decision-making process. He notes that, consistent with recent accounts of presidential policy making, the staff "plays an integral role in formulating and managing policy information while protecting the president's political interests."

Like other current literature on the inputs into the presidential decision-making process, Ponder concludes that the institutionalized domestic policy-making process serves as the locus of the president's decision structure. While the president may utilize other structures such as the bureaucracy, kitchen cabinet, task forces, or other advisory structures, the information from these structures continues to be funneled through the central White House clearinghouse. In the Carter example, that central White House clearinghouse was the Domestic Policy Staff. Ponder astutely notes in this research that the president might not have always taken the advice of the Domestic Policy Staff, due to lack of interest in policy matter, political pressures, or bureaucratic opposition, but he always used the Domestic Policy Staff as the first line of decision making.

One of the many strengths of Ponder's analysis is his conclusion that presidential decision making is multifaceted and largely dependent upon the political climate. Although the domestic policy staff may carefully analyze the policy options and present what appear to be the most politically astute policy options, the president often may move in another direction as a result of strong interest group or congressional political pressure.

The analysis would have been strengthened with stronger comparisons to later administrations. For example, did the domestic policy staffs in the Reagan, Bush, and Clinton administrations continue to operate in the same manner for policy advice as in the Carter administration? What are the similarities and differences? If this research is intended to serve as a model, broader comparisons would be helpful. This comment in no way detracts from the work, however, for it stands as a significant contribution to our understanding of the advisory structures of presidents.

SHIRLEY ANNE WARSHAW

Gettysburg College
Pennsylvania

REED, ADOLPH, JR. 1999. *Stirrings in the Jug: Black Politics in the Post Segregationist Era.* Pp. xiii, 303. Minneapolis: University of Minnesota Press. $47.95. Paperbound, $18.95.

Adolph Reed Jr. proffers a long-overdue analysis of "when the [black] revolution comes, came and went." *Stirrings in the Jug*, a collection of essays written between 1986 and 1998, is a concise overview of African American political development and the evolution of contemporary black politics. This book unabashedly answers vexing questions heretofore inadequately addressed or neglected by scholars, policy analysts, pundits, and black leadership. Why have urban black regimes (black mayors of predominantly black cities) failed to deliver the policy mandates of the black masses that elected them? What are the causes of growing economic and social inequality both between blacks and whites and within the black population after desegregation? What were the gains from civil rights activism of the 1960s? Who benefited and why? Why have left-leaning critical tendencies in black politics failed to secure institutional niches? How should black politics be pursued in order to advance the mandates and interests of the African American petite bourgeoisie as well as elites?

Reed answers these questions by incisive and compelling examination and codification of the primary scholarship, process, and practice of black politics and, thereby, makes an important step toward filling the theoretical void in black politics and black studies. Although Reed stirs up important ideas and concepts—and very likely much debate—in black politics, the most cogent propositions concern patterns of leadership legitimacy, interests accommodation, and co-optation; reconstitution of domination and sources of demobilization; costs of passive acceptance of political symbols, mythology, and iconology; urban black regimes' shift to "the pro-growth" imperative; and the marginalization of radicalism. From the politics of Isaiah T. Montgomery, the only black delegate to the Mississippi state convention in 1890, to the contemporary urban black regimes of Coleman Young, Maynard Jackson, and Andrew Young, Reed identifies and analyzes the historically custodial, accommodationist, and brokerage character of black politics. "The result was a default mode of politics in which individual 'leaders' could determine and pursue agendas purportedly on the race's behalf without constraint by either prior process of popular deliberation or subsequent accountability."

Among others, Reed delineates the detrimental effects of the common practice by black elites of appointing themselves as leaders and spokesmen for the black masses—most notably, the self-nomination of Jesse Jackson in the 1984 and 1988 presidential campaigns. Reed posits that racial authenticity as the basis for intellectual and political judgment was always problematic and begs questions of how authenticity is determined and who chooses its guardians. He points out the failures and consequences of black politics with regard to treating African American interests and needs as undifferentiated and African Americans as unstratified by class, income, or color. Reed also maintains that jettisoning black debate and discourse to preserve appearances of black unity on pivotal issues and strategies both deradicalized black politics and brokered, if not sold out, the interests and mandates of the African American petite bourgeoisie.

Without the standard of authenticity appeals to unity as a means to resolve conflicts or as an explanation of failure appear all the more clearly as the wish fulfillment and platitudes that they are. . . . Stripping away the complex of mystification also removes layers of ideological evasion that have obscured the partial, class-skewed program that has dominated black politics for a century. (49)

Despite these strengths, *Stirrings in the Jug* has some weaknesses. Foremost, this book does not define or discuss the one concept that is pivotal to each of these essays, social injustice and its requisites. This omission is a serious failing of black politics, American politics, and media or scholarly debates on affirmative action, redistributive social policy, reparations, and a "public apology" for state-sponsored slavery and discrimination. Presumption of common understanding or agreement on the meaning of social justice and its requisites engenders the endless cycling around and around on these issues—not unlike the flaws of the underclass paradigm that Reed elucidates so graphically.

Although Reed's critique exposes the tautological determinism and inherent racism of the underclass thesis by delineating many of its pitfalls, misuses, and deleterious effects on black political activity, he neglects discussion of the role of conflicting methodological expectations and assumptions between the disciplines of political science and sociology. By restricting underclass discourse to structural analyses, Reed and black politics scholarship, in general, ignore the limits and biases inherent in both structural and behavioral research methods, units and levels of analysis, and the central foci of these two disciplines. How the individual navigates and is affected by society is a legitimate and necessary area of sociological inquiry. Surely, it is neither "playing into the hands of white folks' black agenda" nor counterintuitive to find that some poor African Americans—as well as other poor people—respond to oppression, segregation, discrimination, and marginalization in ways deviant from the norm, dysfunctional or pathological ways that are harmful to themselves, others, or black progress. As Reed asserts, it is imperative that we "reject all assumptions that poor people behave different," but it is also imperative that we ascertain the societal and individual behavioral costs of both marginalization (systematic denial of access to full rights and benefits of citizenship by either or both economic and political discrimination) and poverty in order "to open opportunity structures."

Undoubtedly, some scholars and black politicians may pan Reed's *Stirrings in the Jug* as yet more heretical stirrings from a seasoned philosophical provocateur. To the contrary, Adolph Reed Jr. exposes the weaknesses of black politics,

as practice and theory, in order to improve the process and outcomes and to advance the field. This book is a valuable contribution that is useful as a textbook in black politics, American politics, public administration, and public policy, and it makes good general reading. Many who value Reed's scholarship still await his writing of a comprehensive, systematic, and theoretically grounded book that chronicles African American political development and evolution of contemporary black politics.

MARILYN E. LASHLEY

Howard University
Washington, D.C.

RHEA, GORDON C. 2000. *To the North Anna River: Grant and Lee, May 13-25, 1864*. Pp. xviii, 505. Baton Rouge: Louisiana State University Press. $34.95.

Gordon C. Rhea's series on the 1864 campaign in Virginia continues with this well-written account of 13-25 May. As in his previous studies, Rhea once again provides a gripping and detailed narrative.

After Ulysses S. Grant's failure to secure victory at Spotsylvania, he decided on a new approach of attacking Robert E. Lee's weakest positions in an attempt to force the Army of Northern Virginia into a defensive counterposition. Such a tactic was necessary to force Lee out of his entrenchment since "stalemate meant Union defeat." Grant's only hope was to change the fate of his predecessors. The war turned to a match between Grant's bold sacrifice of Union manpower and Lee's maneuvering to repel the onslaught. A battle of wits between Lee and Grant provided both armies with opportunities and disappointments. Union disillusionment after

Meadow Bridge and Myers Hill led Grant's troops to question his leadership, saying, "Grant as a general is no match for Lee."

By 18 May, Grant decided against any further attack at Spotsylvania. He swung southward, and Lee countered and won the race to the North Anna River by way of Harris Farm, Jericho Mills, Ox Ford, and Doswell Farm. As Grant prepared to attack on 23 May, Lee corrected the drawbacks that had plagued him at Mule Shoe. Finally deciding on a formation of an inverted V, Lee hit upon an ingenious strategy that would create an opportunity to defeat Grant at the North Anna. By pulling his forces back to form the wings of the V, it would appear as a retreat, thus pulling Grant's forces across the river in pursuit and into a trap. Grant's dispatch to Washington confirmed Lee's strategy had worked. It said, "The enemy have fallen back from North Anna, we are in pursuit."

As Lee stood ready to deliver the decisive blow of the campaign, however, he became so ill he was confined to his tent. His inability to command in the field proved extremely unfortunate for the Southerners. His desire to attack the Union army while it was divided and defeat it failed to materialize because the window of opportunity remained open only briefly. Once Grant realized the danger of his position and entrenched his men, Lee's advantage was lost.

Although historians have considered Lee's lost opportunity on 24 May one of major proportions, Rhea argues that Grant would have viewed a defeat of Winfield Hancock's corps at the North Anna as only a tactical reversal as he had seen previous setbacks at the Wilderness and Spotsylvania, and the campaign would have continued. Traditionally, historians have contrasted Grant's and Lee's styles of command, but Rhea presents a sound argument that the two, at least in

this campaign, were surprisingly similar. Both were aggressive and unorthodox. Grant's strength lay in his tenacity to see the destruction of Lee's army, viewing stalemates as only reverses and never allowing setbacks to discourage him as his predecessors had done. Lee's strength lay in his ability to turn unfavorable situations into advantages. He also benefited from his adversary's numerable mistakes. In the end, Lee had won most of the battles through improvisation, but Grant was winning the campaign through perseverance, and the Army of the Potomac was closer to Richmond.

Rhea's use of published and unpublished sources is comprehensive, and his notes section and bibliography include the latest material available. His clarity, attention to detail, perceptiveness, and evaluation are outstanding. To the scholar and casual reader alike, this book is a must for understanding the 1846 Virginia campaign.

THOMAS D. COCKRELL

Blue Mountain College
Mississippi

SMITH, KIMBERLY K. 1999. *The Dominion of Voice: Riot, Reason, and Romance in Antebellum Politics*. Pp. viii, 318. Lawrence: University Press of Kansas. $40.00.

The Dominion of Voice explores major transitions in American ideas "about how the people should participate in politics" between the early Republic and the antebellum years to argue against today's "almost unchallenged consensus that rational public debate" is the proper model for democratic decision making. The book has substantial virtues, not the least of which is pondering a social science truism in the maelstrom of historical evidence. Smith, a political scientist, brings extraordinary richness of data and seriousness of research to her historical quest. Her conclusion is also wholly convincing: that rational public debate is not and should not be the whole of the process by which a polity stumbles toward its policies. Smith's historical study is intelligent but often puzzling and unconvincing, too. She argues that the Jacksonian era rejected both riot and oratory to pursue "Enlightenment rationalism," represented best in its political press, determinedly "dispassionate, rational, and animated solely by the desire to discover the truth." Her claim that this partisan press eschewed rabid attack, personalities, or dishonest ploys is quite mistaken.

Even odder is Smith's position on oratory, where her title is much more accurate than her text. She contends that press developments and the problematics of "neo-classical oratory" led to "the replacement of the dominion of voice with the rule of reason." Thus she neglects almost all "voice" in the nation's great age of public oratory and debate, when speeches in Congress and on the stump and at lyceums, churches, and celebrations were great national/neighborhood events. Smith's oppositional structure between oratory/passion and press/reason is untenable. The press overflowed with reports of speeches, including endless verbatim ones from Congress, and these often offered the best reasoned arguments to appear there.

These central chapters are bookended by two on riots and two on abolitionists. Smith's handling of colonial and early Republic riots is stronger than her treatment of antebellum mobs, though the former ends in the astoundingly inaccurate conclusion that riot was "for a long time after the founding a more obvious vehicle for democratic politics than was debate."

Smith argues that mobs in the Jacksonian era were wholly condemned and excluded from a role in democratic politics. In fact, rioting of some kinds drew more support and extenuation in this era in the free states than ever before or since. For a good while, few condemned anti-abolition mobs; the Jacksonian party found little wrong with anti-black riots and noted only the glorious "will of the people" in many others; and abolitionists always praised and sometimes plotted fugitive slave mobs. Smith's mistake is to see attitudes toward riot as set, when they actually fluctuated in response to specific issues and actions.

Smith's final chapters argue "that the abolitionists rescued the arts of rhetoric by Christianizing politics." Her chief documents here are handled well enough, but several of her general points are very dubious, especially in regard to abolition's unconcern for truth, politics, and reasoned argument. Some of this misinterpretation again comes from Smith's dismissal of the "voice" of the orators that early gave abolition its foothold through tightly reasoned argument.

On the abstract issue, my casual opinion is that Smith cogently disembowels a straw man. Perhaps lots of people, or political scientists, truly believe that democracy depends on closely reasoned public debate by a wholly rational citizenry, but I would guess that most such calls involve merely a yearning for a modicum of data, deliberation, and decency in the inevitably manipulative and messy process. Historical data little support Habermas's golden age of civic discourse, or Smith's of "Enlightenment rationalism" during the nation's time of high Romanticism.

DAVID GRIMSTED

University of Maryland
College Park

WATERS, MARY C. 1999. *Black Identities: West Indian Immigrant Dreams and American Realities.* Pp. xii, 413. Cambridge, MA: Harvard University Press. $35.00.

Those who have gone to any recent annual conference of the Caribbean Studies Association would have been able to attend sessions dealing with variations on the theme of black West Indian identity in North America. The papers, and especially the discussions that follow, nearly always range from frustration to anger over the withering racism that black West Indian professors and students experience in the United States. Caribbean peoples have for decades known of American structural racism, so they attempt to ready themselves before coming north. But no one can prepare for direct insults, and perhaps worse, the subtleties of voice inflection, facial expression, and body language that occur in countless daily encounters and which, taken altogether, reinforce the interracial hostilities that are so much a part of the contemporary United States.

These testimonies are entirely consistent with findings emphasized by Harvard sociologist Mary Waters in her compelling *Black Identities.* Her study focuses on the attitudes and experiences within the black West Indian community in New York City in an attempt to understand better their well-known successes when compared with mainstream African Americans. Waters reaches conclusions very different from those of others who suggest that Caribbean blacks are simply reliving the traditional American immigrant experience and bypassing American blacks whose dysfunctional cultural characteristics account for their relative poverty. She argues, rather, that over time the distinct elements of West Indian culture the immigrants are most proud of—a willingness to work hard, a lack of attention to radicalism, a high value on education, and strong interests in saving for the future—are undermined by the realities of life in the United States. (8)

Waters bases her study on scores of information-rich personal interviews, most of which she conducted herself, of white, African American, and West Indian employees at a New York food-service company and teachers, administrators, and students at two inner-city high schools. (The methodology appendix describing the harrowing contexts for "sample surveys" and "objectivity" within the realities of the New York City public school system is must reading.) Letting the interviewees speak for themselves, Waters reveals—in graceful, jargon-free prose—their past experiences, daily lives, and ambitions. Initially, black West Indian immigrants usually identify themselves by their particular islands of origin. Many associate little with American blacks. Their children face the ambivalence between what they learn at home and the culture of the New York city streets. Waters asserts that, unlike in the traditional European American immigrant model, time is not on the side of second- and third-generation black West Indians because they are ultimately judged by outsiders as undifferentiated "blacks" and thereby relegated to the lowest level of a color-coded society.

Other immigrant groups appear only briefly in *Black Identities.* Many of Waters's interviewees were transplanted black Trinidadians and Guyanese, and it would be fascinating to know how their fellow countrymen, the descendants of indentured laborers from India, who have themselves immigrated into North American by the thousands, are in comparison. Also, it is unfortunate that her study obviously went to press before she could include the information from Winston James's *Holding Aloft the Banner of Ethiopia: Caribbean Radicalism in*

Early Twentieth Century America (1998), which shows that many of her conclusions from New York in the 1990s were true in the 1920s. The point, of course, is that the improvement of U.S. race relations—perhaps our most important social goal—is an ongoing, multidisciplinary work in progress. Mary Waters's impressive scholarship suggests that understanding, and maybe even a start to a solution, will probably come to those who care enough to stop and listen.

BONHAM C. RICHARDSON

Virginia Polytechnic Institute and State University
Blacksburg

SOCIOLOGY

CARBY, HAZEL V. 1998. *Race Men*. Pp. 228. Cambridge, MA: Harvard University Press. $24.00.

No intellectual movement has had a greater effect within black studies over that last 20 years than feminism, and no scholar has had more to do with this than Hazel Carby. Despite this fact, and in a sense because of it, Carby makes the controversial claim in *Race Men* that black women still do not receive their due from powerful black men in the field, who pay only lip service to their causes. She attributes this unfortunate circumstance to the self-serving and self-defeating willingness of these scholars to promote an old and powerful myth: the automatic equation of blackness, maleness, blacks' political assertion, and intellect. On its own, this myth seems bad enough, but for Carby it is even worse for serving as a dark crippled sidekick for white male hegemony. To this problem, Carby offers *Race Men* not only as an academic analysis but also as an act of political resistance.

Rather than a systematic historical account of ideas about black masculinity, Carby offers a series of six interconnected essays focused on a range of twentieth-century black figures, including W.E.B. Du Bois, Paul Robeson, the blues singer Huddie Ledbetter (Leadbelly), C.L.R. James, Miles Davis, Samuel Delaney, and Danny Glover. Using these individual figures for focus, Carby shows how discourse of race, gender, and nation reflect and refract each other in a variety of cultural contexts ranging from highbrow arts and letters, to photography, to folk music, to the movies. Of course, her main interest is in gender. In one way or another, whether in Du Bois's *Souls of Black Folks*, in artistic depictions of Paul Robeson's body, or in the music of Miles Davis, Carby shows how accounts of black masculinity prove crucial in providing the rhetorical and symbolic power of several widely accepted narratives of race and nation.

For example, in her treatment of Miles Davis's autobiography, she argues that the jazzman's self-presentation as a consummate musician and as a symbol of black freedom depends heavily on his construction of an all-male world of artists like him. This construction hinges as much on his hatred of women as on his ability to repress the homoeroticism and dependency implicit in his relations with other jazz artists and with his male friends. Thus, to produce himself as a genius and a maverick, as a black man strong enough to live free on the edge of society, Davis pulls off an interpretive trick both on his audience and on himself. Carby extends this analysis to an examination of his music, especially his collaboration with John Coltrane, which she reads as a revelation of what Davis represses. Thus she shows that Davis's musical "insight" depends on his personal "blindness."

While Carby's account of homoerotic desire in Miles Davis's autobiography seems plausible, it is also a blunt instrument for engaging the peculiar complexities of his musical creations. Throughout *Race Men*, Carby gives the impression of regarding all exclusive relations between men as homoerotic. But if all exclusively male relations are homoerotic, then the term cannot distinguish contexts of male interaction well enough to explain anything about them. To make her argument more powerful, Carby needed to distinguish sexually charged interactions from others. Without this, homoeroticism, which recurs in all of her essays, gives the distinct impression of convenience rather than explanation.

In *Race Men*, Hazel Carby has succeeded in offering a challenging but by no means flawless account of black masculinity. To her credit, she pursues a worthy political goal, but at times she sacrifices nuance. Still, her bold book will make other scholars take note of an important area that deserves further study.

JEFFREY B. FERGUSON

Amherst College
Massachusetts

LOW, SETHA M. 2000. *On the Plaza: The Politics of Public Space and Culture*. Pp. xx, 274. Austin: University of Texas Press. $40.00. Paperbound $18.95.

Setha Low uses two plazas in San José, Costa Rica, to illustrate how the built environment is socially constructed and experienced. Arguing that public spaces are the necessary stages for successful democracy, Low applies an anthropological lens to architectural and urban planning histories to reveal how political ideals are inscribed in the urban landscape. These plazas, like similar spaces outside Latin America, have become contested territory between the haves and have-nots. As Costa Rica has

become more involved in the global economy, the society has become more stratified; resulting inequalities are manifested by the simultaneous existence in the plazas of, on the one hand, crime and prostitution and, on the other hand, legitimate commerce, conversations, and children's games. Parque Central and Plaza de la Cultura are only one block apart, yet, Parque Central has a traditional design, and Plaza de la Cultura is in the modernist architectural genre. Low describes in detail how these fundamental differences affect the types of activities on these plazas, the gender and age of those who use the plazas, and surveillance by the authorities.

The first section of the book includes notes from Low's 25 years of fieldwork in Costa Rica and a description of her methodology. The second section describes the history of specific plazas in San José, followed by the European and indigenous versions of plaza history. Low abandons the false dichotomy between formal and vernacular architecture by demonstrating how the Spanish American plaza is a hybridization of both indigenous and colonial influences. Part 3 consists of ethnographies of the social production of space, the construction of difference and its inherent boundaries, and the tensions between the plaza as art or commodity. Low draws heavily on the works of LeFebvre, Bourdieu, and Foucault to interpret the meanings of the plazas for their users, the professionals who designed them, and the politicians who sponsored them. The final section addresses the plazas as imagined places (through literature) and remembered places (through memoirs). Low concludes that public spaces like the plaza

are one of the last democratic forums for public dissent in a civil society. They are places where disagreements can be marked symbolically and politically or personally worked out. Without these significant central public spaces, social and cultural conflicts are not clearly visible, and individuals can not directly participate in their resolution. (240)

Not surprisingly, Low rejects cyberspace as an alternative to real places.

On the Plaza contains a visually rich collection of photographs, diagrams, and maps of users' movements. Among issues Low might have addressed more thoroughly are the implications for plaza use of Costa Rica's nearly universal literacy rate, its strong Catholic heritage, and the concentration of nearly half the country's population in the capital of San José. The book breaks with the typical organizational tradition by combining the author's narrative with the voices of Costa Rican novelists, notes from the author's trips to San José, and conversations with users of the parks. Many of the chapters are self-contained and could be read in any order. This book would be good reading for undergraduate and graduate students in Latin American studies, anthropology, and urban studies.

DAPHNE SPAIN

University of Virginia
Charlottesville

RIGGSBY, ANDREW M. 1999. *Crime and Community in Ciceronian Rome.* Pp. xii, 249. Austin: University of Texas Press. $40.00. Paperbound, $19.95.

There is no reason to doubt that Ciceronian Rome was a city with an extremely high incidence of crime. Assaults, thefts, and murders by individuals or groups motivated by "private" considerations—such as anger, desire for revenge, hope of financial or other type of gain—would surely have been as common in the first century B.C. Rome as in any other city approaching a population of 1 million. Various factors would have made such crimes more common, such as the darkness of the city at night and the fact that the carrying of weapons, such as a sword or knife, was apparently quite common. Furthermore, during this period there existed no formal police force.

Not only were private crimes more common, but political violence in the first century had become nearly constant, contributing to the eventual breakdown of the republican system and its conversion into the quasi-monarchical dictatorship of Caesar and the principate of Augustus. From the time of the tribunate of Tiberius Gracchi onward (133 B.C.), not only was rioting frequent, but organized political violence was a common strategy of politicians and military leaders. We might, therefore, expect a study like Andrew Riggsby's to set out the ways in which Romans like Cicero conceptualized crime and attempted, by means of law and persuasion, to provide solutions to its corrosive effect on society. But, in fact, Riggsby's conclusion is that during this period, " 'crime' . . . never became a distinctively articulated topic of discourse or area of action." According to Riggsby, crime—as a conceptual category in the modern sense of the word—seems scarcely to have existed.

Riggsby undertakes a complex, carefully researched, and valuable study of the so-called *iudicia publica* of the Ciceronian period—that is, the "public courts" that prosecuted acts of wrongdoing that were in some sense considered to have been directed against the overall interests of the state and therefore not tried in the civil courts. The line between civil and criminal law, as Riggsby points out, was often difficult to discern and changed over time, but by Cicero's day, a number of areas were subsumed under *iudicia publica*, including *ambitus* (electoral malfeasance, especially bribery); murder; violence; and *res repetundae* (malfeasance in provincial office).

Riggsby's strategy is to focus in each chapter on the extant speeches of Cicero that deal with each of these categories in order to extract a sense of how the jury, and the population at large, would have understood the nature of the crimes being tried.

The work, which began as a dissertation, in some senses betrays its origin, as it is exhaustively researched and often concerned with matters of scholarly debate by specialists in Roman political, legal, and social history. There is much here, however, that would repay the general reader for the effort of working through the book. Most important is Riggsby's insight that the *iudicia publica* "were simultaneously about specific offenses and the general political order." Following Riggsby's persuasive reasoning, then, if we want to understand how Cicero and his contemporaries saw the roots of criminal behavior we ought not to be looking at the *De Legibus* but rather the *De Republica*, for it was their belief that what was really at issue in criminal trials was the constitution and security of the Roman state.

ANN VASALY

Boston University
Massachusetts

STIVERS, CAMILLA. 2000. *Bureau Men, Settlement Women.* Pp. xi, 187. Lawrence: University Press of Kansas. $29.95.

Years ago, as Camilla Stivers reflects, "Waldo saw the field of public administration as grounded in fundamental tension between scientific, efficient, businesslike management of public agencies and the political implications that permeate the substance of agency work." This tension, while only partly true, makes public administration different from other forms of administration. In her book, Stivers addresses the tension by proposing basically a feminist, social work, postmodern paradigm that leaves behind the masculine trappings that have misguided the field to date. These masculine trappings are scientific reasoning and science, deductive analysis, theory, hypothesis testing, statistical analysis, values of economy and efficiency, and budgeting. Stivers's solution is to drop scientific reasoning and base public administration on social work, experiential learning, participative research, and feminist values.

The "paradigm" Stivers proposes is as off the mark as was the public choice paradigm proposed several years ago by Vincent Ostrom, only where as Ostrom's proposal was extremely economically conservative and constitutional, Stivers's proposal is extremely liberal, and more important, epistemologically dangerous. As Stivers states,

My argument is that at least part of the reason for public administration's preference for scientific administration over the values that animated municipal housekeeping—for efficiency over caring—was the threat to municipal reformers posed by the gender accusations of party politicians: specifically, the risk to their masculinity that lay in associating themselves with women's benevolent activities. (125)

She sees men as concerned about proudly reporting "the length of their poles and the quickness with which they raised," science, efficiency, and a fear of feminist values. Women, however, impart "beauty, virtue and refinement" and are concerned about morality and social betterment. She also cites such male-degrading support for her arguments as: " 'Male-administration of government is maladministration of government' " or "Katherine B. David . . . declared . . . that she would run her agency 'exactly as a man would.' The question facing women as they began to move toward the mainstream of public life was whether this was the best they could hope for." Unfortunately, Stivers asserts that these gender differences remain.

Besides portraying gender stereotypes, she falsely presumes that the field is developing much too scientifically (is becoming too masculine). In reality, little public administration research is based on true experimental analysis, and the quasi-experimental analysis that is done tends to be relatively simple. Most scholars ask exploratory questions that can be reasonably addressed through case studies; prompting feminist values is rarely the driving force. Statistical and econometric analyses are conducted, but usually nonexperimentally and not with masculine overtones. Some scholars even generate theories. Unfortunately, few scholars feel comfortable enough to conduct analyses of all types, and some condemn or fear research they do not understand.

The implications of fear are too significant to overlook. Following Stivers's suggestion, public administration students will not have to be concerned with either understanding the value of social science research or engaging in—let alone understanding—statistical, economic, or budgetary analysis. Such knowledge and its application are feminist heresy. Budgeting and finance will no longer be required courses; statistics and economics courses will become optional; and research methods courses will not be recognizable. Indeed, these changes are occurring in M.P.A. programs today. We cannot let the fear of science and math that has so dramatically affected our youths affect us as well.

Lastly, Stivers's assumption that public administration is based on *the* business model and that it should be based on *the* "old" social work model (before it became masculine) is simply inconceivable. Budgeting theories and practice, for

instance, draw on disciplines ranging from accounting to political theory. There is a place for feminist study, postmodernism, and social work in public administration, but that place is not as a guiding philosophy. Our field is much too rich for that.

JOHN FORRESTER

University of Missouri
Columbia

WILSON, BOBBY M. 2000. *America's Johannesburg: Industrialization and Racial Transformation in Birmingham.* Pp. xi, 274. Lanham, MD: Rowman & Littlefield. $60.00. Paperbound, $27.95.

This book describes the "race-connected practices" of planters and industrialists in Alabama from the time of slavery through the "entrepreneurial regime" of recent years. The author, an associate professor of geography and public affairs at the University of Alabama at Birmingham, situates race in the context of "historical materialism," drawing also upon French "regulationist school," the theory of the Kondratieff cycle, and numerous other historical concepts and philosophies. Although Wilson believes that he has freed himself from the rigid constraints of orthodox Marxist theories, in practice this eclectic mixture means that neither the research nor the interpretations advanced are governed by any consistent method or perspective.

Despite the high-level abstract terminology, the chapters sketch a relatively conventional political-economic interpretation of regional economic history. The oppressive slave regime created great wealth for the slave owners, but the "extensive regime of accumulation" also left a poor, underdeveloped economy. For a brief moment, radical reconstruction held out hope for a "dictatorship of the proletariat," but after its collapse, "indebtedness combined with the commissary system gave the former slaveholders almost the same control over labor as had existed under slavery." Even though postwar Alabama moved into a "planter-based industrial regime" in the late nineteenth century, the initial effect of industrialization was to undermine the traditional racial order (chapter 11). Ultimately, however, industrialists determined that "capital derives advantages from racism" because of the latter's role in disguising the structural realities of the capitalist system and dividing the working class. Although the antagonism of white workers for blacks cannot be denied, the white working class nonetheless "paid dearly for permitting the ruling class to instigate economic competition between the races."

This brief synopsis makes the book seem more rigid and formulaic than in fact it is; it is nothing if not flexible. The problem is not merely that many of its formulations have long since been refuted but that they are refuted by the very works that Wilson cites and draws upon. Indeed, they are often refuted by evidence that he himself presents. For example, despite the "heavy price" they were paying for their racism, when unionization came to Birmingham Steel in the 1930s, "unions did not move whites to accept black demands for an end to race-based wage differentials, discriminatory seniority systems, and segregated facilities." Instead, the unions "installed all white officers and gave work preferences to whites." Some heavy price.

The best parts of the book are those in which Wilson assembles new evidence from primary sources. The section on convict labor, for example, presents several informative (and quite chilling) tables from state prison reports on race, coal production, gross state earnings, and

death rates of convicts (116, 117, 119, 123). This evidence could form the basis for a valuable monographic study of this South African–like southern institution.

GAVIN WRIGHT

Stanford University
California

ECONOMICS

SERVON, LISA J. 1999. *Bootstrap CAPITAL: Microenterprises and the American Poor*. Pp. v, 150. Washington, D.C.: Brookings Institution. $39.95.

In *Bootstrap CAPITAL*, Lisa Servon offers a thoughtful examination of U.S. microenterprise development (MED) programs and the people who participate in them. Building on major studies of such programs, she examines how these programs operate, their economic development and social welfare functions, and their unique approach to alleviating persistent poverty. Using a case study approach, Servon examines five programs: the Women's Initiative for Self Employment, Acción New York, Working Capital, the Institute for Social and Economic Development, and the Women's Housing and Economic Development Corporation. Servon interviews program staff and 80 participants, as well as field experts and policy makers.

To provide a context for her analysis, Servon traces the evolution of MED programs in the United States. She discusses their predecessors in the developing world and early U.S. business development efforts targeting disenfranchised groups. While similarities exist between these initiatives and current U.S. programs, Servon cautions against comparisons.

Servon situates the MED strategy within the context of the changing U.S.

economy and welfare reform policy. She asserts that "the fundamental structure of the economy has changed" and that poverty alleviation strategies, like job training, often develop skills that may not be useful in the near future. She contends that strategies like MED are needed that help people "manage the constraints of the new economy, which means gaining access to information technology, economic literacy, and more flexible working conditions." Servon identifies welfare reform policies as constraining factors in the success of the MED strategy. Barriers to entrepreneurs' maintaining welfare benefits while they grow their businesses is one of several examples.

Servon also locates MED programs for disenfranchised populations in the context of economic development and social welfare programs. Acknowledging that MED programs are a hybrid of the two, Servon delineates the economic development and social welfare goals of these programs and explains why it is inappropriate to measure their success based solely on common standards of evaluation for programs belonging squarely in either of these fields.

Servon's analysis reveals that building social capital is an important outcome of MED programs. For individuals, networks develop between program participants and between participants and organizations. These networks increase individuals' access to information, support services, and credit, thus building their social capital. Additionally, intraorganizational networks develop that build communities' social capital, a community development outcome.

Servon concludes with five recommendations for using lessons learned from the U.S. MED experience to inform antipoverty policy. These include maintaining local versus federal control of programs, acknowledging the diversity of the groups to be served, changing indicators for evaluating program success, improving policy coordination, and providing better options for exiting welfare. Servon provides frequent reminders that MED is not the silver bullet for poverty alleviation but rather one option that is important to integrate within a broader strategy for addressing the complex issues of poverty in the United States.

A unique contribution of *Bootstrap CAPITAL* is the insight it provides into MED programs from the perspective of those who operate and participate in them. Servon gives voice to those closest to these programs. Every aspect of her analysis and her policy recommendations is informed by the experiences of low-income entrepreneurs and program staff. The human side of MED is apparent as Servon tells of microentrepreneurs' pride in their own businesses or their struggles with welfare policies that present barriers to their success. The common goal of these programs—to serve disenfranchised populations—as well as their diversity are revealed as program staff articulate the philosophy of their programs and the outcomes each is attempting to achieve. *Bootstrap CAPITAL* presents a well-informed analysis of microenterprise development in the United States. It is a valuable addition to the literature on this new poverty alleviation strategy.

SALOME RAHEIM

University of Iowa
Iowa City

INDEX

VISIT SAGE ONLINE AT: WWW.SAGEPUB.COM

Find what you are looking for faster!

Our advanced search engine allows you to find what you are looking for quickly and easily. Searches can be conducted by:

- Author/Editor
- Keyword/Discipline
- Product Type
- ISSN/ISBN
- Title

Payment online is secure and confidential!

Rest assured that all Web site transactions are completed on a secured server. Only you and Sage Customer Service have access to ordering information. Using your Visa, MasterCard, Discover,
or American Express card, you can complete your order in just minutes.

Placing your order is easier than ever before!

Ordering online is simple using the Sage shopping cart feature. Just click on the "Buy Now!" logo next to the product, and it is automatically added to your shopping cart. When you are ready to check out, a listing of all selected products appears for confirmation before your order is completed.

WE'RE ONLINE!

Visit our Web site at: http://www.sagepub.com